☆☆ **Forbes**

TRAVEL GUIDE

Formerly Mobil Travel Guide

COASTAL
SOUTHEAST

2011

ACKNOWLEDGMENTS

We gratefully acknowledge the help of our representatives for their efficient and perceptive inspections of the lodgings listed. Forbes Travel Guide is also grateful to the talented writers who contributed to this book.

Front Cover image: ©Veer.com
All maps: Mapping Specialists

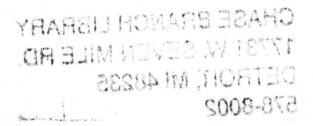

CONTENTS

STAR ATTRACTIONS

If you've been a reader of Mobil Travel Guide, you will have heard that this historic brand partnered in 2009 with another storied media name, Forbes, to create a new entity, Forbes Travel Guide. For more than 50 years, Mobil Travel Guide assisted travelers in making smart decisions about where to stay and dine when traveling. With this new partnership, our mission has not changed: We're committed to the same rigorous inspections of hotels, restaurants and spas—the most comprehensive in the industry with more than 500 standards tested at each property we visit—to help you cut through the clutter and make easy and informed decisions on where to spend your time and travel budget. Our team of anonymous inspectors are constantly on the road, sleeping in hotels, eating in restaurants and making spa appointments, evaluating those exacting standards to determine a property's rating.

What kinds of standards are we looking for when we visit a property? We're looking for more than just high-thread count sheets, pristine spa treatment rooms and white linen-topped tables. We look for service that's attentive, individualized and unforgettable. We note how long it takes to be greeted when you sit down at your table, or to be served when you order room service, or whether the hotel staff can confidently help you when you've forgotten that one essential item that will make or break your trip. Unlike any other travel ratings entity, we visit each place we rate, testing hundreds of attributes to compile our ratings, and our ratings cannot be bought or influenced. The Forbes Five Star rating is the most prestigious achievement in hospitality—while we rate more than 5,000 properties in the U.S., Canada, Hong Kong, Macau and Beijing, for 2011, we have awarded Five Star designations to only 54 hotels, 23 restaurants and 20 spas. When you travel with Forbes, you can travel with confidence, knowing that you'll get the very best experience, no matter who you are.

We understand the importance of making the most of your time. That's why the most trusted name in travel is now Forbes Travel Guide.

STAR RATED HOTELS

Whether you're looking for the ultimate in luxury or the best value for your travel budget, we have a hotel recommendation for you. To help you pinpoint properties that meet your needs, Forbes Travel Guide classifies each lodging by type according to the following characteristics:

★★★★★These exceptional properties provide a memorable experience through virtually flawless service and the finest of amenities. Staff are intuitive, engaging and passionate, and eagerly deliver service above and beyond the guests' expectations. The hotel was designed with the guest's comfort in mind, with particular attention paid to craftsmanship and quality of product. A Five-Star property is a destination unto itself.

★★★★These properties provide a distinctive setting, and a guest will find many interesting and inviting elements to enjoy throughout the property. Attention to detail is prominent throughout the property, from design concept to quality of products provided. Staff are accommodating and take pride in catering to the guest's specific needs throughout their stay.

★★★These well-appointed establishments have enhanced amenities that provide travelers with a strong sense of location, whether for style or function. They may have a distinguishing style and ambience in both the public spaces and guest rooms; or they may be more focused on functionality, providing guests with easy access to local events, meetings or tourism highlights.

Recommended: These hotels are considered clean, comfortable and reliable establishments that have expanded amenities, such as full-service restaurants.

For every property, we also provide pricing information. All prices quoted are accurate at the time of publication; however, prices cannot be guaranteed. Because rates can fluctuate, we list a pricing range rather than specific prices.

STAR RATED RESTAURANTS

Every restaurant in this book has been visited by Forbes Travel Guide's team of experts and comes highly recommended as an outstanding dining experience.

★★★★★Forbes Five-Star restaurants deliver a truly unique and distinctive dining experience. A Five-Star restaurant consistently provides exceptional food, superlative service and elegant décor. An emphasis is placed on originality and personalized, attentive and discreet service. Every detail that surrounds the experience is attended to by a warm and gracious dining room team.

★★★★These are exciting restaurants with often well-known chefs that feature creative and complex foods and emphasize various culinary techniques and a focus on seasonality. A highly-trained dining room staff provides refined personal service and attention.

★★★Three Star restaurants offer skillfully prepared food with a focus on a specific style or cuisine. The dining room staff provides warm and professional service in a comfortable atmosphere. The décor is well-coordinated with quality fixtures and decorative items, and promotes a comfortable ambience.

Recommended: These restaurants serve fresh food in a clean setting with efficient service. Value is considered in this category, as is family friendliness.

Because menu prices can fluctuate, we list a pricing range rather than specific prices. The pricing ranges are per diner, and assume that you order an appetizer or dessert, an entrée and one drink.

STAR RATED SPAS

Forbes Travel Guide's spa ratings are based on objective evaluations of more than 450 attributes. About half of these criteria assess basic expectations, such as staff courtesy, the technical proficiency and skill of the employees and whether the facility is clean and maintained properly. Several standards address issues that impact a guest's physical comfort and convenience, as well as the staff's ability to impart a sense of personalized service. Additional criteria measure the spa's ability to create a completely calming ambience.

★★★★★ Stepping foot in a Five Star Spa will result in an exceptional experience with no detail overlooked. These properties wow their guests with extraordinary design and facilities, and uncompromising service. Expert staff cater to your every whim and pamper you with the most advanced treatments and skin care lines available. These spas often offer exclusive treatments and may emphasize local elements.

★★★★ Four Star spas provide a wonderful experience in an inviting and serene environment. A sense of personalized service is evident from the moment you check in and receive your robe and slippers. The guest's comfort is always of utmost concern to the well-trained staff.

★★★ These spas offer well-appointed facilities with a full complement of staff to ensure that guests' needs are met. The spa facil ties include clean and appealing treatment rooms, changing areas and a welcoming reception desk.

TOP HOTELS, RESTAURANTS AND SPAS

HOTELS

★★★★★FIVE STAR
The Cloister *(Sea Island, Georgia)*
The Fearrington House Country Inn
(Pittsboro, North Carolina)
Four Seasons Hotel Atlanta
(Atlanta, Georgia)
The Lodge at Sea Island Golf Club
(St. Simons Island, Georgia)
The Sanctuary at Kiawah Island
(Kiawah Island, South Carolina)
The Umstead Hotel and Spa
(Cary, North Carolina)
Woodlands Inn
(Summerville, South Carolina)

★★★★FOUR STAR
The Ballantyne Hotel & Lodge
(Charlotte, North Carolina)
The Carolina Hotel
(Pinehurst, North Carolina)
Charleston Place
(Charleston, South Carolina)
The Inn at Harbour Town
(Hilton Head Island, South Carolina)
Inn on Biltmore Estate
(Asheville, North Carolina)
The Inn at Palmetto Bluff
(Bluffton, South Carolina)
InterContinental Buckhead
(Atlanta, Georgia)
The Mansion on Peachtree, A Rosewood
Hotel *(Atlanta, Georgia)*
Old Edwards Inn and Spa
(Highlands, North Carolina)
The Ritz-Carlton, Buckhead
(Atlanta, Georgia)
The Ritz-Carlton Lodge, Reynolds
Plantation *(Greensboro, Georgia)*
The St. Regis Atlanta *(Atlanta, Georgia)*

RESTAURANTS

★★★★★FIVE STAR
The Dining Room at the Woodlands Inn
(Summerville, South Carolina)
Georgian Room *(Sea Island, Georgia)*

RESTAURANTS

★★★★FOUR STAR
Bacchanalia *(Atlanta, Georgia)*
Carolina Crossroads
(Chapel Hill, North Carolina)
Charleston Grill
(Charleston, South Carolina)
Circa 1886 *(Charleston, South Carolina)*
The Fearrington House Restaurant
(Pittsboro, North Carolina)
Gallery Restaurant
(Charlotte, North Carolina)
Herons *(Cary, North Carolina)*
Park 75 *(Atlanta, Georgia)*
Peninsula Grill
(Charleston, South Carolina)
The Ocean Room
(Kiawah Island, South Carolina)
Quinones at Bacchanalia
(Atlanta, Georgia)

SPAS

★★★★★FIVE STAR
The Cloister Spa *(Sea Island, Georgia)*
Spa at The Sanctuary
(Kiawah Island, South Carolina)

★★★★FOUR STAR
29 Spa at The Mansion on Peachtree
(Atlanta, Georgia)
Remède Spa, St. Regis Atlanta
(Atlanta, Georgia)
The Ritz-Carlton Lodge Reynolds
Plantation Spa *(Greensboro, Georgia)*
The Spa at Ballantyne
(Charlotte, North Carolina)
The Spa at Old Edwards Inn
(Highlands, North Carolina)
Spa at Palmetto Bluff,
Inn at Palmetto Bluff
(Bluffton, South Carolina)
The Spa at Pinehurst, The Carolina Hotel
(Pinehurst, North Carolina)
The Umstead Spa,
The Umstead Hotel and Spa
(Cary, North Carolina)

WELCOME TO GEORGIA

IMAGINE THE TASTE OF SWEET TEA AND PERFECT PEACHES.
with Georgia on your mind, there's no limit to the travel experiences offered up by the Peach State.

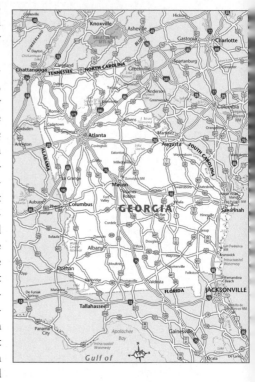

Tourism is one of Georgia's primary industries, and the state boasts many wonders, from its Blue Ridge vacation lands in the north—where Brasstown Bald Mountain rises 4,784 feet—to the deep "trembling earth" of the ancient Okefenokee Swamp bordering Florida. The coastal Golden Isles, set off by the Marshes of Glynn, feature moss-festooned oaks that grow down to the white sandy beaches. Historical attractions also abound, from the world's largest brick fort near Savannah to the Martin Luther King Jr. Historical District in Atlanta. There is the infamous Confederate prison at Andersonville and the still lavish splendor of the cottage colony of the 60 millionaires of the Jekyll Island Club, now a state-owned resort. Most towns in the state have historical homes and museums offering perspectives on our nation's history.

The state was one of the country's original 13 colonies and the fourth state to join the Union (January 2, 1788), but the fifth of the 11 Confederate states to secede during the Civil War. Georgia's capital city, Atlanta, is the center of the New South, alive with culture and history and teeming with business—the city boasts headquarters for Coca-Cola, Delta Airlines and Home Depot, among others.

BEST ATTRACTIONS

GEORGIA'S BEST ATTRACTIONS

ATLANTA

A visit to the state's capital provides the best of all worlds: There's history, sports, theater and music, outdoor activities, fine dining, shopping, museums, the Olympic park and much more. The largest city in the state, Atlanta is a must-see for all visitors to the Peach State.

COASTAL CITIES

Georgia offers a variety of pursuits and if it's water you love, then the coastal cities of Georgia are for you. Golf is plentiful here but so are water sports, resorts, fine dining and culture. Explore islands or stroll through downtown Savannah and relax by the Atlantic.

BLUE RIDGE MOUNTAINS

Take in the majesty of the Blue Ridge Mountains in Georgia. This is the great outdoors; hiking trails abound, as does fishing and white water rafting.

MASTERS GOLF

Each year Augusta plays host to the Masters Golf Tournament, one of four major golf championships. Played at the Augusta National Golf Club, golf fans clamor to the course, named number one last year in Golf Digest's list of America's 100 greatest courses.

ATLANTA

It's easy to think of Atlanta as merely a city of slogans. After all, the city's founders have done a bang-up job at promoting the city as a land of opportunity, from the prewar days when it was a bustling rail center to the years after the war, when locals rebuilt Atlanta into a booming metropolitan area and state capital, eventually to become an international hub for all manner of Fortune 500 businesses.

The birthplace of 24-hour news giant CNN and headquarters for Delta Airlines has called itself everything from "The Capital of the New South" to "The City

Too Busy to Hate." Billboards—including enormous futuristic video signs—and modern skyscrapers abound in this city where creep-and-crawl traffic is the norm (most locals simply don't bother with the limited public transportation). But if you look past the city's knack for brassy self-promotion, you'll find a history-rich destination full of charming neighborhoods, lush green parks, splurge-worthy shopping and major points of civic pride, among them a multimillion-dollar aquarium and stunning buildings designed by world-class architects such as Renzo Piano.

It's a little-known secret that Atlanta has a vibrant, varied restaurant scene. From nationally acclaimed burger joints to authentic ethnic food of all varieties to temples of haute cuisine, this city has it all when it comes to dining. Visitors will want to enjoy a traditional Southern "meat and three" spread (referring to, for instance, a platter of fried chicken with a choice of three sides); for a more international experience, bring those taste buds to the Vietnamese, Korean and Mexican restaurants that line Buford Highway.

And if you're hoping to see tourist attractions such as CNN Center, stay in the heart of Downtown or Midtown. Traffic can be a bear in Atlanta, depending on the time of day, so ditch your car and walk or take public transportation such as the MARTA train. Businessmen might try the smaller, high-end hotels throughout the city, or spots to the north, west and south of town that are closer to corporate headquarters. Buckhead hotels are a great place for luxury shoppers or spa-goers.

WHAT TO SEE

BUCKHEAD
ATLANTA HISTORY CENTER
130 W. Paces Ferry Road N.W., Buckhead, 404-814-4000; www.atlantahistorycenter.com

This museum and research center features papers and exhibits that illuminate Atlanta's—and the Southeast's—history. Learn how the 1996 Olympic Games changed Atlanta forever in an extensive, interactive exhibit that chronicles the history of how the city won the bid to host the games and goes into day-by-day detail of the 16 days of the Games through multimedia presentations. Go further back in history to deepen your understanding of the Civil War through photos and personal stories of the soldiers, as well as exhibits of cannons, uniforms and other artifacts. Other exhibits focus on golf legend Bobby Jones, the evolution of folk art and the history of Atlanta. You won't want to miss the elegant Swan House and the Tullie Smith Farm, a working farm where you can see re-creations of 19th-century activities like blacksmithing.

Admission: adults $15, students and seniors $12, children 4-12 $10, children under 4 free. Monday-Saturday 10 a.m.-5:30 pm., Sunday noon-5:30 p.m. Swan House and Tullie Smith Farm open Monday-Saturday 11 a.m.-4 p.m., Sunday 1-4 p.m.

GOVERNOR'S MANSION
391 W. Paces Ferry Road N.W., Buckhead, 404-261-1776; www.gov.georgia.gov

The three-story Greek Revival-style mansion has been home to the state's governors for 40 years, and you can check out the lavish interior during a walking tour. Be sure to notice the federal period furnishings, which were selected by a fine-arts committee while the mansion was being built. They represent one of the best collections of this period in the country (the canopy

HIGHLIGHTS

WHAT ARE THE TOP THINGS TO DO IN ATLANTA?

VISIT THE MARTIN LUTHER KING JR. NATIONAL HISTORIC SITE

If you're curious about the civil-rights leader and the indelible mark he made on history, spend an afternoon wandering around the Old Fourth Ward and the buildings that make up King's historic site, including King's home.

HAVE SOME FUN AT THE GEORGIA AQUARIUM

The world's largest aquarium features an enormous collection of fish and other aquatic animals, with more than 100,000 animals of 500 different species in all. Don't miss the Ocean Voyager, where you pass through a 100-foot tunnel beneath the aquarium's largest exhibit and get a chance to see the four whale sharks and more.

TOUR THE JIMMY CARTER PRESIDENTIAL LIBRARY AND MUSEUM

Thumb through 27 million pages of documents and correspondence from Carter's White House years. Afterward, check out the former president's 2002 Nobel Peace Prize, which is on display.

PERUSE THE WORKS AT THE HIGH MUSEUM OF ART

One of the premier art museums in the Southeast, the High boasts more than 11,000 pieces of art housed in crisp, white modern buildings designed by Renzo Piano and Richard Meier. Permanent collections include European paintings, folk art, photography and modern pieces by Mark Rothko, Frank Stella and Robert Rauschenberg.

and four-poster beds in the guest rooms are particularly elegant, as is the twinkling crystal chandelier suspended over the dining-room table). It's easy to imagine past governors attending to state business in the wood-paneled study, then relaxing with a mint julep in a rocking chair on the vast front porch. *Tours: Tuesday-Thursday 10-11:30 a.m.*

DOWNTOWN

CENTENNIAL OLYMPIC PARK

265 Park Ave. West N.W., Downtown, 404-222-7275; www.centennialpark.com

The large, five-ring fountain in the heart of this 21-acre park is a reminder that it was originally built as a gathering spot for visitors to the 1996 Olympic Games. The Games might be long over, but visitors and locals alike still enjoy the park for its large expanse of sunny lawn (which is often host to craft shows, outdoor movies and concerts); its shady water garden, which simulates a stream tumbling soothingly over rock formations; and two side-by-side playgrounds. In the summer, the park lights up with one of the city's several Fourth of July celebrations and fireworks shows. Come winter, you can practice your Olympics-worthy triple axel on Atlanta's only outdoor ice-skating rink, which is part of the park's Holiday in Lights festival.

Daily 7 a.m.-11 p.m.

CNN CENTER

1 CNN Center, Downtown, 404-827-2300; www.cnn.com/StudioTour

You'll need advance reservations for a tour of the world's most famous 24-hour news network. The 45-minute walking tour gives you a chance to peek at the control room, mull over journalism ethics at an exhibit and even make a video of yourself reading the day's top stories in the newsroom. At the end of the tour, head for the light-filled CNN Center atrium, where you can load up on souvenirs branded with CNN, Cartoon Network and Braves logos and grab a snack in the building's food court, where you can munch on everything from Mexican to Chinese to salads from both local and national fast-food chains. You might end up eating a burger next to Anderson Cooper.

Tour admission: adults $12, seniors $11, children 4-18 $9, children under 4 not permitted on the tour. Tours: daily 9 a.m.-5 p.m., departing every 10 minutes.

GEORGIA AQUARIUM

225 Baker St., Downtown, 404-581-4000; www.georgiaaquarium.org

When this ship-shaped spectacle opened several years ago, crowds waited for hours for the chance to check out the world's largest aquarium and its enormous collection of fish and other aquatic animals: more than 100,000 animals of 500 different species in all. Don't miss the Ocean Voyager, where you pass through a 100-foot tunnel beneath the aquarium's largest exhibit and get a chance to see the four whale sharks as well as rays, groupers, zebra sharks, humphead wrasses and more. There are also exhibits devoted to tropical fish, cold-water creatures (including three graceful beluga whales), river-dwelling animals and underwater critters native to Georgia. For an extra fee, you can also check out a fun multimedia show, "Deepo's Undersea 3-D Wondershow," and a behind-the-scenes tour. The aquarium is undergoing a multimillion-dollar expansion that will add a dolphin exhibit and show, both of which will open sometime in 2011.

Admission: adults $26, seniors $21.50, children 3-12 $19.50, children under 3 free. Sunday-Friday 10 a.m.-5 p.m., Saturday 9 a.m.-6 p.m. Hours vary during winter holidays; check website for details.

GEORGIA DOME

1 Georgia Dome Drive, Downtown, 404-223-4636; www.gadome.com

The Georgia Dome is worth a visit for its architectural brilliance alone; it's the largest cable-supported domed stadium in the world and was built with more iron and steel than the Eiffel Tower in Paris. It even withstood a recent tornado that swept through downtown Atlanta with nary a scratch. All of which makes this massive venue a fitting home for the NFL's Atlanta Falcons who, despite having made it to the Super Bowl only once in their 42-year history, are still beloved by their hardcore fans. The Falcons share the Dome with Arena Football's Georgia Force and the occasional college bowl event. You can also catch marching bands strutting their stuff in showcases, cheerleaders showing some spirit in competitions and even motocross events with bikers performing amazing stunts.

IMAGINE IT! THE CHILDREN'S MUSEUM OF ATLANTA

275 Centennial Olympic Park Drive N.W., Downtown, 404-659-5437; www.imagineit-cma.org

If you want to sneak in some education for your little ones, bring them to Imagine It!, which is geared toward children ages 8 and under. Pint-sized shoppers can fill shopping baskets with play fruits and vegetables in a simulated supermarket, then cook them up in the kitchen. Toddler visitors have their own enclosed space filled with soft blocks and toys, while older kids can splash in the water-play area (little raincoats are provided), mold sand sculptures or play dress-up in front of a video camera. A rotating schedule of exhibits has included themes like Bob the Builder, the circus, Curious George and Sesame Street. You can treat the kids to a memento of their visit in the small but well-selected gift shop, which has one of the city's best selections of educational toys.

Admission: adults and children $11 (plus tax), children 1 and under free. Monday-Friday 10 a.m.-4 p.m., Saturday-Sunday 10 a.m.-5 p.m.

PHILIPS ARENA

1 Philips Drive, Downtown, 404-878-3000; www.philipsarena.com

Join the locals as they cheer on their hockey team (the National Hockey League's Atlanta Thrashers) and basketball teams (the NBA's Atlanta Hawks and the WNBA's Atlanta Dream), all of whom play at this cavernous arena. Before games, you can see if you've got what it takes to be a pro player in an interactive area where you can shoot baskets or goals. And of course, with its location next door to CNN Center, you're never too far from a television blaring breaking news from CNN or funny Cartoon Network clips. Not into hockey or hoops? You can also catch ice shows, circuses and rock concerts. It's where big names such as U2, Bruce Springsteen and Madonna play when they're in town.

STATE CAPITOL

214 State Capitol, Downtown, 404-656-2844; www.sos.georgia.gov

Built in the late 1800s, this neoclassical building was modeled after the Capitol in Washington, D.C., and its gleaming dome is gilded with gold from Dahlonega, a mining community in the north Georgia mountains. The residents of Dahlonega donated the gold to cover the dome not once, but twice, when the leaf flaked off less than 20 years after its original application. The Capitol Museum isn't just filled with stale information about Georgia's governmental

KNOW BEFORE YOU GO

ARRIVING AND DEPARTING

The world's busiest airport, Hartsfield-Jackson Atlanta International Airport (*6000 N. Terminal Parkway, College Park, 404-209-1700; www.atlanta-airport. com*) serves more than 80 million passengers each year (providing people watching at its finest). The airport is split into two terminals, North and South, with South used for Delta, Delta Connection flights, Aero Mexico and Air France, and North used for all other airlines. The Atrium is at the center of the airport and has restaurants and shopping. Hartsfield airport is 10 miles from downtown Atlanta, and is serviced by Metropolitan Atlanta Rapid Transit Authority (or MARTA, as locals call it), Atlanta's public transportation system (see below).

HOSPITALS

In the case that you need medical care while in Atlanta, there are numerous hospitals to choose from. A pioneer in patient care, Piedmont Hospital (*1968 Peachtree Road, N.W., Buckhead, 404-605-5000; www.piedmonthospital.org*) located in Buckhead, is a private hospital specializing in a wide-range of services. Staffed by the Emory School of Medicine faculty, the renowned Emory University Hospital (*1364 Clifton Road, Emory, 404-712-2000; www.emoryhealth-care.org*) is a national leader in cardiology, cardiac surgery and transplants, among other things. Grady Memorial Hospital (*80 Jesse Hill Jr. Drive S.E., Little Five Points, 404-616-6689; www.gradyhealthsystem.org*) is a public hospital and is part of one of the largest public health care systems in the country. Atlanta's oldest hospital, Saint Joseph's (*5665 Peachtree Dunwoody Road, N.E., Dunwoody, 678-843-7001; www.stjosephsatlanta.org*) was founded in 1880 by the Sisters of Mercy and is still respected as an innovator in health care today.

WEATHER

There's a reason the city is called "Hot-lanta." Blistering summer heat often sets in as early as mid-April and doesn't abate until the end of September or early October. The unrelenting humidity is what makes the scorchers so tough. But fall brings fair weather, and the winters are mild and generally don't get cold until February. Season changes are somewhat unpredictable, but generally March and October are the mildest months (and therefore perhaps the nicest times to visit). When you're packing, bring layers so you're prepared for whatever the weather throws at you.

PANHANDLING

There is no way around it: Atlanta has a panhandling problem. A law was passed in 2005 banning panhandling in the Downtown tourism district, but the law is ambiguous and rarely enforced. The good news is that most of the panhandlers are not dangerous, and some are downright jovial. The bad news is that others are belligerent, and sometimes follow you if you don't give them any money. For the most part they just want a little respect and a friendly "hello," so if you decide not to fork over some change, politely saying you're fresh out is generally a better option than ignoring them.

PEACHTREE STREET

You don't have to spend much time in Atlanta to notice that there is an over-abundance of streets with "Peachtree" in their names. Locals could probably name 10 off the top of their heads. They are all separate streets, though there's one major exception. Peachtree Street is the central thoroughfare in Mid-town Atlanta that stretches from Downtown all the way through Buckhead. It is Peachtree Street from Downtown through Midtown, and then becomes Peachtree Road shortly after 26th Street on through Buckhead. Though the name changes, it's still the same road.

PUBLIC TRANSPORTATION

Although the powers that be in Atlanta are in what seems to be a constant state of planning to improve the city's sluggish and inconvenient public transportation, sometimes it's just easier to rent a car in this auto-loving town. Most tourist sights provide plenty of parking, and in Midtown, you'll find some metered street parking and plenty of pay-to-park lots. If you want to avoid the hassle of driving, take the Metropolitan Atlanta Rapid Transit Authority (MARTA) (*www.itsmarta.com*), which runs north and south from Hartsfield-Jackson Atlanta International Airport to North Springs, and east and west from Indian Creek to Hamilton E. Holmes Drive. Tickets can be purchased as a single one-way fare, in increments of 10 or 20 trips, or as a seven-day or 30-day pass or a multi-day visitor pass with unlimited rides for from one to four days. Discounts are available for groups and conventions. Trains typically run every 10 minutes during peak morning and evening hours, and every 15 to 20 minutes on weekends and holidays. Monday through Friday, trains run from 5 a.m. to 1 a.m., and on weekends and holidays from 5 a.m. to 12:30 a.m. Taxis can be found around the city, particularly on weekends around the city's hot spots. The Buckhead Uptown Connection (*www.bucride.com*), or "buc," buses provide free rides between hotels, restaurants and office buildings in the Buckhead area. Buses leave every eight to 20 minutes Monday through Friday and every 30 minutes on Saturdays. Stops and schedules can be found on the website.

history; it also offers exhibits on the state's flora and fauna, thanks to a long-ago directive by the Georgia General Assembly for the state geologist to collect samples of minerals and soils. Since there wasn't a place for those samples, they ended up in the hallways of the Capitol building and eventually became the backbone of the museum. In terms of government exhibits, check out the one on the scandalous "three governors" incident in 1946-47, when governor-elect Eugene Talmadge died before taking office, and a power struggle between three political factions led to three men commandeering the governor's office and refusing to relinquish it to either of the others. If you want more insight into this historic building, join the tour, which stops in the public galleries of the House of Representatives and the Senate and gives a brief overview of the Capitol's history.

Monday-Friday 8 a.m.-5 p.m. Tours: Monday-Friday 10 and 11 a.m.; 1, 2 and 3 p.m.

TURNER FIELD
755 Hank Aaron Drive S.W., Downtown, 404-577-9100; www.atlantabraves.com

The Atlanta Braves have been hitting it out of the Ted, as locals call it, since the ballpark's opening in 1997. Bring the brood to this family-friendly baseball stadium; younger Braves fans can "run the bases" on a simulated baseball path in the Coca-Cola Sky Field, practice their pitching with foam balls and play baseball-related video games in the Cartoon Network-sponsored Tooner Field, which also features kid-friendly food and souvenirs. You'll have plenty more than just peanuts and Cracker Jacks to choose from in the way of seventh-inning refreshments; the teeming concession stands feature everything from barbecue to burritos to pizza. After you fill up on delicious junk, head to the year-round museum, which houses more than 600 artifacts and photos from the baseball franchise's history, dating back to when the Braves were based in Boston and Milwaukee. The Hall of Fame honors players and others such as Hank Aaron and Skip Caray. Take an hour-long tour of the stadium and you'll get a glimpse of a luxury suite, the press box, the team locker room and dugout.

Museum admission: $5 (or $2 with ticket admission). October-March, Monday-Saturday 10 a.m.-2 p.m.; April-September, Monday-Saturday 9 a.m.-3 p.m., Sunday 1-3 p.m. Tours: adults $12, children 3-13 $7, military $7 (includes museum admission).

UNDERGROUND ATLANTA
50 Upper Alabama St., Downtown, 404-523-2311; www.underground-atlanta.com

In its heyday during the 1960s, it was on par with Bourbon Street for live music and entertainment. After years of decline, Underground Atlanta is now mostly a tourist destination, complete with a worthwhile guided tour that explains how early Atlanta was a thriving railway hub. An offbeat assortment of shops ranges from clothing and footwear stores to souvenir shops offering everything from personalized key chains to photos taken with an Atlanta backdrop to regional candies. When the sun goes down, Kenny's Alley turns into a hopping late-night club scene. Eight nightclubs include an Irish pub; the upscale Motion, where you can dance to Top 40 and hip-hop; and The House. On New Year's Eve, the Underground is the site of the Peach Drop, the local twist on Manhattan's Times Square ball-dropping celebration. During baseball season, it's a convenient place to catch the shuttle to Turner Field to watch the Atlanta Braves hit it out of the park.

Admission: $2 entry required for Kenny's Alley on Friday and Saturday after 9 p.m. Mall hours: Monday-Saturday 10 a.m.-9 p.m., Sunday 11 a.m.-7 p.m.

THE WORLD OF COCA-COLA

121 Baker St. N.W., Downtown, 404-676-5151; www.woccatlanta.com

This museum dedicated to the soft drink reopened in a massive new building in early 2007. There you'll find the world's largest collection of Coke memorabilia, including pop-culture art created by the likes of Andy Warhol and Norman Rockwell; a fully-functioning bottling line that produces 8-ounce souvenir bottles; and more than 60 different cola products from around the world to sample, such as Beverly, a strangely addictive bitter quaff that's sold in Italy. The displays walk you through the entire history of the carbonated beverage that originally was said to cure everything from headaches to morphine addiction. There's even a 3-D movie presentation that follows a scientist on his quest to find the coveted secret formula.

Admission: adults $15, seniors $13, children 3-12 $9, children under 3 free. Sunday-Thursday 10 a.m.-6:30 p.m., Friday-Saturday 9 a.m.-6:30 p.m., hours vary during holidays.

DRUID HILLS

FERNBANK MUSEUM OF NATURAL HISTORY

767 Clifton Road N.E., Druid Hills, 404-929-6300; www.fernbankmuseum.org

This museum is serious about fossils, from the tiny ammonites and belemnites in the prehistoric limestone floor tiles to the 47-foot fossil cast of a Giganotosaurus looming in the Great Hall. You'll also find plenty of rocks and shells here, but for a human touch, check out the examples of clothing and adornments from ancient cultures from around the world, such as Indonesia, Nepal and China. Two children's discovery rooms teach little ones everything from urban development to environmental diversity. While the fossils, jewelry and other artifacts in the museum's collections might be ancient, there's nothing old-fashioned about the museum's IMAX movies (screened several times a day as well as during special "Martinis & IMAX" events on most Friday nights) or the technology used in many of the museum's special exhibits, which employ multimedia presentations, interactive computer kiosks and other modern-day accoutrements.

Admission: adults $15, students and seniors $14, children 3-12 $13, children 2 and under and museum members free. Monday-Saturday 10 a.m.-5 p.m., Sunday noon-5 p.m.

FERNBANK SCIENCE CENTER

156 Heaton Park Drive N.E., Druid Hills, 678-874-7102; www.fernbank.edu

This combined museum, planetarium and observatory may focus on the beauty in the skies, but you can find land-based beauty in the adjacent rose garden and a nearly 70-acre forest full of trails and plants labeled for you to identify. You'll also find exhibits on volcanoes, earthquakes and other natural phenomena inside the Fernbank, as well as gems, a weather station, fossilized trees and replicas of dinosaurs that lived in prehistoric Atlanta. In fall biologists from the museum take birders on guided walks through the woods. Astronomy buffs will go starry-eyed for the observatory; under the 30-foot dome sits the largest telescope in the Southeast, and you can peek at the universe for free on Thursday and Friday nights, weather permitting. The planetarium, too, is a stargazer's dream; it offers rotating shows throughout the year for children and

WHAT ARE ATLANTA'S NEIGHBORHOODS?

ATLANTIC STATION

If the name Atlantic Station sounds like a steel mill, that's because it once was. This 130-plus acre swath of land in the middle of the city was a forgotten, blighted mass. But some visionary developers—spurred by federal funds for cleaning up contaminated land—turned a virtual dumping ground into a gleaming, sparkling, almost Disney-like city-within-a-city. Atlantic Station now boasts hundreds of shops, including chains like Dillard's and Ann Taylor as well as only-in-Atlanta stores, such as K-La and Taste Clothing Boutique. Top-notch restaurants, a spa, a movie theater, trendy hotels, city markets and sleek urban living round out the mini-community. A free shuttle connects the center to the transit line, so you can leave if you want, although everything you need is right there.

BUCKHEAD

Nothing screams Atlanta money—both the old and the new kinds—like Buckhead. Home to sprawling estates and glittering high-rises, the Beverly Hills of the South is probably the most famous—and infamous—neighborhood in the city. Residents include politicians and captains of industry, so it's no surprise that Buckhead sports the best of the best when it comes to shopping, dining and hotels. It also has been known as a wild party scene; but that's changing to make room for—what else?—more stores, fancy restaurants and elite residences. An ambitious upcoming development includes some of the most luxe stores around, such as Hermès and Van Cleef & Arpels.

DECATUR

This quirky little neighborhood is really its own city. In fact, it's older than Atlanta. It has retained its charm and small-town feel, complete with a town square and county courthouse, but don't equate small town with boring. Decatur is a bustling, thriving area with cute outdoor cafés, funky boutiques, haute cuisine (get real Southern fare at Watershed, which is co-owned by an Indigo Girl) and happening bars. It's also home to live-music mecca Eddie's Attic, where you can always find quality bands and cold brews.

DOWNTOWN

Downtown has seen a marked resurgence over the last few years as more young residents and suburban empty-nesters have discovered the perks of living close to the action. Some of the top tourist attractions in the city are there, such as the Georgia Aquarium, the World of Coca-Cola, CNN Center and Philips Arena (home of the beloved Hawks, though the venue also hosts other major sporting events and mega-concerts). As residents moved back to the city center, more bars and restaurants followed, including high-end sports bar Stats. At the area's core is Centennial Olympic Park, with its sparkling fountains. The park hosts a number of music and art festivals during the year as well as an ice-skating rink in the winter and Fourth of July fireworks.

DRUID HILLS/EMORY

Leafy Druid Hills and neighboring Emory University boast some of the finest examples of Georgian architecture in the city. Residents have stayed true to the historic neighborhood's roots in renovations so you'll feel like you took a step back in time in this picturesque area (drive right through the heart of it en route to nearby Decatur). You'll find some adorable boutiques and coffee shops, as well as Fernbank, a top-notch natural history museum with a must-see IMAX theater (and if you're there on a Friday, catch the Martinis and IMAX party). Known for its exclusive private country club and estates, it is also the backdrop for the 1989 film Driving Miss Daisy; drive past 822 Lullwater Road for a glimpse of Miss Daisy's two-story red-brick abode.

GRANT PARK

One of the city's oldest neighborhoods is a well-shaded enclave of Craftsman bungalows and pastel-hued Victorian houses centered around a 131-acre park designed by the Olmsted Brothers, sons of Frederick Law Olmsted, who designed Central Park in New York City. East of downtown, Grant Park was once downright dangerous, but it has been reinvigorated with the influx of families who painstakingly renovated the aging but classic houses in the area. Now Grant Park is popular with both tourists and residents alike. The core of the neighborhood is—no surprise—the actual park inside the same-monikered neighborhood. As beautiful as the green space is, that's not what draws people here. The real attractions are Zoo Atlanta, a world-class facility complete with pandas, and Atlanta Cyclorama, a cylindrical painting that comes to life and depicts the Battle of Atlanta during the Civil War.

LITTLE FIVE POINTS/CANDLER PARK/INMAN PARK/PONCEY-HIGHLAND

These close-by neighborhoods are some of the quirkiest in the city. Bounded by Ponce de Leon and Euclid Avenues, Little Five Points has no shortage of funky bars—dive, music, alternative and otherwise. There are also nifty restaurants serving everything from sushi to burgers, terrific shopping, rocking live music venues and beautiful architecture. Inman Park, in particular, boasts a cluster of some of the best examples of restored Victorian homes you'll find. This neighborhood, which also hosts one of the most hopping spring street festivals in the city, was once the first Atlanta "suburb." It fell on hard times, but over the last 30 years it has been rejuvenated and renovated.

ATLANTA'S NEIGHBORHOODS...*continued*

MIDTOWN/CHESHIRE BRIDGE/WESTSIDE

Once a haven for hippies, Midtown is fast becoming the hippest neighborhood in the city. A sophisticated plan has enabled controlled development along the main Peachtree Street artery, which runs from the Amtrak station at the north end to Ponce de Leon Avenue at the south. In between, you'll find eclectic shopping, fine dining and The Fox Theatre, a nicely restored ornate theater that hosts concerts, shows and the perennial classic The Nutcracker. The western part of Midtown, known alternatively as Midtown West or the Westside, is an up-and-coming area of reclaimed warehouses that happen to house some of the best shopping and most spectacular dining in town. Finally, as you head east, you'll run into Cheshire Bridge Road, known locally as the "street zoning forgot." Here you'll find unique antique stores sandwiched between strip clubs, and fine-dining establishments next to old-time Southern meat-and-three joints. This street is a local institution.

OLD FOURTH WARD/KING HISTORIC DISTRICT

Nestled along Auburn Avenue just to the east of downtown, this historically African-American part of the city is best known as the birthplace of Martin Luther King, Jr. The heart of the neighborhood is Ebenezer Baptist Church, where Martin Luther King Jr. preached. Stop by The King Center and pay homage to King's tomb, which seems to float in a pool of crystal-clear water. The area also boasts a terrific farmers' market, the Sweet Auburn Curb Market. Neighboring Old Fourth Ward is one of the hottest emerging areas in the city, teeming with hip restaurants and charming cafés. There you'll find Dad's Garage, one of the funniest improv theaters around.

OUTSIDE THE PERIMETER (OTP)

If you go outside the city—not very affectionately known as OTP here for Outside the Perimeter of Interstate 285—there's a handful of things to do and places to go. First is the Verizon Wireless Amphitheatre in Alpharetta, a new outdoor concert venue. Likewise, the Cobb Energy Performing Arts Center just outside the city in Smyrna is spectacular; it's the home of the Atlanta Ballet and the Atlanta Opera. If you want to do some shopping, head to The Forum on Peachtree Parkway, a terrific shopping spot in Norcross.

VININGS

Vinings is a little enclave just on the outskirts of Buckhead. Technically it's in the suburbs, but close enough to the city that it's usually considered "in town." It's near the rambling Chattahoochee River, where several restaurants such

ATLANTA'S NEIGHBORHOODS...*continued*

as Canoe line the riverbank and offer lovely views of the water. There's also ample shopping, including the all-encompassing Vinings Jubilee, an outdoor shopping and dining center with both chain and local specialty stores.

VIRGINIA HIGHLAND

Sitting snugly between Emory and Downtown, Virginia Highland is marked by two roads: Virginia Avenue and Highland Avenue (hence the name). It's easy to find. These two long blocks are home to some of the most fun establishments in the city. Pubs, cool clubs and dive bars line the streets, which makes it easy to do your own pub or bar crawl. But there's more to do here than get bar hop. Sumptuous spas, funky stores and casual and fine-dining establishments are all nestled in this lovely residential neighborhood that's filled with lovingly restored Craftsman bungalows. This area is one of the nicest in Atlanta and it's easy to spend an afternoon and evening here.

adults. Recent shows have examined Mars and our knowledge of the night sky through the ages.

Exhibit hall: Monday-Wednesday noon-5 p.m., Thursday-Friday noon-10 p.m., Saturday 10 a.m.-5 p.m. Forest: Monday-Friday 2-5 p.m., Saturday 10 a.m.-5 p.m. Closed for school holidays. Planetarium shows: adults $4, students and seniors $3. Schedule varies.

MICHAEL C. CARLOS MUSEUM

571 S. Kilgo Circle, Druid Hills, 404-727-4282; www.carlos.emory.edu

You might feel as if you've stumbled onto the set of a horror flick, with all the coffins, mummies and tombs that are in this museum located on Emory University's campus. They're all part of the largest collection of ancient art in the Southeast. Time-travel to the days of Cleopatra as you take in lavishly painted coffins, granite sculptures, bronze figurines and beautiful carved amulets, and then visit the oldest Egyptian mummy in the Americas. Egypt isn't the only region represented here; there's also a great collection of sub-Saharan African masks, gorgeous Greek and Roman sculptures and ceramics, and ancient pieces from the Incan and Mayan civilizations. The museum's curators don't only dwell in the past; one of the museum's recent temporary exhibits was a showcase of Andy Warhol's Polaroid portraits, including snapshots of skater Dorothy Hamill and Sylvester "Rocky" Stallone.

Admission: $7 suggested donation. Tuesday-Saturday 10 a.m.-5 p.m., Sunday noon-5 p.m. Closed university holidays.

GRANT PARK

ATLANTA CYCLORAMA & CIVIL WAR MUSEUM

800 Cherokee Ave. S.E., Grant Park, 404-624-1071; www.atlantacyclorama.org

The largest oil painting in the world, the Cyclorama jumps off the page. Plop down in the plush seats and sit back while the historic Battle of Atlanta comes alive, as depicted in the cylindrical painting and a diorama that further sets the scene. Your seat revolves to view the entire painting as narration, music and sound effects tell the story of one of the Confederacy's most crushing defeats. Afterward, a guide tells the fascinating tale of the painting's creation and history, pointing out details such as the image of dashing actor Clark Gable, who is depicted as a dying soldier. After the show, check out the Civil War artifacts, which include weapons, uniforms and documents, as well as the locomotive Texas, which chased and recaptured a train stolen by Union soldiers.

Admission: adults $8, seniors $7, children 6-12 $6, children under 6 free. Tuesday-Sunday 9 a.m.-4:30 p.m.

HISTORIC OAKLAND FOUNDATION

248 Oakland Ave. S.E., Grant Park, 404-688-2107; www.oaklandcemetery.com

What began as a 6-acre garden cemetery blossomed into an 88-acre burial ground for thousands of Confederate soldiers, 25 former Atlanta mayors, six Georgia governors, golfer Bobby Jones and beloved local author Margaret Mitchell, who penned the Southern classic—required reading in these parts—*Gone with the Wind*. Enveloped by majestic oaks and bejeweled with all different kinds of sculpture, the cemetery sits on a hill overlooking the Atlanta skyline. Its twilight walking history tours cover topics from architecture to African-American history and more.

Guided tours: adults $10, students and seniors $5. Daily dawn-dusk. Tours: March-November, Saturday 10 a.m. and 2 p.m., Sunday 2 p.m.; March-October additional twilight tour at 6:30 p.m.

ZOO ATLANTA

800 Cherokee Ave. S.E., Grant Park, 404-624-9453; www.zooatlanta.com

A few steps from the Cyclorama is Zoo Atlanta, where you'll find nearly 200 animal species spread across 40 acres of natural habitats. The zoo is one of only four zoos in the United States to have a giant-panda exhibit; residents Lun Lun and Yang Yang and their two cubs are among the most-visited creatures in the zoo. Don't miss the playful meerkats or the majestic elephants, which you can occasionally spot playing ball with their zookeepers. When the kids have had their fill of giraffe-spotting, they can blow off steam by scaling giant rock-climbing walls, going round and round on an endangered-species carousel, running around in indoor and outdoor play spaces, and hopping aboard the Georgia Natural Gas Blue Flame Express train.

Admission: adults $18.99, seniors, military and college students $14.99, children 3-11 $13.99, children under 3 free. Daily 9:30 a.m.-5:30 p.m.

MIDTOWN

ATLANTA BOTANICAL GARDEN

1345 Piedmont Ave. N.E., Midtown, 404-876-5859; www.atlantabotanicalgarden.org

Some talk of urban sprawl in this metropolitan area of more than 5 million people. But they tend to overlook this urban oasis, which includes an orchid center bursting with the purple-hued florals; gorgeous sculptures at every turn, including several by glassblower artist Dale Chihuly; and a giant greenhouse that displays plant life, multicolored birds and frogs in environments ranging from desert to the tropics. Little ones will stay busy in the enormous, interactive children's garden, which mingles slides and tunnels with real beehives, vegetables and other interesting flora. If you have extra time, enroll in one of the classes and learn about everything from sketching orchids to planting a drought-resistant garden, or stay for cocktails and live music on Thursday nights from May until October, when the garden stays open late for themed happy hours. You'll be so immersed in nature, you'll forget the urban sprawl outside.

Admission: adults $12, seniors and children 3-17 $9, children under 3 free. April-October, Tuesday-Sunday 9 a.m.-7 p.m.; November-March, Tuesday-Sunday 9 a.m.-5 p.m.

GEORGIA INSTITUTE OF TECHNOLOGY
Midtown, ramblinwreck.cstv.com

Georgia Tech—or just Tech, as the locals call it—is an NCAA Division I-A school, smack-dab in Midtown. Founded in 1885, Tech is one of the top science and engineering universities in the country, but crowds come out to cheer on its athletic teams in the Atlantic Coast Conference. Tech has teams in numerous men and women's fields, but football and men's basketball are the big spectator sports. Tech football games are played at the legendary Bobby Dodd Stadium at Historic Grant Field (*155 North Ave. N.W.*). This stadium, built in 1913 and the oldest on-campus stadium in NCAA Division I, presents one of the most unusual football settings in the country: It's nestled beneath Atlanta's towering skyline, which makes night games particularly spectacular. The stadium recently underwent a major renovation, increasing the capacity to 55,000 and adding luxury boxes. A word of warning: Don't even try to get tickets when rival University of Georgia comes to town. Tech's basketball games are held at Alexander Memorial Coliseum (965 Fowler St. N.W.), nicknamed "The Thrillerdome," where students stand behind each basket to heckle the visiting team. Whether you go for some pigskin or b-ball, you'll have to partake in an Atlanta sporting tradition: tailgating. It's almost as important as the game and should be done before and after just down the street at The Varsity, the world's largest drive-in. The Varsity has been serving chili dogs, onion rings and Cokes since 1928. Just make sure you have your order ready when servers yell, "What'll ya have," or you'll be put to the back of the line.

Tickets: football $25 and $40, basketball $20 and up. Football: August-November. Basketball: November-March.

HIGH MUSEUM OF ART
1280 Peachtree St. N.E., Midtown, 404-733-4444; www.high.org

One of the premier art museums in the Southeast, the High boasts more than 11,000 pieces of art housed in crisp, white modern buildings designed by Renzo Piano and Richard Meier. Permanent collections include European paintings, folk art, photography and modern pieces by Mark Rothko, Frank Stella and Robert Rauschenberg. The extensive American-art collection is a standout with pieces by John Singer Sargent, Georgia O'Keeffe, William Merritt Chase and other 19th- and 20th-century artists. Fans of African art won't want to miss the museum's collections of sculptures, masks, beadwork and paintings from ancient to contemporary times, including a Baga sculpture from Guinea that was donated to the museum by Helena Rubinstein in the 1950s. The museum regularly partners with other museums around the world. For example, the museum's partnership with the Louvre in Paris brought in everything from Egyptian and Roman antiquities to paintings by Vermeer and drawings by Michelangelo. If you like your art set to music, stop by on the third Friday of every month, when the museum stays open until 10 p.m. and live jazz echoes through the galleries.

Admission: adults $18, students and seniors $15, children 6-17 $11, military personnel and children under 5 free. Tuesday-Wednesday 10 a.m.-5 p.m., Thursday 10 a.m.-8 p.m., Friday-Saturday 10 a.m.-5 p.m., Sunday noon-5 p.m.

MARGARET MITCHELL HOUSE AND MUSEUM
990 Peachtree St., Midtown, 404-249-7015; www.gwtw.org

Margaret Mitchell penned the bulk of her Civil War epic *Gone with the Wind* when she lived in an apartment in this grand, turn-of-the-century home in the 1930s. The building is now on the National Register of Historic Places, and the museum inside gives you a look—courtesy of a docent-guided tour—at the place where Mitchell dreamt up the dastardly but dashing Rhett Butler and the coquettish, fierce Scarlett O'Hara. You can also learn about Mitchell's pre-*Gone With the Wind* work and get the inside scoop on the making of the Academy Award-winning movie. The in-house literary center offers lectures, writing classes and readings from authors such as Candace Bushnell and Anne Rivers Siddons. You might leave wondering if Mitchell would approve of the view of glossy high-rises and hip restaurants that can now be seen from the leaded-glass window through which she looked while penning her famous novel.

Admission: adults $12, students and seniors $9, children 4-12 $5, members and children under 4 free. Monday-Saturday 9:30 a.m.-5 p.m., Sunday noon-5 p.m.

PIEDMONT PARK
Piedmont Avenue and 14th Street N.E., Midtown, 404-875-7275; 1071 Piedmont Ave., Midtown (Visitor Center); www.piedmontpark.org

A mecca for runners, Rollerbladers and dog walkers—not to mention countless corporate softball teams—this 189-acre spot is the city's answer to New York's Central Park. It was redesigned in the early 20th century by Frederick Law Olmsted's sons, whose father created the aforementioned Manhattan green space. Feed the ducks at the scenic lake, hit some balls at the tennis center or flip some burgers on one of the 22 public grills scattered throughout the park. Kids will enjoy checking out the two playgrounds: a retro, Isamu Noguchi-designed play area completed in 1976, which boasts super-tall swings and a climbing mound, and a newer playground designed to help children explore all of their senses through interactive play structures. The park buzzes with events, including a Saturday-morning farmers' market and weekly summer outdoor movies, but it's also just a great place to lie back on the vast lawn and admire the city's skyline, just like in that other Olmsted-designed park.

Daily 6 a.m.-11 p.m.

WOODRUFF ARTS CENTER
1280 Peachtree St. N.E., Midtown, 404-733-4200; www.woodruffcenter.org

Located in the same arts complex as the High Museum, this center includes a symphony hall and is home to the Atlanta Symphony Orchestra and the Alliance Theatre. The Alliance hosts local and touring productions of plays and musicals, such as the annual chestnut A Christmas Carol and a gospel version of the rock musical Jesus Christ Superstar, while musicians both classical and contemporary grace the stage of Symphony Hall, including Joshua Bell, The Blind Boys of Alabama, Wynton Marsalis and Big Bad Voodoo Daddy. Music and visual art aren't the only masterpieces at Woodruff, however: The center's restaurant, Table 1280, is also acclaimed for its high-end, American brasserie fare.

OLD FOURTH WARD/KING HISTORIC DISTRICT
APEX MUSEUM
135 Auburn Ave., King Historic District, 404-523-2739; www.apexmuseum.org

This 30-year-old museum celebrates the rich, often-untold history of African-Americans (the name is an acronym for the African-American Panoramic Experience). Check out "Hall of Achievement," which focuses on musicians, artists, businesspeople, Olympic athletes and others who have pioneered in their respective fields. Another exhibit, "Black Inventors," celebrates black inventors and entrepreneurs, such as boxer Jack Johnson, who also invented a patented wrench design. You'll step inside a replica of the Yates & Milton Drug Store, one of the city's first black-owned businesses, and a theater showing videos about the African-American experience is housed inside a trolley car, just like the ones that used to chug along Auburn Avenue, where the museum is located.

Admission: adults $4, students and seniors $3, children 3 and under free. Tuesday-Saturday 10 a.m.-5 p.m.

EBENEZER BAPTIST CHURCH
407 Auburn Ave., King Historic District, 404-688-7300; www.historicebenezer.org

Across the street from the original church where Dr. Martin Luther King, Jr. preached about nonviolence stands a newer, bigger house of worship that was born out of that legacy. Come here Sunday for one of its two morning services and you'll be moved by the ethereal gospel choir and the rousing, timely sermons from Pastor Raphael G. Warnock.

Sunday services: 7:45 and 11 a.m.

JIMMY CARTER PRESIDENTIAL LIBRARY AND MUSEUM
441 Freedom Parkway, Old Fourth Ward, 404-865-7100; www.jimmycarterlibrary.org

If you're looking for some light reading, head to this museum, where you can thumb through 27 million pages of documents and correspondence from Carter's White House years. Afterward, check out the former president's 2002 Nobel Peace Prize, which is on display. Despite its name, the museum isn't all about the 39th president. Traveling exhibits based on documents and items from museums from around the world often revolve around presidential or political themes, such as a recent exhibit about the education of the United States presidents. Plus, the museum often hosts book talks and lectures from prominent authors and public figures as diverse This American Life contributor Sarah Vowell, adopted Atlantan Ted Turner and novelist Salman Rushdie. Occasionally Carter will swing by to check on his namesake library and give a talk, too.

Admission: adults $8, seniors, military personnel and students $6, children under 17 free. Monday-Saturday 9 a.m.-4:45 p.m., Sunday noon-4:45 p.m.

MARTIN LUTHER KING JR. NATIONAL HISTORIC SITE
450 Auburn Ave. N.E., King Historic District, 404-331-5190; www.nps.gov/malu

If you're curious about the civil-rights leader and the indelible mark he made on history, spend an afternoon wandering around the Old Fourth Ward and the buildings that make up King's historic site. Start out at the visitor's center, where younger visitors can learn about children's role in the civil-rights movement and you can sign up for a tour of King's birth home, located a few blocks away. King's home, where his family lived until 1941, is furnished with period pieces, as well as a few items that actually belonged to the family, such as the set of dishes on the dining-room table. Don't miss a peek inside the historic Ebenezer Baptist Church, where King was baptized, ordained and where he served as co-pastor along with his father. It's also the church where his funeral was held after he was assassinated in 1968. Finally, pay your respects to King at the King Center, where his tomb appears to float on a serene, aqua-blue reflecting pool.

Visitor center: mid-August-mid-June, daily 9 a.m.-5 p.m.; mid-June-mid-August 9 a.m.-6 p.m. Same-day tickets for the birth-home tour are issued at the visitor center beginning at 9 a.m.

SOUL FOOD MUSEUM
372 Auburn Ave. N.E., King Historic District, 678-508-9478; www.naacaha.com

It takes about a half-hour to tour this oddly charming and hunger-inducing former convenience store, which is filled with packaged foods that have been developed by or marketed to African-Americans. The more than 600 treats on display include Rap Snacks potato chips, Isaac Hayes barbecue sauce and James Brown Cookeez. At the museum, you'll also learn that an African-American man, John Standard, was responsible for inventing a non-electric icebox and an oil stove and that George Crum created the potato chip when a guest at the restaurant for which he was a cook complained that his French fries were too thick. If the exhibits make you peckish, you can purchase some of the snacks on display in the gift shop.

Admission: adults $5, seniors and children $3. Daily 9 a.m.-7 p.m.

ARTS AND CULTURE

ART
BILL LOWE GALLERY
1555 Peachtree St. N.E., Buckhead, 404-352-8114; www.lowegallery.com

Bill Lowe Gallery just relocated to this space, where Buckhead meets Midtown in a gleaming office building. Don't let the corporate exterior fool you—this is a serious gallery run by a serious expert. The new space features soaring ceilings, a wrap-around mezzanine, a catwalk and small, intimate rooms for showing multiple exhibitions. Famous artists such as glass master Dale Chihuly have showed their wares here. There is one corporate-like aspect of the art space: The brand also has a gallery in Los Angeles.

Tuesday-Friday 10 a.m.-5:30 p.m., Saturday 11 a.m.-5:30 p.m., Sunday-Monday by appointment.

FAY GOLD GALLERY
764 Miami Circle, Buckhead, 404-233-3843; www.faygoldgallery.com

Fay Gold Gallery, in Buckhead's Miami Circle, has been around for more than 25 years and has earned a reputation for representing A-list Southern and nationally known artists. You won't see boring still-lifes here. Go check out the gallery's cutting-edge pieces in a variety of genres, including painting, sculpture, glass and works on paper. Don't miss the black-and-white photography from Robert Mapplethorpe.

Tuesday-Saturday 9:30 a.m.-5:30 p.m.

JACKSON FINE ART

3115 E. Shadowlawn Ave., Buckhead, 404-233 3739; www.jacksonfineart.com

Housed in a Buckhead bungalow, Jackson Fine Art features three exhibition rooms that showcase everything from sculpture to photographs with works and shows by notable names such as Horst P. Horst, Ansel Adams and Diane Arbus. The gallery rotates collections every six weeks and works with private collectors—including part-time Atlanta resident Sir Elton John—as well as corporations and institutions such as the Metropolitan Museum of Art. The gallery also boasts a library with more than 1,000 research books and a framing room where you can prep your souvenir so that it's ready to hang when you get home.

Tuesday-Saturday 10 a.m.-5 p.m.

MASON MURER FINE ART

199 Armour Drive, Midtown, 404-879-1500; www.masonmurer.com

Mason Murer was opened by two men just a few years ago and has become one of the top galleries in the city. It's located near Midtown, but off the beaten path in a warehouse district, so it can be hard to find for non-locals. The space is massive, but it doesn't feel overwhelming because art is thoughtfully and carefully exhibited among smaller spaces that were carved out in the cavernous building. As such, the gallery showcases all sorts of art in all sorts of styles and sizes—from small-format works to larger paintings, sculpture and even installation pieces—and nothing gets lost. If you can't get enough of Mason Murer, visit smaller sister gallery Mason Murer Projects (*325 E. Paces Ferry Road, Buckhead, 404-551-3900*).

Tuesday-Saturday 10 a.m.-5 p.m., Sunday noon-5 p.m. and by appointment.

SWAN COACH HOUSE GALLERY

3130 Slaton Drive N.W., Buckhead, 404-266-2636; www.swancoachhouse.com

This Buckhead gallery is part of Atlanta's legendary Swan Coach House, a sprawling place that also includes an eatery and a gift shop. The gallery is housed in the carriage house, on the historic Edward Inman estate. Both the estate and coach house are on the grounds of the Atlanta History Center so you can make a day of visiting the whole complex. After you fill up on sweet tea and tasty, dainty tea sandwiches at Swan Coach House Restaurant, check out the work of contemporary Southeastern artists in a variety of media.

Tuesday-Saturday 10 a.m.-4 p.m.

COMEDY

ATLANTA'S ORIGINAL UPTOWN COMEDY CORNER

800 Marietta St., Midtown, 404-881-0200; www.uptowncomedy.net

For 20 years, the Uptown Comedy Corner in downtown has been the place in Atlanta for urban comedy shows. This has been the proving ground for many African-American comedians, including Chris Tucker, Damon Wayans and Mike Epps. And because it's well known among the African-American comic circuit, many top performers have been known to drop by, including Wanda Sykes, D.L. Hughley and Chris Rock. There is a full dinner menu (it's standard bar fare; try the wings, they come in flavors like garlic pepper and Thai peanut and are great for sharing) and bar, and a two-item or $5 minimum purchase, not including the

ticket price. So order a brew and get ready for some sidesplitting chuckles.
Ticket prices vary and are sold through Ticketweb (www.ticketweb.com).

THE PUNCHLINE
280 Hilderbrand Drive, Outside the Perimeter, 404-252-5233; www.punchline.com

When it comes to comedy, The Punchline is no joke. It's the oldest and best-known laugh house in Atlanta, as well as the largest. Located in a suburban strip mall just outside of Atlanta, the club has heard one-liners from top comics such as Eddie Murphy, Chris Tucker, Tim Allen, Jerry Seinfeld, Dave Chappelle and Jeff Foxworthy. The Punchline serves a full dinner menu, so you can make a night of it. It gets quite crowded here and not all the seats are great, but the comedy is usually worth it.
Prices and show times vary.

WHOLE WORLD IMPROV THEATRE
1216 Spring St., Midtown, 404-817-7529; www.wholeworldtheatre.com

Whole World Improv is just as its name suggests, an improv house. Well at least that's how it started. The improv comedy troupe has expanded into traditional drama, but its core is the improv shows, which can get pretty risqué during weekends as the rowdy emcee eggs on the late-night audience to participate in the bawdy fun. Entry is general admission and shows sell out quickly; it's best to buy tickets to weekend shows in advance. Whole World also offers kids' shows, classes and improv workshops to train your future little improv comedians.
Tickets: $16 and up. Tuesday-Sunday 8 and 10:30 p.m.

DANCE
ATLANTA BALLET
404-873-5811; www.atlantaballet.com

The Atlanta Ballet has been pirouetting across Atlanta for more than 78 years. Founded in 1929 by Dorothy Alexander, the company was one of the first to be formed in a smaller city community. She held the first rehearsals for the Dorothy Alexander Concert Group in her garage and as the troupe grew, it eventually became the Atlanta Ballet. She led the company for more than 30 years. Today the Atlanta Ballet is one of the country's premier professional dance companies. It is known for both its classical renditions—the annual *Nutcracker* is a must—as well as innovative programs, often with a local twist; the company partnered with OutKast's Antwan "Big Boi" Patton to premiere *Big* and also produced *Shed Your Skin*, a project with Indigo Girls.
Tickets: $15 and up. October-May, Nutcracker in December.

MUSIC
THE ATLANTA OPERA
404-881-8801; www.atlantaopera.org

The Atlanta Opera is a relatively young company but has developed a following among opera aficionados for its high quality and elaborate staging. Over the last three decades, the opera has done 75 different productions and seen attendance reach nearly 1 million. It generally runs traditional programming, including works by Puccini, Rossini, Verdi and Wagner. If you're a hardcore opera patron, snag tickets to the opening night fund-raising ball, a highlight of

the Atlanta social calendar.
Tickets: $27.50 and up. October-May.

ATLANTA SYMPHONY ORCHESTRA

1280 Peachtree St. N.E., Midtown, 404-733-4900; www.atlantasymphony.org

The Atlanta Symphony Orchestra is part of the huge Woodruff Arts Center in Midtown, the largest arts center in the Southeast and fourth largest in the country. The ASO, in its 64th season, is worthy of its grand digs, as it's one of the country's top orchestras known for its live performances, choruses and Grammy Award-winning recordings. Director Robert Spano is hailed as one of the top conductors in the business and the ASO's glowing reviews show it. You can catch Yo-Yo Ma, Itzhak Perlman and more at the ASO's main concert venues: the Symphony Hall in Woodruff, Verizon Wireless Amphitheatre in Alpharetta and Chastain Amphitheatre. The orchestra does the classics, but also dabbles in different genres, like a jazz collaboration with Wynton Marsalis.
Tickets: $15 and up. September-June, Tuesday-Sunday.

BLIND WILLIE'S

828 N. Highland Ave., Virginia Highland, 404-873-2583; www.blindwilliesblues.com

Named for influential bluesman Blind Willie McTell, Blind Willie's is a legendary blues house. You'll find local acts like Francine Reed, who belts it out so hard she practically doesn't need a microphone, as well as major bands Lazy Lester and Rufus Thomas, who love to play at this venue for its focus on the three sources of blues sound: Chicago, Memphis and New Orleans. Once you hear Reed's robust voice, you won't need any other evidence that sound is a good one.
Cover charges vary.

DONNA AND MARVIN SCHWARTZ CENTER FOR PERFORMING ARTS, EMERSON CONCERT HALL

1700 N. Decatur Road N.E., Emory, 404-727-5050; www.arts.emory.edu

Located on the bucolic Emory University campus, the Donna and Marvin Schwartz Center hosts more than just amateurish college bands. You'll find pros such as the Warsaw Philharmonic and the Atlanta Opera filling the hall with music. You'll also see dance and theatric performances there. The Cherry Logan Emerson Concert Hall is the cherry on top, featuring a custom-built, Daniel Jaeckel Opus 45 pipe organ. The hall, modeled after Boston's Symphony Hall and Vienna's Musikverein, is long and narrow and has a soaring ceiling, making the acoustics pitch-perfect.
Ticket prices vary.

EDDIE'S ATTIC

515-B N. McDonough Road, Decatur, 404-377-4976; www.eddiesattic.com

One of Atlanta's most hopping live music venues, Eddie's Attic has long been a favorite for nationally known artists, some of whom are local acts who got their start here, including John Mayer, Indigo Girls, Sugarland and The Black Crowes. The main stage "Listening Room" only seats 185 people and has a great acoustic stage, making it an intimate experience. Maybe a little too intimate, if you're claustrophobic. In that case, head out to the adjacent rooftop grill, where you can spread out and still hear the music. Both rooms offer good food and

drinks, but the draw here is the indie folk music.
Prices and hours vary.

NORTHSIDE TAVERN

1058 Howell Mill Road, Westside, 404-874-8745; www.northsidetavern.com

No pretense here—this isn't a restaurant with a stage. This is just a good old-fashioned dive blues bar. Housed on a street corner in what was once a gas station, the building looks dilapidated, in fact abandoned, from the outside. Inside, it's not much better, but that's what makes the blues the blues. For more than 30 years, Northside Tavern has entertained everyone from neighborhood drunks to Buckhead businessmen and college students to housewives with blues every night of the week. Try to catch regular Mudcat Dudeck, a local fave.
Admission: Sunday-Thursday free, Friday, Saturday $10.

SMITHS OLDE BAR

1578 Piedmont Ave., Little Five Points, 404-875-1522; www.smithsoldebar.com

The granddaddy of Atlanta music bars, Smiths Olde Bar is a labyrinth of music, with five rooms devoted to the three major recreation groups: drinking, eating and listening to live music. Go to the downstairs bar first for a cold beer, stop in the dining room for some classic bar grub, then head to the music room and Atlanta room, the crown jewels. Here, you'll catch diverse acts from the famous (David Bowie played here) to local bands, from bluegrass to punk. Come nightly to get your fill of the holy live music trinity.
Prices vary. Monday-Saturday 5 p.m.-3 a.m., Sunday 4 p.m.-12 a.m.

STAR COMMUNITY BAR

437 Moreland Ave., Little Five Points, 404-681-9018; www.starbar.net

When you get bored of pretentious bars, drinks and people, it's time to get back to basics. Head to Little Five Points' Star Bar, as it's known, one of the greatest dive bars in Atlanta. Its grunginess belies its roots as a great honky-tonk venue—both in music and mood (though bands can run the gamut from country to punk). Stop by the Grace Vault, a room with a window that is an elaborate shrine to Elvis, complete with a golden toilet, various Elvis statues and of course, a velvet painting. You can kneel and pay homage to the King. But kitsch isn't what makes it a dive; any dive bar worth its grime must have just one factor: cheap beer. And Star Bar delivers, as Pabst Blue Ribbon is the brew of choice here—and it's always $2.
Cover charges and hours vary.

TABERNACLE

152 Luckie St. N.W., Downtown, 404-659-9022; www.tabernacleatl.com

The Tabernacle downtown is a sanctuary of music. It started the 20th century as a Baptist church—hence the name—and ended the era as a House of Blues when Atlanta hosted the Olympics. Since the Games, it has become one of the top music venues in Atlanta, with Elvis Costello, Prince and Elton John all stopping by to preach to the choirs. The Tabernacle holds 2,600 people; downstairs is general admission, standing room only, but you can snag a seat upstairs in one of two balconies. The building has retained its church charm, with soaring ceilings, a giant organ, a crystal chandelier and stained glass windows adding to the aura and atmosphere. Explore the other rooms in this historic building; they are now used for lounges. If you want a more intimate vibe, go to The Cotton Club in the basement, where you can catch local bands. It'll make you a believer.

Prices vary.

VARIETY PLAYHOUSE
1099 Euclid Ave., Little Five Points, 404-524-7354; www.variety-playhouse.com

Some great musicians hit up this theater-style venue in Little Five Points, including everyone from Gnarls Barkley to Squeeze. But Atlantans in the know come to see Kingsized, a local Elvis Presley tribute band that has developed a cult-like following. Kingsized, with sidekick dancing girls Dames Aflame, doles out some jailhouse rock during three concerts a year here—for Elvis' birthday, death day and a holiday concert. These events are almost as legendary as the King himself; people have been known to scalp tickets outside. All shows are general admission and include standing areas, seats and tables. Just don't forget your blue suede shoes.

Prices vary.

THEATER
ALLIANCE THEATRE AND HERTZ STAGE
1280 Peachtree St. N.E., Midtown, 404-733-4650; www.alliancetheatre.org

Locals take pride in the Alliance, especially since it won the Regional Theatre Tony Award in 2007. Here you'll find a lot of plays with distinctive local flavor, from the tissue-box-worthy debut of Alice Walker's *The Color Purple* musical to the world premiere of *Aida* by Tim Rice and Atlanta's honorary native son Elton John. Many prominent Atlanta playwrights, such as Alfred Uhry (who wrote the play *Driving Miss Daisy*), have launched their careers at the theater. It also is one of the few leading regional theaters in the country that produces full-scale productions for both adults and children. Housed in the sprawling Woodruff Arts Center, the Alliance also holds the Hertz Stage, a black box theater that presents a variety of shows, including original plays. Every year, the season takes a holiday break so the Alliance can stage that perennial chestnut *A Christmas Carol*.

Tickets: $15-$65. August-April.

CENTER FOR PUPPETRY ARTS
1404 Spring St. N.E., Midtown, 404-873-3089; www.puppet.org

Your kids will have a blast here, but you'll be too busy re-creating scenes from *Fraggle Rock* to notice. This is the place to check out puppets, or rather Muppets, from Jim Henson's workshop. The center is the largest organization in the U.S. dedicated to puppetry and opened in 30 years ago with a ribbon cutting by Mr. Green himself, Kermit the Frog. You can take classes or browse the museum to see classic dolls like puppeteer Wayland Flowers' Madame. But children will want hit one of the two stages to watch puppet shows such as *The Ugly Duckling, Brer Rabbit & Friends* and *Jack & The Beanstalk*. You could catch one of the adult-themed shows, such as *Don Quixote*, or go back and play with the Fraggles.

Admission: $6-$10. Tuesday-Saturday 9 a.m-5 p.m., Sunday 11 a.m.-5 p.m. Free Thursday after 1 p.m.

THE COBB ENERGY PERFORMING ARTS CENTRE

2800 Cobb Galleria Parkway, Outside the Perimeter, 770-916-2800; www.cobbenergycentre.com

One of the newest venues in Atlanta, The Cobb Energy Centre is just outside the city center, but still in the confines of the metro Atlanta area. It's just off the interstate, so getting in and out is easy. Plus, parking is plentiful and free—a rarity in most of the city's concert venues. But the draw isn't the convenience. The centerpiece of the Centre is the John A. Williams Theatre, a state-of-the-art facility that features remarkable acoustics and a breathtaking design that is a modern take on classic theaters and opera houses. It is adorned in opulent dark wood, red, purple and gold, and the ceiling features gold and silver metals that create a shimmering, intimate canopy. For a classic experience, book one of the 14 private boxes to get a primo view of the Atlanta Ballet (but you won't see *The Nutcracker* here) or the Atlanta Opera, both of which call the Centre home. Or catch one of the Broadway Series shows such as *Spamalot* and numerous concerts and shows, from Jon Stewart to Alanis Morissette.

Ticket prices vary.

DAD'S GARAGE

280 Elizabeth St., Inman Park, 404-523-3141; www.dadsgarage.com

Grab a bucket of beer and catch an off-color puppet show or the not-so-traditional annual twisted holiday tale, A Very Merry Unauthorized Children's Scientology Pageant. This Inman Park theater is staffed by more than 300 performers and volunteers, which contributes to the passion people feel about this place. Hipsters and soccer moms alike crowd the theater to see comedy, puppet shows—R- and G-rated versions—and original plays. Besides such gems as *The Song of the Dead: A Zombie Musical*, Dad's Garage hosts *Scandal!*, a weekly show featuring the Southeast's only improv soap opera team. If that weren't enough, there's an itty-bitty black box theater, Top Shelf, which is a great place to meet someone, since you'll practically sit on his or her lap.

Admission: Mainstage and Top Shelf $10-$28, Improv $10-$15. Thursday-Saturday 8, 10:30 p.m.

FERST CENTER FOR THE ARTS

349 Ferst Drive N.W., Midtown, 404-894-9600, www.ferstcenter.gatech.edu

While Georgia Tech is known for producing a bevy of engineering and math geeks, the university also has become a hub for the arts. The Ferst Center, right in the middle of the campus, plays host to several big-name acts every year, including The Capitol Steps. The theater features a proscenium stage and a full orchestra pit, enabling a wide array of performances, including music, theater, dance and opera. There's something for everyone here, from blues to classical, ballet to flamenco, and several Atlanta performing arts companies call the arts hub home, including the Ballethnic Dance Company and the Atlanta Gay Men's Chorus.

Tickets: $15-$100. September-May.

THE FOX THEATRE

660 Peachtree St., Midtown, 404-881-2100; www.foxtheatre.org

The Fox is a theater, a movie house, a concert hall and an event space all in one. It's one of Atlanta's most beloved venues, even though it did not host the big-screen premiere of *Gone with the Wind*, as some people think. This ornate building was erected in the 1920s as the Yaarab Temple Shrine Mosque and reflects Americans' fascination with all things Egyptian (which became all the rage when King Tut's tomb was discovered in 1922); the interior's elaborate, exquisite mosaics in bold, beautiful jewel tones are worth seeing even without taking in a show. The theater, which hosts 300 performances and attracts 750,000 visitors per year, is a source of pride among Atlantans as the impetus for historic restoration and preservation. But it's what's on the stage that'll make you come here. The Fox hosts two Broadway series, which is unusual for any theater: Broadway Across America and Theater of the Stars bring hot plays such as *Wicked* and *Mamma Mia!* to the theater house. During the holidays, the Atlanta Ballet prances onto the stage to present *The Nutcracker*—a tradition for generations of Atlantans who come dressed to impress, particularly aspiring little ballerinas. Don't miss The Fox's crowning glory, "Mighty Mo," a custom-made Möller pipe organ that was built for the theater's opening in 1929. With 3,622 pipes in five chambers, it is the second-largest theater organ in the world after Radio City's in New York. Hear the live organ blare during its own shows during the Coca-Cola Summer Film Festival, where you can catch current and classic movies, and *The Nutcracker*.

Ticket prices vary. Guided tours: $5-$10 Monday, Wednesday, Thursday 10 a.m., Saturday, 10 and 11 a.m. through the Atlanta Preservation Center (404-688-3350; www.preserveatlanta.com).

WHERE TO STAY

BUCKHEAD
★★★GRAND HYATT ATLANTA
3300 Peachtree Road N.E., Buckhead, 404-237-1234; www.hyatt.com

The Japanese garden landscaped with statuary, a sprinkling of trees and tumbling waterfalls, sets the mood for a stay at this Buckhead hotel. Rooms follow suit in the relaxation department: Pillow-top mattresses, high-thread-count sheets and down blankets top the beds. Take advantage of the hotel's complimentary transportation to any destination within two miles, a radius perfect for exploring Buckhead's restaurants and nightclubs. Or settle into a plush armchair at the Onyx bar for an appetizer such as the truffled lobster martini.

438 rooms. Restaurant, bar. Fitness center. Pool. Business center. Pets accepted. $151-250

★★★★INTERCONTINENTAL BUCKHEAD
3315 Peachtree St. N.E., Buckhead, 404-946-9000; www.intercontinental.com

Shopaholics will adore the InterContinental's prime location in the heart of Buckhead's high-end shopping district. The hotel is known for its in-house spa (try a personal facial analysis or reflexology foot treatment), its posh rooms with sweet blue-and-white floral bedspreads and marble bath, and its top-notch concierges. After you check in, head to the French brasserie Au Pied de Cochon for a bowl of to-die-for French onion soup to fuel up before hitting the shops. After your shopping spree, reward yourself for the bargains you scored by sipping a snifter of Hennessy at the hotel's XO Bar, known for its long list of specialty cognacs.

422 rooms. Restaurant, bar. Fitness center. Pool. Spa. Business center. Pets accepted. $151-250

★★★JW MARRIOTT HOTEL BUCKHEAD ATLANTA

3300 Lenox Road, Buckhead, 404-262-3344; www.marriott.com

Connected to Buckhead's Lenox Square Mall and across the street from a MARTA station, this hotel is also a short walk from luxury shopping and some of the city's best restaurants. But who says you'll want to leave? It'll be tempting to just hole up in your room, which brims with details like pillow-top mattresses and a separate porcelain soaking tub and shower. Be sure to visit the onsite Dass spa; it's just the place for a seaweed scrub or a hot-stone massage. Most convenient of all is that after your blissful treatment, your room is just a few steps away.

367 rooms. Restaurant, bar. Fitness center. Pool. Spa. Business center. $251-350

★★★★THE MANSION ON PEACHTREE, A ROSEWOOD HOTEL

3376 Peachtree Road, Buckhead, 404-995-7500; www.rwmansiononpeachtree.com

You'll feel like you live in a mansion when you check into this hotel. Opened in May 2008, this ritzy spot in the heart of Buckhead is the tallest hotel in the neighborhood. Made from limestone and cast stone, the structure soars 580 feet above the traffic on Peachtree Road. The service is just as grand as its hulking exterior; you'll get your own professionally trained butler, and housekeeping will tidy up your room twice a day and turn down your sheets at night. And what a room it is: The gray and tawny space is spiced up by a dark-paneled accent wall flanked by mirrors, a velvety slate-colored armchair and fresh flowers daily. You'll also get free deliveries of breakfast, snacks and hors d'oeuvres. Be sure to visit the enormous 29 Spa, where Lydia Mondavi—as in the Mondavi wine family—offers her trademark antioxidant-rich grapeseed treatments, and the Tom Colicchio-owned restaurant Craft Atlanta, which began serving its hearty American fare in late 2008. You'll feel right at home in this manse.

127 rooms. Complimentary breakfast. Restaurant, bar. Fitness center. Pool. Spa. Business center. Pets accepted. $351 and up

★★★★THE RITZ-CARLTON, BUCKHEAD

3434 Peachtree Road N.E., Buckhead, 404-237-2700; www.ritzcarlton.com

Those who love tradition will fit right in as they sweep by the uniformed doorman at this regal Buckhead hotel into a dazzling lobby laden with chandeliers, antique rugs and comfortable furniture. The pale peach and green rooms also pack a punch with marble and granite accents, down pillows and soft linens. The Lobby Lounge is a favorite afternoon-tea destination for locals, so if you think you'll be in need of a late-day pick-me-up, make reservations as soon as possible to enjoy a spread of scones and clotted cream, delicate finger sandwiches and divine pastries. Or, save your appetite for The Café at the Ritz-Carlton, a restaurant known for its delicious regional cuisine and its equally impressive wine selection. It's just the thing after a shopping spree at the nearby Phipps Plaza mall.

517 rooms. Restaurant, bar. Fitness center. Pool. Business center. Pets accepted. $351 and up

★★★★THE ST. REGIS ATLANTA

88 West Paces Ferry Road, Buckhead, 404-563-7900; www.starwoodhotels.com

The sweeping grounds alone are enough to convince you never to leave this elegant Buckhead property. Wait until you set your sights on the guest rooms. Floor to ceiling windows, original art work and ebony finishes provide a sense of upscale luxury, while state-of-the-art flat-screen TVs and iPod sound docks keep rooms in line with the newest tech trends. Butler service ensures that you won't want for anything. Rejuvinate at the Remede Spa or spend the afternoon in the 40,000-square-foot pool piazza. Dining options run the gamut from casual bistro fare to elegant afternoon tea in the Long Gallery.

151 rooms. Restaurant, bar. Fitness center. Pool. Spa. $351 and up

★★★W ATLANTA – BUCKHEAD

3377 Peachtree Road N.E., Buckhead, 678-500-3100; www.starwoodhotels.com

To stand out from its posh Bucktown surroundings, this hotel gives a funky Southern twist to the usually more subdued W chain. Enter the lobby and see an antler chandelier dangle above rainbow-zigzag striped chairs and a mirror in the shape of a girl's silhouette on a wall. Design doctor Thom Filicia (of *Queer Eye for the Straight Guy* fame) brings a similarly eclectic retro vibe to the rooms, whose feather beds are framed by a light teal padded headboard that reaches the ceiling and spreads above the goose-down duvets to give a modern take on a canopy bed. The rooms get a lived-in feel with mismatched chairs, colorful art covering the walls and splashes of bold color such as a pumpkin desk. But the hotel isn't all retro-hip—rooftop bar Whiskey Blue provides a trendy respite. Head to the mid-century-modern-inspired joint, sink into a couch and order up a yummy Clementine Crush (Svedka Clementine vodka, fresh orange juice, tonic, ginger root and sugar). Although the photos of old-school rockers like David Bowie and Bob Dylan on the walls and the beautiful people sipping martinis will capture your attention, the gorgeous view of Buckhead is the main attraction at this hotel.

291 rooms. Restaurant, bar. Fitness center. Pool. Business center. Pets accepted. $251-350

★★★THE WESTIN BUCKHEAD ATLANTA

3391 Peachtree Road N.E., Buckhead, 404-365-0065; www.starwoodhotels.com

The Westin of course touts its Heavenly beds and cribs, both of which live up to their names with plush mattresses and pillows. You'll be so wrapped up in the cushy bed you won't even notice the modern dark-wood furniture, the rich browns and little bursts of blue from the curved loveseat and the stripes on the underside of the curtains. If Fido's in tow, he'll get to enjoy a Heavenly dog bed. The Westin takes the Heavenly moniker one step further with its Heavenly bath; the double-headed shower fixture offers more water, more power and adjustable spray options. Other details that will help you reach cloud nine include in-room massage services, a babysitting service and an indoor heated pool and sauna. Though concierges could easily point you to some fine-dining options in the area, instead head for the hotel's onsite restaurant, The Palm, part of the New York City-based restaurant empire. Order one of the oversized lobsters for which the restaurant is famous—it's, dare we say, heavenly.

365 rooms. Restaurant, bar. Fitness center. Pool. Business center. Pets accepted. $151-250

DOWNTOWN

★★★ATLANTA MARRIOTT DOWNTOWN

160 Spring St. N.W., Downtown, 404-688-8600; www.marriott.com

At this conveniently located downtown hotel, the luxurious down comfort-ers and super-fluffy pillows will guarantee a good night's rest so that you'll be recharged and ready to explore Atlanta when daylight breaks. The hotel puts you in the middle of the attractions; Georgia Aquarium, The World of Coca-Cola, Imagine It! Children's Museum and Centennial Olympic Park are all within walking distance. It's also a popular place among business travelers, thanks to two floors of meeting space, a well-equipped business center and Web TV in the guest rooms. After hitting all of the tourist spots, grab a late-night cocktail at the lobby bar, Liquid Lounge, where you can into one of the plush sofas and ottomans. It's just the thing before settling back into that comfy bed.

312 rooms. Restaurant, bar. Fitness center. Pool. Business center. $151-250

★★★ATLANTA MARRIOTT MARQUIS

265 Peachtree Center Ave., Downtown, 404-521-0000; www.marriott.com

If you have an eye for detail, this centrally located hotel will give you plenty to look at. A recent renovation upgraded the guest rooms with sleek granite coun-tertops in the bathrooms, Bath & Body Works toiletries and contemporary, sculptural lamps. The indoor/outdoor pool feels as hip as one in South Beach, with its airy cabanas and modernistic lounge chairs. Pulse Bar, too, has a see-and-be-seen feel, with its central bar that looks almost like a gleaming modern sculpture, and dizzying views of the hotel's central atrium.

1,663 rooms. Restaurant, bar. Fitness center. Pool. Spa. $151-250

★★★THE ELLIS HOTEL

176 Peachtree St. N.W., Downtown, 404-523-5155;
www.ellishotel.com

If you're a woman traveling alone, this boutique hotel in the heart of downtown is for you. The Women Only floor offers secured entry, and rooms feature amenities like slippers and curling irons. But guys and gals alike will dig the spare, elegant rooms decorated in chocolate, white and other neutral hues, not to mention the 32-inch LCD televisions, iPod docking stations, beds with fine linens and ostrich headboards, and bathrooms with white limestone floors and walls. If you're hungry, head to the e Street Grill for Southern-style fare, including addictive fried peach pie and Bourbon pecan bread pudding—anyone with a sweet tooth will have trouble deciding between these two delicious treats.

127 rooms. Restaurant, bar. Fitness center. Business center. Pets accepted. $151-250

★★★THE GLENN HOTEL

100 Marietta St. N.W., Downtown, 866-404-4536;
www.glennhotel.com

If you crave some Manhattan chic down South, head to the city's first boutique hotel, part of Marriot's new Autograph Collection of hotels. Each room comes with a flat-screen TV, a rain-flow shower, a pillow-top mattress and 400-thread-count linens. If you're here for business, you'll easily settle into the room's nicely sized desk and its ergonomically designed chair. It's all the better to burn the midnight oil in the warm room with ivory bedspreads and sheer curtains. Corporate types will also like the two conference rooms, the 24-hour business center, and the PurDigital technology, which transmits voice, video and data files in a snap. What's more, the onsite Maxim Prime Steakhouse is perfect for entertaining clients. Whether your visit involves business or pleasure, The Glenn's central location, makes it easy to get wherever you need to go and enjoy everything the city has to offer.

110 rooms. Restaurant, bar. Fitness center. Business center. Pets accepted. $151-250

★★★HILTON ATLANTA

255 Courtland St. N.E., Downtown, 404-659-2000; www.hilton.com

You'll have plenty of room to stretch at this downtown hotel, which features extra-large guest rooms and spacious bathrooms with full-sized tubs. Rooms are basic (think beige and burgundy) but comfortable, with flat-screen TVs, triple-sheeted beds topped with duvets, and Crabtree & Evelyn toiletries. For dinner, head to Nikolai's Roof, a fine-dining restaurant on the hotel's 28th floor, where you'll have a fantastic view of the sparkling skyline to complement your heavy French-Russian meal (be sure to end with the signature Grand Marnier soufflé with orange almond crème fraîche). Or, sip a Mai Tai at Trader Vic's, the onsite tiki-themed watering hole. If you're ambitious, go to the fitness center, one of the biggest among the downtown area's hotels, to work off your supper on the jogging track or the tennis courts.

1,242 rooms. Restaurant, bar. Fitness center. Tennis. Pool. Business center. Pets accepted. $151-250

★★★HYATT REGENCY ATLANTA

265 Peachtree St. N.E., Downtown, 404-577-1234; www.hyatt.com

One of the nation's top convention and trade show facilities, this downtown hotel adjacent to the Mall at Peachtree Center has extensive ballroom, exhibit and meeting spaces. It's also ideally situated for leisure travelers who want easy access to attractions such as the Georgia Aquarium, High Museum of Art and the King Center. But there are other perks aside from the location; this hotel offers chic rooms decorated with soft neutral bedding, marble-topped bedside tables and dark wood furnishings with brushed chrome hardware. Nice touches like a morning newspaper and an in-room coffee maker will make it easy to get your day going. If you want to do some jogging after a sedentary day of sitting in meetings, stop by the Stay Fit at Hyatt fitness center and borrow a GPS armband. Not only will it make sure you don't get lost in Atlanta's tangle of Downtown streets, but it'll also track your heart rate and distance, giving you one less thing to stress about after a busy day at work.

1,260 rooms. Restaurant, bar. Fitness center. Pool. Business center. $251-350

★★★OMNI HOTEL AT CNN CENTER

100 CNN Center, Downtown, 404-659-0000; www.omnihotels.com

If you want to be in the thick of things, check into the Omni, which is part of CNN Center. You can beat the crowds by just rolling out of bed and catching the first CNN Studio Tour of the day. But it isn't all about location at this hotel; you'll also get lovely views of the city's skyline and Centennial Olympic Park from your room, which invites lingering with a comfortable leather armchair, a bed piled high with pillows, a desk overlooking that stunning view, and a marble and granite bathroom. Health nuts will be pumped about the Get Fit rooms, which come equipped with treadmills and healthy snacks, and the onsite location of Natural Body Spa, one of Atlanta's most popular spa chains. After all, you do want to look your best in case you get an impromptu close-up on your CNN Center tour.

1,070 rooms. Restaurant, bar. Fitness center. Pool. Spa. Business center. Pets accepted. $151-250

★★★THE RITZ-CARLTON, ATLANTA

181 Peachtree St. N.E., Downtown, 404-659-0400; www.ritzcarlton.com

Stay at this luxury hotel and you'll be treated to skyline views and easy access to the city's top destinations, among them Turner Field, Philips Arena and The World of Coca-Cola. Beyond the spectacular view, enjoy your recently renovated room's marble floors, Frette linens, flat-screen TV and iPod docking station. If the vista and the fine linens aren't posh enough for you, snag a reservation for afternoon tea with scones and pretty pastries in the Lobby Lounge, or enjoy the upscale Southern fare at the Atlanta Grill, which has views of Peachtree Street.

444 rooms. Restaurant, bar. Fitness center. Business center. $251-350

★★★SHERATON ATLANTA HOTEL

165 Courtland St., Downtown, 404-659-6500; www.sheratonatlantahotel.com

After a redesign not too long ago, the downtown hotel looks less like a ho-hum chain and more like an Art Deco boutique masterpiece. The artsy mood begins with the mod, geometric white awning stretching over the hotel's entryway and continues through to the gleaming marble floor in the lobby and the luxurious pool area, which has a retro Southern California feel, with lush potted plants, a retractable roof and bistro tables for alfresco cocktails. Although the guest rooms and suites are of a traditional styling, they echo the art deco feel, with angular contemporary sofas and armchairs, and graphic artwork dotting the walls.

763 rooms. Restaurant, bar. Fitness center. Pool. Business center. Pets accepted. $151-250

★★★TWELVE HOTEL & RESIDENCES CENTENNIAL PARK

400 W. Peachtree St., Downtown, 404-418-1212; www.twelvehotels.com

This boutique hotel is like your super-chic home away from home. In fact, some people do get to call this soaring tower home, since it has a residential area. Each suite comes with skyline views, full-size kitchens with stainless-steel appliances, a living room area and private balcony. And of course, you'll get the latest technology: flat-panel televisions, DVD players and complimentary wireless Internet, as well as a computerized concierge system that allows you to do everything from order room service to check your email on an in-room monitor and keyboard. As if that weren't enough, the hotel partnered with a local car dealer to offer a Bed & Beemer package, which includes your choice of BMW to drive around town.

102 suites. Restaurant, bar. Fitness center. Pool. Business center. Pets accepted. $151-250

★★★THE WESTIN PEACHTREE PLAZA, ATLANTA

210 Peachtree St., Downtown, 404-659-1400; www.starwoodhotels.com

This glistening, circular 73-story tower is a dominant part of Atlanta's skyline and is considered to be one of the Western Hemisphere's largest hotels. The sweeping city view is the star in your room, which has floor-to-ceiling windows, so be sure to request a high floor when you make your reservation. But the view inside the room is just as nice, particularly that of your bed, a soothing white oasis of soft cotton sheets, a fluffy comforter and a down pillow, all atop a designer mattress. But if you really want an amazing vista, take the glass elevator up to the spinning rooftop bar, The Sundial, for a 360-degree panorama of the city to accent your Peachy Keen Daiquiri or Atlanta Hurricane.

1,068 rooms. Restaurant, bar. Fitness center. Pool. Business center. Pets accepted. $151-250

★★★W ATLANTA - DOWNTOWN

45 Ivan Allen Jr. Blvd., Downtown, 404-582-5800; www.starwoodhotels.com

Opened in January 2009, this Downtown hotel marks the fourth and newest outpost of the W chain in Atlanta. The Downtown location is looking to outdo its sister hotels, offering the city's first hotel rooftop heliport. Plus, it's the second of the W quadruplets to have an ahh-inducing Bliss spa (the Midtown branch also has one). This hotel goes for sleek and chic, with rooms done up in inviting chocolate browns—such as the padded headboards—dark wood and silver accents, like the skinny bedside lamps. But what makes the youngest W stand out is its central location: It's only steps away from tourist favorites such as the World of Coca-Cola, the Georgia Aquarium, Imagine It! The Children's Museum of Atlanta and Centennial Olympic Park.

237 rooms. Restaurant, bar. Fitness center. Pool. Spa. Pets accepted. $151-250

MIDTOWN

★★★★★FOUR SEASONS HOTEL ATLANTA

75 14th St., Midtown, 404-881-9898; www.fourseasons.com/atlanta

At this hotel, you get just what you need when you need it. If your kids are restless, there are board games and other goodies to engage them. If you're congested, an attendant will bring you a humidifier or an ionizer. If you're feeling stressed, the spa's detox massage uses a blend of essential oils to help frequent travelers release tension. Plus, there's your serene room, with a crisp white comforter adorned with a simple border, rich dark wood furniture and a DVD player with a DVD library. There isn't any need that's not covered. The hotel even rents laptops and pagers to harried business types who've left their portable devices behind. Limousine service is always available here, but the hotel is in walkable Midtown, so stretch your legs and visit the High Museum of Art or any of the eateries along nearby Crescent Avenue.

244 rooms. Restaurant, bar. Fitness center. Pool. Spa. Business center. $351 and up

★★★GEORGIA TECH HOTEL AND CONFERENCE CENTER

800 Spring St. N.W., Midtown, 404-347-9440; www.gatechhotel.com

Leave it to a technology school to have a state-of-the-art hotel on the cusp of its campus. Located in the school's Technology Square development, it's decorated like any boutique hotel (mahogany and cherry wood furnishings, posh linens in warm hues) but goosed with techie touches such as flat-screen televisions, laptop-ready desks and wireless technology. With a lap pool, restaurant, business center and meeting space, this spot is an ideal place to stay and host your annual tech-geek convention, or any other conference, for that matter.

252 rooms. Restaurant, bar. Fitness center. Pool. Business center. $151-250

★★★THE GEORGIAN TERRACE HOTEL

659 Peachtree St. N.E., Midtown, 800-651-2316; www.thegeorgianterrace.com

Clark Gable and Vivien Leigh stayed at this Flatiron-style hotel back in 1939, when it hosted the premiere reception for the Atlanta classic *Gone with the Wind*. Built in 1911, this National Register of Historic Places-listed hotel has also lent its rooms to old-time celebrities such as F. Scott Fitzgerald, Tallulah Bankhead, Rudolph Valentino and many other famous folks throughout its history. Though it is rooted in the past, it has also planted itself in the future with a multi-million-dollar renovation on guest rooms, adding modern and antique touches—like wood furniture with old-fashioned handles, full-size refrigerators and stoves with ovens—as well as a junior Olympic rooftop pool, among other things. As you admire the elegant pillars, sparking crystal chandeliers and graceful arched windows in the spacious lobby, you can almost imagine Gable sipping a mint julep and greeting his fans.

326 rooms. Restaurant, bar. Fitness center. Pool. Business center. $151-250

★★★W ATLANTA - MIDTOWN

188 14th St. N.E., Midtown, 404-892-6000; www.starwoodhotels.com

Within walking distance of Piedmont Park, the High Museum of Art and Midtown's offbeat eateries and nightclubs, this was the first W hotel to open in Atlanta. Pick from six levels of accommodation, ranging from the Wonderful Room (outfitted in 350-thread-count bedding, great Bliss bath products and a 37-inch HDTV with plug-in for your laptop), all the way up to the very roomy Extreme Wow Suite, where you'll enjoy panoramic views of distant Stone Mountain, a dining area for eight and a 42-inch LCD TV with DVD/CD player (and a collection of CDs for your listening pleasure). If you can drag yourself away from your posh digs, the hotel features plenty of New York City imports, including Bliss spa, Jean-Georges Vongerichten's Spice Market (with a menu inspired by Southeast Asian street food) and nightclub impresario Rande

Gerber's Whiskey Park (and, as a W guest, you'll get to sweep past the long line at the velvet rope).

433 rooms. Restaurant, bar. Fitness center. Pool. Spa. Business center. Pets accepted. $151-250

WHERE TO EAT

BUCKHEAD

★★★ANTHONY'S FINE DINING

3109 Piedmont Road, Buckhead, 404-262-7379; www.anthonysfinedining.com

A gracious 200-year-old mansion, relocated brick-by-brick from its original site 117 miles east of the city, is now an ideal place for weddings, proms and tourists eager to experience the Old South. While it's predominantly an event venue, the restaurant is open for à la carte dining. The house's various dining areas include a cozy brick kitchen, rooms with fireplaces, and a sunny porch overlooking the lovely landscaped lawn and gardens. The old-school menu holds no surprises or innovations, just well-prepared classics like Châteaubriand for two, Dijon-crusted rack of lamb and crab-stuffed grouper fillets. Desserts are a must, particularly the fantastic Bananas Foster for two, which is showily flambéed tableside, a retro touch that surely the mansion's old ghosts would appreciate.

American. Dinner. Closed Sunday. Reservations requested. $36-85

★★★ARIA

490 E. Paces Ferry, Atlanta, 404-233-7673; www.aria-atl.com

You'll have to vie for a seat on the cushy red sofas in Aria's cramped bar—order an aperitif from the well-curated wine list (which includes a nice selection of half-bottles) to make the wait bearable—before being ushered into an airy dining room. The entire space is a study in black and white, from the aforementioned bar, painted a claustrophobic black, to the contrastingly spacious white-and-black dining room. Sister to Canoe restaurant, Aria offers a menu that similarly embraces high-quality and seasonal ingredients, like farm-raised duck and beef, locally caught trout and farmers' market vegetables. Organic pork from a local farm is braised and served with collard greens and black-eyed peas. Don't miss the comforting yet upscale desserts, which might include a dense semolina pudding strewn with figs and served with pink pepper ice cream, or a warm and satisfying chocolate cheesecake in a crisp walnut crust.

American. Dinner. Closed Sunday. Bar. Reservations recommended. Outdoor seating. $36-85

★★★ATLANTA FISH MARKET

265 Pharr Road N.E., Buckhead, 404-262-3165; www.buckheadrestaurants.com

The space is cavernous, but tourists and locals still find themselves waiting for a table at this always-packed seafood favorite. Fresh-as-can-be seafood is lovingly displayed in glass cases; have the fish of your choice made with one of several preparations, such as Hong Kong-style (steamed, with Asian sauce and sticky rice) or blackened. You can also match your fish to a vintage from the lengthy wine list—try lesser-known discoveries or an unusual Spanish macabeo. When your party finally secures a table, order the tower of seafood; its chilled Maine lobster, iced mussels, oysters and jumbo shrimp are perfect for a crowd.

Seafood. Lunch, dinner. Bar. Reservations recommended. $36-85

★★★AU PIED DE COCHON

InterContinental Buckhead, 3315 Peachtree Road N.E., Buckhead, 404-946-9070;
www.aupieddecochonatlanta.com

If you feel like you've stepped into a posh Parisian brasserie when you enter Au Pied de Cochon, don't be surprised. It's related to a 62-year-old restaurant of the same name in Paris, opened by a pig butcher to accommodate the erratic hours of the meat trade by operating 24-7. Like the Paris location, Atlanta's version serves the same menu day and night, so whether you're craving cheesy French onion soup at 3 a.m. or a rich but surprisingly light foie gras terrine at 3 p.m. (both favorites on the classic French menu), you'll be in luck. The oil-on-canvas murals of cherubs, maidens and, yes, pigs, that cover the walls and ceiling were hand-painted by a Mexican artist, and stunning Murano glass chandeliers add drama. True foodies can partake of a multicourse chef's-choice meal at a special table overlooking the kitchen, and lovebirds or privacy-craving celebrities can hole up in one of three "lover's booths" fully enclosed by heavy red velvet curtains—a very Parisian touch, indeed.

French. Breakfast, lunch, dinner. Open 24 hours. Bar. Reservations accepted. Outdoor seating. $36-85

★★★BLUEPOINTE

3455 Peachtree Road, Buckhead, 404-237-9070; www.buckheadrestaurants.com

Soaring ceilings, swooping architectural details and a stunning backlit bar area give Bluepointe a hip, urban feel. The Asian-tinged menu offers plenty of options for the statuesque wannabe models who crowd the bar area and fill the banquettes. Start your meal with creative sushi rolls or a platter of bracingly fresh oysters, then choose an entrée from the seafood-heavy main courses like peanut-crusted grouper in Massaman curry or a perfectly seared tuna steak. The temptingly creative accompaniments (think somen noodle cakes, shiitake and wild leek spring rolls, and coconut-infused sticky rice) make it even harder to make a decision. The swanky bar area is the place to see and be seen, particularly on Martini Night (Tuesday), when locals are three-deep at the bar, sipping the restaurant's famous green apple martini.

American, Asian. Lunch (Monday-Friday), dinner. Bar. Reservations recommended. $36-85

★★★BONE'S RESTAURANT

3130 Piedmont Road N.E., Buckhead, 404-237-2663; www.bonesrestaurant.com

Many a deal has been sealed over tender, dry-aged steaks at this old-school steakhouse, where the walls are festooned with caricatures of regulars and black-and-white photos of historic Atlanta and celebrity diners like the senior George Bush and the late Bob Hope. Hobnailed red leather chairs, stag lanterns and wood paneling complete the masculine decorating scheme, while more romantic tables for two are arrayed along the brick-walled wine gallery, overlooking the glassed-in chambers that house the impressive wine selection. The menu is straightforward: Carnivores' choices range from 10-ounce petit fillets to 28-ounce T-bones, alongside à la carte vegetables like grit fritters or sautéed greens. If you've got room, the Mountain High Pie, towering layers of three kinds of ice cream on an Oreo crust and crowned with meringue topping, is a good way to celebrate that sealed deal.

Steakhouse. Lunch (Monday-Friday), dinner. Bar. Reservations recommended. $36-85

★★★THE CAFÉ AT THE RITZ-CARLTON BUCKHEAD

The Ritz-Carlton, Buckhead, 3434 Peachtree Road N.E., Buckhead, 404-237-2700; www.ritzcarlton.com

As hotel restaurants go, the café in the Ritz-Carlton Buckhead's lobby is exceptional. The simply furnished, elegant area, open to the buzz of the lobby lounges, is a relaxed setting to enjoy everything from a quick but impeccably prepared breakfast, like poached eggs on corned beef hash with asparagus and hollandaise sauce, to lavish lunchtime sandwiches featuring fillings such as grilled halibut with Cajun rémoulade or slow-roasted brisket. Dinner is a more formal affair, with silky lobster bisque swirled with chive cream and accompanied by lobster hush puppies; fork-tender Kobe beef flat-iron steak; and perfectly seared diver scallops bathed in truffle butter. The restaurant pulls out all the stops for its legendary Sunday buffet, a jaw-dropping presentation of gorgeously prepared foods, including a chocolate fountain, made-to-order omelets and a vast raw bar.

American. Breakfast, lunch, dinner, Sunday brunch. Bar. Reservations recommended. Outdoor seating. $36-85

★★★CHOPS/LOBSTER BAR

70 W. Paces Ferry Road, Buckhead, 404-262-2675; www.buckheadrestaurants.com

The Rat Pack would have been right at home in Chops' elegantly appointed dining room, with its polished marble bar and floors, ornately paneled wooden ceiling, and brass and frosted glass light fixtures. Expense-account types, well-heeled regulars from the surrounding tony Buckhead neighborhood, and people celebrating a special occasion feast on classic surf-and-turf fare, from prime aged steaks and chops to lobster, crab and fresh fish that's flown in daily. Steak tartare is prepared tableside with all the fixings, and the half-pound center-cut filet mignon, served with a lobster tail fried in an ethereally light batter, is as rich as Sinatra's croon. The Lobster Bar downstairs has the same exact menu, but the more intimate space is modeled after New York City's fabled Grand Central Oyster Bar, with a domed subway-tile ceiling, mosaic tile floors and a curved bar overlooking the display of fresh seafood.

American. Lunch (Monday-Friday), dinner. Bar. Reservations recommended. $36-85

★★★JOËL

3920 Northside Parkway, Buckhead, 404-233-3500; www.joelrestaurant.com

Atlanta bluebloods still flock to Joël for excellent, if not inventive, fine French fare. The recently revamped dining room now boasts warm ochre walls, tan velvet-upholstered booths and banquettes, and a vaulted ceiling, with red accents in the form of a tiled wall and tabletop votives. The menu also has been freshened. More unusual options include a salmon sashimi appetizer topped with a tiny scoop of mustard ice cream, and baked John Dory accompanied by fried, tapenade-filled rissolé. Although no longer in the kitchen, chef Joël Antunes still is a partner in his eponymous restaurant, and the kitchen continues to turn out food that makes its high-society diners marvel.

French. Lunch (Monday-Friday), dinner. Closed Sunday-Monday. Bar. Reservations recommended. Outdoor seating. $36-85

★★★KYMA

3085 Piedmont Road, Buckhead, 404-262-0702; www.buckheadrestaurants.com

One of Atlanta's best Greek restaurants (and certainly one if its most luxe), Kyma offers a modern take on both cuisine and atmosphere. Focusing on seafood, particularly from the Aegean Sea, Kyma's menu includes whole fish, as well as seafood prepared in traditional specialties, such as skate in a fisherman's stew and whole prawns prepared saganaki-style. The menu is rounded out with a small selection of chicken and meat dishes, not to mention a nice assortment of classic Greek appetizers and sides. The beautifully designed space boasts a striking deep blue and white color scheme, with a constellation-studded midnight-blue ceiling, pristine white pillars, blue slip-covered chairs and carpeting, and gauzy white curtains.

Greek. Dinner. Closed Sunday. Bar. Reservations recommended. Outdoor seating (covered patio). $36-85

★★★LA GROTTA RISTORANTE ITALIANO

2637 Peachtree Road, Buckhead, 404-231-1368; La Grotta Ravinia, Crown Plaza Hotel, 4355 Ashford Dunwoody Road, Dunwoody, 770-395-9925; www.lagrottaatlanta.com

For years, La Grotta has been the prime spot for proposals, anniversaries and other romantic celebrations. And for good reason: The cuisine, warm service and well-appointed dining room all make for a fabulous evening. A vaulted, burgundy ceiling makes the spacious room seem intimate and cozy, divided banquettes are spaced widely enough apart to allow for private conversations. The professional but friendly servers glide between the tables, bearing authentic Italian dishes, such as tortellini filled with a mixture of braised onions, prosciutto, thyme and mascarpone cheese; pillowy herbed gnocchi with a wild mushroom sauce finished with truffle oil; and roasted quail with Italian sausage, creamy polenta and a just-tart-enough balsamic sauce.

Italian. Dinner. Closed Sunday. Bar. Reservations recommended. Outdoor seating. $36-85

★★★NAVA

3060 Peachtree Road, Buckhead, 404-240-1984; www.buckheadrestaurants.com

Buckhead socialites get tipsy on strong, fruity margaritas on the crowded patio at Nava, while inside the adobe walls and rough-hewn beams channel Santa Fe. So does the menu: Posole and smoked chicken taquitos are among the appetizers, while entrées boast Latin and Southwestern ingredients like pepitas, chilies, black beans, corn and roasted peppers. For a sweet (and spicy) finish, try the Mexican chocolate bread pudding or the flavorful Tequila Caramel Mexican Flan.

Southwestern. Lunch (Monday-Friday), dinner. Reservations recommended. Outdoor seating. $36-85

★★★PANO'S & PAUL'S

1232 W. Paces Ferry Road, Buckhead, 404-261-3662; www.buckheadrestaurants.com

With its elegant supper-club feel and uniformed waitstaff, Pano's & Paul's harkens to a more formal time. The stunning space features a starburst of polished wood radiating out from the center of the room; under the nexus is a towering floral arrangement. Couples canoodle on romantic red-velvet banquettes, enjoying dishes like the restaurant's signature lobster tail, encased in a crisped batter and served with drawn butter, or the meltingly tender filet mignon in a mushroom ragout with cracked peppercorns. In another nod to the genteel dining traditions of yore, grilled whole fish are deftly filleted tableside. The separate bar area, swathed in heavy bronze satin drapes and furnished in pillow-strewn sofas and damask armchairs, gets melodic with live piano music on the weekends, but it's a chic place to grab a cocktail just about any night of the week.

American. Dinner. Closed Sunday. Bar. Reservations recommended. $36-85

★★★RESTAURANT EUGENE

2277 Peachtree Road, Buckhead, 404-355-0321; www.restauranteugene.com

This small, sleek space dressed in warm neutrals with burnt-orange accents is an understated foil for the ever-changing culinary creations put forth by chef Linton Hopkins. He sources his ingredients from local and artisanal purveyors. On any given night, you might find on the menu sautéed foie gras with crumbled biscuit and kumquat marmalade; Alaskan halibut (with Georgia white shrimp, carnaroli risotto, wild ramps, parmigiano-reggiano, sake-shellfish broth and parsley oil); or rabbit from Mississippi, with baby carrots, Georgia English peas, Hakurei turnips and roasted spring onions. An equally impressive wine list curated by the restaurant's master sommeliers offers options from half-bottles of Billecart-Salmon Brut Rose Champagne to a luscious (and spendy) bottle of 2003 Domaine Serene "Monogram" Pinot Noir from Oregon's Willamette Valley. Join the regulars who crowd the restaurant for its well-priced, three-course Sunday Suppers. Although that menu changes as well, the stellar fried chicken is a mainstay.

American. Dinner. Bar. Reservations recommended. Outdoor seating. $36-85

DECATUR

★★★WATERSHED

406 W. Ponce de Leon Ave., Decatur, 404-378-4900; www.watershedrestaurant.com

Co-owned by an Indigo Girl and chef Scott Peacock, this cozy Decatur restaurant is worth the short trek from downtown Atlanta for the glimpse it offers into yet another interpretation of the Deep South's signature cuisine. Peacock learned a thing or two from his longtime friendship with Southern cook Edna Lewis, and his take on the regional fare is understated and fresh. Dishes like salmon croquettes, okra pancakes with yellow squash and cucumber salad, and oven barbecued chicken with corn on the cob and creamy coleslaw are all familiar and comforting, but elevated with organic, local ingredients and Peacock's deft hand. You won't be able to pass up home-style desserts like warm chocolate chip cookies and milk or crumbly fruit buckle.

Southern. Lunch (Monday-Saturday), dinner (Monday-Saturday), Sunday brunch. Bar. $36-85

DOWNTOWN

★★★CITY GRILL

50 Hurt Plaza, Downtown, 404-524-2489; www.citygrillatlanta.com

One of the most beautiful restaurants in Atlanta, City Grill resides in a marble-clad 1912 office building, in a space that once housed a Federal Reserve Bank. Vaulted ceilings trimmed with gold soar over an elegantly furnished dining room, and walls are painted with forest scenes and blue, cloud-dotted skies.

The clientele ranges from businesspeople to couples and parties celebrating special occasions, and the opulent surroundings have even inspired a fair share of proposals. The menu is suitably sophisticated; standouts include delicate seared monkfish served with lobster and leek rice pilaf and a four pepper Creole sauce, and succulent grilled venison tenderloin with a Dijon demi sauce, orzo and roasted squash. After your meal, grab a seat in the small, comfortable bar area, order a martini or a Manhattan and take in the beautiful scenery.

American. Lunch (Monday-Friday), dinner (Monday-Saturday). Closed most Sundays. Bar. Reservations recommended. $36-85

★★★FRENCH AMERICAN BRASSERIE

30 Ivan Allen Junior Blvd., Downtown, 404-266-1440; www.fabatlanta.com

Atlantans were universally sad when the storied Brasserie Le Coze closed a few years ago, so when the proprietor, Fabrice Vergez, resurfaced with a bigger, better concept in an up-and-coming neighborhood, it was cause for celebration. The vast, four-floor restaurant makes any meal seem like a special occasion, with smooth service (occasionally bordering on obsequious), polished Continental décor like gleaming brass trim and elegant statuary, and a menu of classic French favorites. The cuisine is French comfort food at its best: coq au vin, halibut au pistou and steaks bathed in your choice of luxuriant sauces.

French. Lunch, dinner. Closed Sunday. Bar. Reservations recommended. Outdoor seating. $36-85

★★★NIKOLAI'S ROOF

255 Courtland St., Downtown, 404-221-6362; www.nikolaisroof.com

Tourists and deep-pocketed locals alike can't help but swoon over the views from the floor-to-ceiling windows on the 30th floor of downtown's Hilton Atlanta. If you can tear yourself away from the twinkling skyline, the restaurant itself has a special-occasion feel, with dapper uniformed servers and old-school custom gold-edged china. Choose from the eight-course chef's menu, which begins with the restaurant's signature piroshki pastries and ends with a too-rich-for-words liqueur-infused soufflé, or from the equally sumptuous à la carte menu which features classic preparations like roasted pheasant, rack of lamb and boar tenderloin with foie gras (depending upon the season). Amazing dishes like these will keep your eyes glued to the table rather than the view outside.

French. Dinner. Closed Sunday-Monday. Bar. Reservations recommended. $36-85

LITTLE FIVE POINTS/CANDLER PARK/INMAN PARK/ PONCEY-HIGHLAND

★★★RATHBUN'S

112 Krog St., Inman Park, 404-524-8280; www.rathbunsrestaurant.com

Set in a deserted warehouse district that's now home to design studios, Rathbun's is named for chef-owner Kevin Rathbun, hometown favorite and Iron Chef America winner. The small-plates dishes are the thing to order on the extensive menu, so bring a few hungry friends to share hot and cold plates like eggplant fries dusted with confectioner's sugar, decadently creamy roasted bone marrow to spread on buttered brioche toast, bracingly refreshing tuna crudo and a simple but sublime shaved fennel salad. If you're feeling flush, "Second Mortgage Plates" include a lobster and green chile soft taco, as well as a selection of generously portioned prime meats. The pastry chef obviously has fun with the dessert menu; priced at just over $3, they're meant to be ordered in multiples and shared—a good thing, considering you won't have to make hard choices among the vast and ever-changing selection that might include a banana cream pie or a paper sack full of warm, sugar-coated doughnuts holes.

American. Dinner. Closed Sunday. Bar. Reservations recommended. Outdoor seating. $36-85

★★★WISTERIA
471 N. Highland Ave., Inman Park, 404-525-3363; www.wisteria-atlanta.com

Located in a storefront on a cute block in Inman Park, Wisteria feels like the perfect neighborhood joint. The diminutive dining room gets noisy with the chatter of buzzed locals on their second bottle of wine (and the exposed brick wall doesn't help acoustic matters much), but grab a table at the back, or in the window, and just be prepared to raise your own voice a little. Chef Jason Hill turns out Southern dishes that rival Atlanta's best meat-and-three restaurants. Fried chicken is virtually greaseless and crisp-tender, while shrimp-and-grits swims in a savory broth. Don't miss the green tomato fries as an appetizer, which come with a blue cheese dipping sauce. The restaurant's "four bite" desserts are indeed just big enough to give you a taste of Southern favorites such as pecan pie and fruit cobbler. After dining here, you'll wish you lived in this neighborhood.

American, Southern. Dinner. Bar. Reservations recommended. $36-85

MIDTOWN/CHESHIRE BRIDGE/WESTSIDE

★★★★BACCHANALIA
1198 Howell Mill Road, Midtown, 404-365-0410; www.starprovisions.com

Pass through Star Provisions, a foodie emporium of all things culinary, to reach Bacchanalia's serene dining room, its home since moving from a Buckhead cottage in 1999. Chef-owners (and husband and wife) Clifford Harrison and Anne Quatrano consistently impress with their ever-changing menu entirely composed of organic and seasonal ingredients, many of which come from the owners' own Summerland Farm. The four-course meal is prix fixe (dishes can also be ordered à la carte at the marble bar), but the menu offers a wide range of choices for every course, and each dish an impeccable composition of pristine ingredients and stunning contrasts in flavor and textures. You might find choices such as tender poached Georgia shrimp paired with mouth-puckering kimchee and buttery pork belly, or spring lamb accented with caramelized eggplant and tangy, creamy housemade yogurt. The gleaming, glassed-in kitchen runs the length of the restaurant, so while you enjoy your quiet meal, you'll also get a glimpse of the carefully orchestrated hustle of the chefs at work.

American. Dinner. Closed Sunday. Bar. Reservations recommended. $86 and up

★★★★PARK 75
Four Seasons Hotel Atlanta, 75 14th St., Midtown, 404-253-3840; www.fourseasons.com

Dressed in elegant neutrals, the dining room and terrace of Park 75, in the Four Seasons Hotel, is a tranquil setting in which to enjoy executive chef Robert Gerstenecker's seasonal, artisanal fare. Although the menu is ever changing, the chef is always playful with combinations, pairing such dishes as foie gras with

Grand Marnier French toast, or accenting the richness of scallops with caramelized grapefruit and vanilla parsnip purée. Local or specially procured ingredients are featured prominently on the menu, which has included antelope from Broken Arrow Ranch, cheese from Sweetgrass Dairy and produce from a number of nearby farms. If you're feeling daring, book the chef's table in the kitchen for an unforgettable multicourse extravaganza that really showcases some of these special ingredients. Brunch is a tasting menu of five courses, and afternoon tea on the light-filled marble landing is a particular treat, with delicious scones accompanied by traditional clotted cream, dainty sandwiches and gorgeous petite pastries.

American. Breakfast, lunch (Monday-Saturday), afternoon tea, dinner (Monday-Saturday), Sunday brunch. Bar. Reservations recommended. $86 and up

★★★★QUINONES AT BACCHANALIA

1198 Howell Mill Road, Midtown, 404-365-0410; www.starprovisions.com

Bring your appetite and your taste buds for one of Atlanta's most impressive gustatory experiences. Put yourself in the capable hands of chef-owners Anne Quatrano and Clifford Harrison for the 10-course prix fixe menu (no choices allowed) at Bacchanalia's smaller, more lavish sister. In-season ingredients inspire each dish, juxtaposed in a manner that reflects not only the chefs' impeccable classic culinary techniques, but also their passion for finding new interpretations and contrasts (think foie gras torchon paired with pickled blackberries and Georgia peanut streusel) that will wow even the most jaded gourmand. A warm and gracious staff will make you feel welcome, and the intimate dining room, with its pretty chandeliers, neutral color scheme and elegant upholstered chairs make for a comfortable setting—a good thing, since your meal will probably last more than three hours.

Contemporary Southern. Dinner (Friday-Saturday). Reservations recommended. $86 and up

★★★ECCO

40 Seventh St., Midtown, 404-347-9555; www.ecco-atlanta.com

Ecco is the poster child for the nouveau-hip Midtown neighborhood it calls home. The open kitchen and the polished dining room, full of exposed ductwork and angular modern furnishings, would be equally at home in New York or L.A., as would the grazing-friendly menu of artisanal cheeses from around the world (helpfully arranged in order of increasing pungency), charcuterie, small plates and wood-fired pizzas. With the exception of a handful of main dishes, the menu is eminently share-worthy, and with so many well-crafted and beautifully prepared choices, ordering as a group is the way to go. Oak-grilled-asparagus-and-tomato salad is briny with a surprise addition of olives, while ethereal puffs of fried goat cheese are drizzled with honey and dusted with black pepper. Cocktails are as interesting as the food, full of intriguing infusions and unexpected ingredients, such as Long Live the Queen—a concoction of Bombay Sapphire gin, elderflower syrup and crushed mint—or the Pink Hangar, which combines vodka, framboise and a float of champagne. They just might be why the hipsters haven't yet moved on to the next hot destination.

European. Dinner. Bar. Reservations recommended. Outdoor seating. $36-85

★★★ONE. MIDTOWN KITCHEN

559 Dutch Valley Road, Midtown, 404-892-4111; www.onemidtownkitchen.com

Whether you're a devoted foodie or a scenester who knows all the right places, you'll fit right in at this chic spot. The gorgeously refurbished former warehouse is lit by bare bulbs that appear to float overhead, casting a flattering glow on diners ensconced on pillow-strewn banquettes. At first glance, the menu seems familiar and traditional, but it's full of thought-provoking contrasts and little surprises, like cubes of watermelon serving as pedestals for crisply-seared scallops (which appears on the summer menu), and tuna steak with juniper, wheat berries and parsnips. There's plenty of food to go around, but you won't be able to resist a delectable side dish of mac 'n cheese elevated with a drizzle of truffle oil, whether you're here for the scene or the cuisine.

American. Dinner. Bar. Reservations recommended. $36-85

★★★VENI VIDI VICI

41 14th St., Midtown, 404-875-8424; www.buckheadrestaurants.com

Once owned by the godmother of Italian cooking, Marcella Hazan, Veni Vidi Vici now is owned by a restaurant consortium but turns out homemade pastas and other authentic specialties just as ably. A slowly turning rotisserie roasts crisp-skinned chicken, duck and suckling pig, while the antipasti selection includes tasty hand-sliced prosciutto and bresaola. The creamy-walled dining room is as warm and inviting as an Italian trattoria, and the long bar, under the command of friendly, swarming bartenders, is the perfect place for dining solo.

Italian. Lunch (Monday-Friday), dinner. Bar. Reservations recommended. Outdoor seating. $36-85

SPAS

BUCKHEAD

★★★★29 SPA

The Mansion on Peachtree, A Rosewood Hotel, 3376 Peachtree Road N.E., Buckhead, 404-995-7529; www.rwmansiononpeachtree.com

Atlanta native Lydia Mondavi (whose name you may have seen on a bottle of cabernet or pinot noir) brings the anti-aging body benefits of wine to 29 Spa. The Mansion on Peachtree is home to the 15,000-square-foot spa where all of the most fabulous Georgia peaches get pampered in the 14 rooms, each complimented with heated waterbed tables, bathed in linen and silk and serving the signature wine. Quench your thirst head to toe with wine and grape seed-infused treatments for the scalp and body, massages and facials, or get primped to the (twenty)nines at home if you grab some goodies from Mondavi's line, 29 Cosmetics.

★★★★REMÈDE SPA, ST. REGIS ATLANTA

The St. Regis Atlanta, 88 West Paces Ferry Road, Buckhead, 404-563-7900; www.starwood.com

Customization is key at this intimate hotel spa, where every service from a brow wax to a Buckhead escape body treatment is personalized and serene. The spa's 10 treatment rooms are comfortable and spacious, stocked with the Remède's exclusive line of amenities. After strolling around the city all day, nothing will feel better on your feet than a micro-exfoliating pedicure, which includes an amino acid peeling mask to smooth and soften tired toes. Or book a hot stone massage for the ultimate in muscle relaxation.

WHERE TO SHOP

BUCKHEAD

ADDICTION

414 E. Paces Ferry Road, Buckhead, 678-927-9383; www.shop-addiction.com

Trendsetter Nikki Salk opened Addiction to satisfy her own need for a store that has it all, from clothing to books. She turned a charming house into a sleek boutique offering a well-edited selection of clothing, accessories and even perfume. Here, you'll find upscale designers, including Badgley Mischka, Found Denim, Ferretti and Basso & Brooke. This place will fuel your addiction for designer duds.

Tuesday-Saturday 11 a.m.-6 p.m., Sunday-Monday by appointment only.

BEEHIVE CO-OP

1831-A Peachtree Road, Buckhead, 404-351-1166; www.beehiveco-op.com

Walk into this narrow boutique on a strip of shops and restaurants in the southern part of Buckhead and you'll think you landed in an artist's studio, with the handcrafted wares displayed like art on easels, shelves, walls and other blank spaces. In fact, you have. Beehive Co-op, located in a former gallery, rents space to local artists and designers to give them a place to sell their work without having to find and rent their own stores. The result is a diverse mix of styles, designs and products, from organic-fiber children's clothes to couture frocks to handmade stationery. The store hosts events and classes, too. It's easy to spend an afternoon here.

Monday-Friday 10 a.m.-6 p.m., Saturday 10 a.m.-7 p.m., Sunday 1-5 p.m.

BOXWOODS GARDENS AND GIFTS

100 E. Andrews Drive, Buckhead, 404-233-3400, www.boxwoodsonline.com

Part nursery, part gift shop, part antique store, this jewel box is full of surprises. It's housed in a cozy cottage in Buckhead's chic boutique section off Roswell Road, and each room is full of treats tucked away in nooks and crannies. You never know what you'll find here—maybe a silver rattle for a baby or a precious plant such as a perfectly manicured boxwood. Holiday time is especially festive with unique gifts, including glittery baubles, that make this jewel of a shop shine.

Monday-Saturday 10 a.m.-6 p.m.

MIAMI CIRCLE

630 Miami Circle N.E., Buckhead, 404-233-6890; www.miamicircleshops.com

Miami Circle is worth seeking out, even though it's not on the corridor of Buckhead proper. Situated alongside railroad tracks, Miami Circle's strip of warehouses and industrial buildings is a mecca for designers, interior decorators and consumers alike. Go there to peruse art galleries, furniture stores, fabric shops and antique dealers. Put Curran Designer Fabrics, Pierre Deux, ART Rugs of Persia, and Foxglove Antiques & Galleries on your list of stops. After browsing, stop at Eclipse di Luna for tapas and sangria—you'll need it after treasure hunting through the sprawling center.

HIGHLIGHT

WHAT ARE ATLANTA'S BEST MALLS?

Lenox Square Mall (3393 Peachtree Road N.E., Buckhead, 404-233-6767; www.simon.com) is one of the largest malls in the Southeast and features several stunning shops, including the flagship Pottery Barn store. Go on a high-end shopping binge at stores such as Hermès, Lacoste, Louis Vuitton and True Religion. Check out one of the mall's latest additions, Lush (404-841-1223; www.lush.com) for deliciously fragrant handmade soaps, lotions and potions. Be sure to pick up one of the bath bombs, fizzes that'll make your soak splendid (try the best-selling jasmine-scented Sex Bomb). When you need to give your feet a rest between shops, try steak and sushi haven Prime (404-812-0555) or upscale American eatery Neiman Marcus Café (404-279-5850). Don't miss the annual Pink Pig train ride during the holiday season; it's a holdover from the old Rich's Department Store days and a tradition for generations of Atlantans. *Monday-Saturday 10 a.m.-9 p.m., Sunday noon-6 p.m.*

As nice a mall as Lenox is, Phipps Plaza (3500 Peachtree Road N.E., Buckhead, 404-262-0992; www.simon.com) is another story entirely. This three-level establishment features the best in designer shopping, from Tiffany to Gucci to Barney's New York Co-op. There are two don't-miss stores. Intimacy (404-261-9333; www.myintimacy.com), the original and flagship shop (the chain has outposts in the Midwest, South and East Coast), hawks prestige lingerie, from slinky wedding trousseaus to functional maternity items. After buying some lacy numbers, check out Jeffrey Atlanta (404-237-9000; www.jeffreyatlanta.com). The shop was founded by Jeffrey Kalinsky, who is so prestigious in the fashion world he was spoofed on Saturday Night Live. It was only after this women's apparel emporium became so successful that he opened an outpost in New York's Meatpacking District, which then turned into the trendy scene it is today. The Atlanta store incorporates Kalinsky's family's Bob Ellis Shoes; they were once separate stores but now are housed in one location called Jeffrey. Jeffrey sales associates dress Atlanta's high-society women—often personally—and always know who is wearing what to which event to avoid any catty conflicts. You'll find only the best clothing and shoe labels here, including Jil Sander, Christian Louboutin, Prada, Chanel and Balenciaga. Dress the part when shopping and you'll get the service reserved for those high-society ladies.

A word of caution about shopping at Phipps: If you go during the holidays, don't even bother trying to get a picture with Santa. Reservations are required and are all snatched up almost immediately. It's something of a status thing to do in Atlanta, and you do not want to battle the Southern soccer moms with their dressed-to-the-nines tots.
Monday-Saturday 10 a.m.-9 p.m., Sunday noon-5:30 p.m.

RAZZLE DAZZLE

49 Irby Ave., Buckhead, 404-233-6940; www.razzledazzleatlanta.com

Part of the Atlanta fashion scene for more than two decades, Razzle Dazzle consistently hits the mark in fashion-forward designs and accessories. You'll find great updated basics, such as Michael Stars shirts and denim, as well as the perfect little black dress for a night out on the town. Check out the vintage Levi's, too. Known for its bold accessories—chunky necklaces, bracelets and stylish belts—this is the perfect place to fine something to give your outfit some razzle-dazzle.

Monday-Saturday 10:30 a.m.-5 p.m.

SUSAN LEE

56 E. Andrews Drive N.W., Buckhead, 404-365-0693

The quintessential ladies-who-lunch boutique is the place to go for formal wear and special-occasion dresses, from mother-of-the-bride to debutante gowns. Colorful confections are big sellers here, owing to Southern belles' tastes. Don't dismiss this shop if you don't have a ball to attend; there are plenty of cocktail dresses and casual looks as well. You'll find impeccable feminine styles from such exclusive and hard-to-find labels as Carol Peretz, Catherine Regehr, Canvasbacks and Alberto Makali in this two-story boutique that screams old money, or rather whispers it in a sugary-sweet Southern drawl.

Monday-Saturday 10 a.m.-6 p.m.

LITTLE FIVE POINTS
CRIMINAL RECORDS

1154-A Euclid Ave. N.E., Little Five Points, 404-215-9511; www.criminal.com

You don't hear the term "record store" much anymore, but Criminal Records is the real deal. Yes, it sells records. It also offers indie-rock items, toys, coffee and comics. And there's an occasional concert there—and not just coffee-shop guy strummer (though there's that, too), but bigger acts such as Rose Hill Drive. This indie musician hangout also buys and sells used cassettes and CDs. Don't be startled if you see a big-time music celebrity such as Bruce Springsteen thumbing through the records next to you—this is often their first stop when they land in Atlanta while on tour or to record at one of the many local studios.

Monday-Thursday 10 a.m.-9 p.m., Friday-Saturday 10 a.m.-10 p.m., Sunday noon-7 p.m.

STEFAN'S VINTAGE CLOTHING

1160 Euclid Ave. N.E., Little Five Points, 404-688-4929; www.stefansvintage.com

Atlanta's oldest vintage store, Stefan's carries immaculate men and women's threads from the 1900s through the '70s. You can pick up a vintage tuxedo, a chiffon confection or an elegant wedding gown here. But this is not a costume shop—fashionistas and well-known rock stars, supermodels and movie stars including Lauren Hutton, Naomi Campbell, Ringo Starr and Cyndi Lauper haunt this store for one-of-a-kind designs, including pristine cashmere cardigans.

Monday-Saturday 11 a.m.-7 p.m., Sunday noon-6 p.m.

WISH ATLANTA

447 Moreland Ave., Little Five Points, 404-880-0402; www.wishatl.com

This sportswear store is unlike any you'll find in a mall or strip center. Housed in a turn-of-the-century library, Wish showcases hard-to-find footwear and apparel by such brands as Puma, Mishka and 10 Deep. These aren't just some old kicks—some of the styles are unavailable anywhere else in the city and include special editions. The store is a visual delight, light and airy upstairs and dark and reminiscent of its library roots downstairs, with hardback books lining the walls. A catwalk made of glass boxes illuminates the entrance and creates a fashion-show vibe, as does the DJ who spins there on the platform. Think of it as sneaker couture.

Monday-Thursday noon-8 p.m., Friday-Saturday noon-9 p.m., Sunday 1-7 p.m.

MIDTOWN

DREW LEWIS
845 Spring St. N.W., Midtown, 404-881-5359; www.drewlewis-atl.com

This nifty boutique is fashioned after a Southern mansion but carries a distinct New York vibe—without the attitude. You'll swoon over its exclusive men's and women's designs. Guys head downstairs to peruse labels such as Rag & Bone, Band of Outsiders, Trovata, Modern Amusement and A.P.C. Ladies go upstairs to see garb by Sass & Bide, Charlotte Ronson, Vena Cava and Milly. The store also carries the largest selection of Tom Ford eyewear in Atlanta. Be sure to snatch up a pair—your New York pals will lust after your hard-to-get shades.

Tuesday-Saturday 11 a.m.-8 p.m., Sunday noon-6 p.m.

FAB'RIK
1114 W. Peachtree St., Midtown, 404-881-8223; www.shopfabrikboutique.com

Almost everything (but premium denim and some jackets) at this trendy little store is priced at less than $100—quite a shock since the store focuses on trendy, cutting-edge clothing for everyone in the family. You can pick up the latest BB Dakota dress, Ben Sherman men's shirts and Kingsley kiddie shirts. You'll find a well-edited collection in limited numbers, ensuring you'll have a unique look. After you rifle through stacks of William Rast, True Religion and Free People denim looking for that perfect pair, take a break at the water bar for complimentary sips of H2O.

Monday-Saturday 11 a.m.-7 p.m., Sunday noon-5 p.m.

H. STOCKTON-ATLANTA
1180 Peachtree St., Midtown, 404-249-7002; www.hstockton.com

It's no surprise that you'll find H. Stockton in Midtown, the location for most of the top law firms in the city. The suits flock to the venerable Atlanta men's store, which has been around for nearly 50 years (there are four locations in the Atlanta area). The secret to its longevity is that it forgoes of-the-moment duds in favor of classic attire, such as pinpoint shirts and refined Ferragamo ties. Dapper fellas can even order custom made-to-measure clothes.

Monday-Friday 9 a.m.-6 p.m.

LUXE
1000 Marietta St., Midtown, 404-815-7470; www.luxeatlanta.com

Housed in BrickWorks at Midtown West, a complex of restored warehouses complemented by some newly constructed buildings, Luxe showcases a fine mix of designer threads at reverse-sticker-shock prices. You'll find Chloé, Diane von Furstenberg, Zac Posen and Jimmy Choo with price tags that are generally 50 percent to 75 percent off retail. The store owners round out the assortment with an extensive line of vintage jewelry, accessories and hand-made arm candy—such as a reptile-embossed bag in regal purple. The sumptuous shopping environment belies the deals you'll find—drenched in rich chocolate and Tiffany blue, Luxe looks like a French salon. Frequent parties and designer trunk shows also make shopping there an event. Afterward, stop at the nearby coffeehouse Urban Grind for a Turtle Mocha (*962 Marietta St., 404-724-0605; www.urbangrindatl.com*) or Toscano & Sons Italian Market (*1000 Marietta St., 404-815-8383; www.toscanoandsons.com*) for a panino to refuel and take another peek at your Luxe loot.

Tuesday-Saturday 11 a.m.-7 p.m.

SID MASHBURN

1198 Howell Mill Road, Midtown, 404-350-7135; www.sidmashburn.com

This genuine men's haberdashery is like a preppy fashion museum, with separates carefully on display. Sid Mashburn had a long career in fashion before opening his classic yet whimsical eponymous store. His focus is entirely on tailored, well-made clothes, shoes and accessories, some of which are not available anywhere else in the United States. His style, which is reflected in the store, is "a fresh interpretation of old standards." The shop sells hard-to-get, good old-fashioned Levi's 501 jeans and timeless Edward Green shoes—if you're prepared to drop $1,400 on a pair of kicks. If you spy some trousers that are almost perfect but don't quite fit, bring them to the full-time, on-site tailor, who also makes made-to-measure clothing. You'll look like a preppy museum piece (in a good way) in no time.

Monday-Saturday 10:30 a.m.-6:30 p.m. and by appointment.

SPROUT

1198 Howell Mill Road, Midtown, 404-352-0864; www.sproutatlanta.com

You'll find something cute and fun for the little ones here. We're not talking just any old play clothes, but haute garb from Zutano, Petit Bateau and Catimini, as well as classically designed furniture. Even better, the store carries a wide assortment of creative books and handcrafted toys, all in a fun shopping environment. No kid—big or small—can resist Bla Bla knit dolls (fancy takes on sock monkeys) and wistfully nostalgic Haba wooden toys. You'll think you're bringing back something for the kids, but you're really just reliving your childhood.

Monday-Saturday 10 a.m.-6 p.m.

STAR PROVISIONS

1198 Howell Mill Road, Midtown, 404-365-0410; www.starprovisions.com

Owned by Clifford Harrison and Anne Quatrano, the star-chef duo behind some of Atlanta's best restaurants, this charming storefront—conveniently situated at the entrance to their fine-dining establishment Bacchanalia— features fresh-baked breads and pastries, locally grown produce, high-quality meats and sumptuous prepared food. Grab a sandwich and a scone for a quick pick-me-up. Be sure to check out the chef-selected array of cookware, tableware and other kitchen goodies, such as Valrhona chocolate and 100-year-old vinegar.

Monday-Saturday 10 a.m.-10 p.m.

YES HOME

921 Peachtree St., Midtown, 404-733-5909; www.yes4me.com

You'll want to redecorate your digs once you see this home furnishings store's great contemporary furniture, art, gifts, lighting and accessories. Maybe you can't take home the white armless mid-century modern Mitchell Gold + Bob Williams sofa, but an exotic Slatkin candle easily fits in a suitcase. You'll enjoy shopping in the beautiful, bright, airy store—and free parking at the building doesn't hurt.

Monday-Friday 10 a.m.-7 p.m., Saturday 10 a.m.-6 p.m., Sunday noon-6 p.m.

VIRGINIA HIGHLAND

BELLA CUCINA

1050 N. Highland Ave., Virginia Highland, 404-347-6476;
www.bellacucina.com

You may have eaten the addictive dips and spreads from this company; its products are sold in gourmet stores around the country. This is where founder Alisa Barry creates and sells her Italian-inspired gourmet goods. Do not go home without the velvety-smooth and somewhat tart Artichoke Lemon Pesto (and Bella's dipping crackers—they're crisp and tasty).

Monday-Thursday 11 a.m.-8 p.m., Friday-Saturday 10 a.m.-9 p.m., Sunday noon-6 p.m.

BELLY GENERAL STORE

772 N. Highland Ave., Virginia Highland, 404-872-1003;
www.bellystore.com

This charming relic hawks gourmet groceries and bakery treats. Inside the exposed-brick building, which looks like an old-time country general store, you'll find artisan cheeses, old-fashioned sodas and even organic fruits. Did we mention the cupcakes? From plain vanilla with buttercream icing to Southern classics such as red velvet, the drool-worthy cupcakes are the icing on this sweet shop.

Monday-Saturday 7 a.m.-7 p.m., Sunday 8 a.m.-5 p.m.

BILL HALLMAN MEN/BILL HALLMAN WOMEN

792 N. Highland Ave., Virginia Highland, 404-876-6055; Bill Hallman Women,
784 N. Highland Ave., Virginia Highland, 404-607-1171; www.billhallman.com

Bill Hallman is a retail pioneer, creating a fashion destination away from the mall and in the heart of Virginia Highland. His men's and women's stores carry designers such as Citizens of Humanity, Izaak, Helmut Lang, John Varvatos and Hype as well as vintage pieces. Stylish and tailored pants meet ultra-short skirts and body-revealing dresses at this longtime Atlanta haunt for female fashionistas, while rocker-chic tees and denim make this a must for the guys.

Both stores: Monday-Wednesday noon-8 p.m., Thursday 11 a.m.-9 p.m., Friday-Saturday 11 a.m.-10 p.m., Sunday noon-7 p.m.

DABBERDOO

1048 N. Highland Ave., Virginia Highland, 404-815-6700;
www.dabberdoo.com

This just might be the perfect gift store. What started as a stationery shop has grown to include just about every present you can imagine, from soaps to purses to luggage tags. Grab great girly gifts here, such as fragrant piña colada-scented hand cream and fluffy ribbon-trimmed towel wraps. There's an extensive collection of items that can be personalized, from wine glasses to koozies to small plaques for your car. The items sometimes look a bit "Southern sorority girl," but it's easy to find something for just about everyone.

Monday-Tuesday 10 a.m.-8 p.m., Wednesday-Saturday 10 a.m.-9 p.m., Sunday noon-6 p.m.

ECO-BELLA

1046 N. Highland Ave., Virginia Highland, 404-815-4280; www.eco-bella.com

In 2005, five moms decided they had had enough of searching for organic and eco-friendly home and children's products, so they opened a store. The ladies practice what they sell by using milk-based paint on the walls and bamboo on the floor in the shop. You'll find everything from paint to baby clothes to skin-care products, not to mention home goods and women's clothes. It's a particularly good spot to buy baby gifts—the organic kimonos and jumpers are standouts that'll give little ones a start on the right low-carbon footprint.

Monday-Thursday 11 a.m.-7 p.m., Friday-Saturday 11 a.m.-9 p.m., Sunday noon-6 p.m.

MITZI & ROMANO

1038 N. Highland Ave., Virginia Highland, 404-876-7228

Mitzi & Romano, along with sister store Mitzi's Shoe Box, caters to the fashionable. This place has style and substance with prices to match. Still, it's not a snooty shop. You can pick up an impeccable little black dress and a perfectly worn-in T-shirt as well as a purse to go with both. It's clear from the assortment at the neighboring shoe boutique that footwear is a passion, not an afterthought. Rummage through the clearance racks for too-good-to-be-true bargains like a Hazel tank top for just 10 bucks—the items are all designer labels.

Monday-Thursday 10 a.m.-9 p.m., Friday-Saturday 10 a.m.-10 p.m., Sunday 11 a.m.-7 p.m.

GREATER ATLANTA

Athens is the ultimate college town—the site of the University of Georgia, chartered in 1785. The landscape here is stunning—set on a hill beside the Oconee River—enhanced by towering oaks and elms, white-blossomed magnolias, old-fashioned boxwood gardens and many well-preserved and still-occupied antebellum houses. Some claim that the university is one of the best college experiences in America, as is the town's lively (some lists even rank it among the top 10) music scene. Bands like REM, the B-52s and the Indigo Girls, among others, all got their start here. Whether you're looking for music festivals, college sports or antebellum history, the home of the Georgia Bulldogs offers up an active mix.

Located outside of Atlanta, you'll find towns like Marietta, with lodging choices and activities for traveling families and those on business, while Cartersville highlights some of Georgia's history and natural beauty with the state park. Wine and dine just north of Atlanta in Braselton, home to the Chateau Elan Winery and Resort, which has a luxurious inn and full winery onsite, as well as an acclaimed equestrian center. Weekend warriors find Lake Lanier in Buford a perfect summer spot while Greensboro boasts a new Ritz-Carlton complex and golfing retreat near Lake Oconee. Find Native American history and antebellum houses in Rome.

WHAT TO SEE

ATHENS
CHURCH-WADDEL-BRUMBY HOUSE
280 E. Dougherty St., Athens, 706-353-1820

Located in the historic north end of Athens, this restored 1820 Federal-style house is believed to be the oldest residence in Athens. It houses the Athens Welcome Center, which has information on all things Athens as well as tour information for other historic buildings and notable spots, such as the University of Georgia.

Monday-Saturday 10 a.m.-5 p.m., Sunday noon-5 p.m.

THE STATE BOTANICAL GARDEN OF GEORGIA
2450 S. Milledge Ave., Athens, 706-542-1244; www.uga.edu/botgarden

The State Botanical Garden is a public educational facility three miles south of the University of Georgia. It is a "living laboratory" for university students and faculty, as well as a public garden for enjoyment by the general public. Occupying 300 acres, visitors will also find nature trails, wildlife, special collections, a café and gift shop.

Admission: $5 (garden tours). Gardens: October-March daily 8 a.m.-6 p.m.; April-September daily 8 a.m.-8 p.m. Visitor Center & Conservatory: Tuesday-Saturday 9 a.m.-4:30 p.m., Sunday 11:30 a.m.-4:30 p.m.

TAYLOR-GRADY HOUSE
634 Prince Ave., Athens, 706-549-8688; www.taylorgradyhouse.com

A National Historic Landmark and restored to a high level of historical accuracy, this 1844 mansion is surrounded by 13 columns, which are said to symbolize the 13 original states. Today, the Junior League of Athens keeps the house open to the public for rentals and tours. The home contains period furniture throughout.

Admission: free. Monday-Friday 9 a.m.-1 p.m., 2-5 p.m.

THE UNIVERSITY OF GEORGIA
College Station and East Campus Roads, Athens, 706-542-0842; www.uga.edu

Consisting of 16 schools and colleges, the main campus extends more than two miles south from the Arch, College Avenue and Broad Street. Historic buildings from the 1800s include Demosthenian Hall; Old College, the oldest building, designed after Connecticut Hall at Yale; Waddel Hall and Phi Kappa Hall.

AUSTELL
SIX FLAGS OVER GEORGIA
275 Riverside Parkway, Austell, 770-948-9290; www.sixflags.com/overgeorgia

This amusement park west of downtown Atlanta has more than 30 rides, one for every temperament. The Georgia Scorcher and Superman: Ultimate Flight are the fastest and most furious rides, where the latter suspends you in a flying position Superman-style and the former has you standing up through a series of stomach-dropping corkscrews and vertical loops at 54 miles per hour. For those with a weak stomach, there are also milder-mannered pleasures such as bumper cars, stage shows and plenty of cotton candy. The park gets mobbed

HIGHLIGHT

WHAT ARE THE TOP THINGS TO DO
IN GREATER ATLANTA?

EXPERIENCE THE MUSIC SCENE IN ATHENS

Home of REM, the B-52s and Indigo Girls, Athens still has a thriving music scene and several festivals during the year highlighting such. It's also a big college town (home to the University of Georgia) so in addition to the sprawling campus, visitors will find the usual intellectual and cultural delights that accompany higher education, such as fun dining, unique coffee shops, art galleries and the like. Of course, there are also plenty of college sports.

LEARN THE HISTORY

This area is rich with Native American history. Visit the sites of New Echota and the Chieftains Museum to see some of the earliest examples of Native American life. Additionally, Civil War buffs will want to visit Resaca Confederate Cemetery and the site of the battle that took place there.

on weekends and when school's out, so try to go during the quieter weekdays, if possible. And if you want a chance to shock your system with those popular 'coasters without a mind-numbingly long wait, plan to hit them either first thing in the morning or after 6 p.m. If you have a very impatient temperament, spring for the $66.99 gold Flash Pass, which reduces your wait time by up to 75 percent.

Admission: adults $39.99, children under 48 inches $29.99, children 2 and under free. Opening days and hours vary. Closed November-February.

BUFORD

LAKE LANIER ISLANDS

7000 Holiday Road, Buford, 770-932-7200; www.lakelanierislands.com

This 1,200-acre, year-round resort offers swimming, waterskiing, a water park with a wave pool, 10 water slides and other attractions, fishing and boating. Landlubbers can enjoy horseback riding, two 18-hole golf courses and tennis.

CARTERSVILLE

ETOWAH INDIAN MOUNDS HISTORIC SITE AND ARCHAEOLOGICAL AREA

813 Indian Mounds Road S.W., Cartersville, 770-387-3747; www.gastateparks.org

The most impressive of more than 100 settlements in the Etowah Valley, this village was occupied from A.D. 1000-1500. It was the home of several thousand people of a relatively advanced culture. Six earthen mounds grouped around two public squares, the largest of which occupies several acres, served as funeral mounds, bases for temples and the residences of the chiefs. A museum displays artifacts from the excavations and crafts. Don't miss the painted white marble mortuary.

Admission: $2.50-$5. Wednesday-Saturday 9 a.m.-5 p.m.

CALHOUN

NEW ECHOTA STATE HISTORIC SITE

1211 Chatsworth Highway N.E., Calhoun, 706-624-1321; www.gastateparks.org

New Echota holds a big place in the history of the Cherokee Nation as it is one of the earliest experiments in a tribe self-governing. Located on the site are 12 original and reconstructed buildings including a legislative hall, a Supreme Court house, a mission and several other buildings.

Admisstion: $3.50-$5. Thursday-Saturday 9 a.m.-5 p.m.

RESACA CONFEDERATE CEMETERY

300 S. Wall St., Calhoun, 800-887-3811; www.gordonchamber.org

This is the site of the Civil War battle that opened the way to Atlanta for Union General Sherman. Stop off at the Civil War markers and cemetery on the Civil War Discovery Trail.

Daily 8:30 a.m.-5 p.m.

DAWSONVILLE

KANGAROO CONSERVATION CENTER

222 Bailey-Waters Road, Dawsonville, 706-265-6100; www.kangaroocenter.com

You don't have to travel to Australia to see kangaroos. Three hundred of the marsupials bounce through an 87-acre nature preserve one hour north of the city. Though the animals are sold to zoos around the world, the owners also run a handful of tours of the center each week. Either ride around the facility in a Jeep or explore it at your own pace; you'll see everything from tiny sugar gliders (tiny Aussie "flying" creatures related to the opossum) to bearded dragons to mulga parrots and, of course, those adorable kangaroos.

Tour prices, dates and times vary. Children under 6 are not permitted in the conservation center.

HAMPTON

ATLANTA MOTOR SPEEDWAY

1500 Highway 19/41, Hampton, 770-946-4211; www.atlantamotorspeedway.com

Just 25 miles south of the city, you'll find the local answer to Talladega Superspeedway. Racing enthusiasts rush here for track tours or NASCAR events that heat up the more than 800 acres of racetrack. There are places for motocross and go-karts, but if you're feeling the need for speed, take a stock-car driving lesson. The Speedway's website lists links to local driving schools that'll give you a crash course on how to be the next Dale Earnhardt, Jr.

LILBURN

BAPS SHRI SWAMINARAYAN MANDIR

460 Rockbridge Road N.W., Lilburn, 404-297-0501; www.swaminarayan.org

The largest Hindu temple of its kind in the United States, it soars above surrounding strip malls and pharmacies at a busy suburban intersection. Made from interlocking blocks of marble, limestone and sandstone, this intricately carved marvel uses no screws, nails or any other metal to hold it together. The amazing architecture isn't the only feature that makes this temple stand out: When you remove your shoes and climb the steps into this dimly lit center of worship, you'll be awed and inspired by the tranquility within.

Daily 9 a.m.-noon, 4-6 p.m.

YELLOW RIVER GAME RANCH

4525 Highway 78, Lilburn, 770-972-6643; www.yellowrivergameranch.com

Two miles east of Stone Mountain, this 24-acre ranch is home to its share of fine feathered and furry friends just waiting to be fed. Stroll along a path past bunnies, sheep, deer, black bears, a cougar and other species indigenous to Georgia, even newborn animals that you can pet, such as fawns, piglets and lambs. Its resident groundhog, General Beau Lee, is 94 percent accurate in predicting the start of spring.

Admission: adults $8, children 2-11 $7, children under 2 free (one child per adult free). Daily 9:30 a.m.-6 p.m.

MARIETTA

SIX FLAGS WHITE WATER

250 Cobb Parkway North, Marietta, 770-948-9290; www.sixflags.com/whitewater

When you need relief from the relentless Georgia sun, head to one of the region's top water parks. Daredevils will be itching to slay Dragon's Tail, a water slide with a scream-inducing 250-foot drop, while the more timid will prefer the tamer Lizard's Tail, which slithers you into a lagoon. You'll stay wet all day long, whether you're drifting lazily on the Little Hooch River, frolicking with toddlers in the safe and shallow Little Squirt's Island or bobbing in the continually moving Atlanta Ocean. If you need to dry off a little, try your hand at video games, skee-ball or a video-dance machine. Then head back out to hang ten on the Tidal Wave.

Admission: adults $36.99, children under 48 inches $26.99, children 2 and under free. Opening days and hours vary. Closed September-May.

ROME

CHIEFTAINS MUSEUM/MAJOR RIDGE HOME

501 Riverside Parkway, Rome, 706-291-9494; www.chieftainsmuseum.org

This is the 18th century house of prominent Cherokee leader Major Ridge, featuring artifacts, exhibits and events with an emphasis on Cherokee history.

Admission: adults $5, seniors $3, students $2. Wednesday-Saturday 10 a.m.-5 p.m.

OAK HILL AND THE MARTHA BERRY MUSEUM

24 Veterans Memorial Highway, Rome, 706-368-6789; www.berry.edu

This antebellum plantation house was owned and occupied by Martha Berry, the founder of Berry College. Manicured lawns, formal gardens and nature trails abound. The museum is located on the grounds of Oak Hill and serves as a visitor center and also includes an art gallery and a temporary exhibit.

Admission: adults $4, students $2. Monday-Saturday 10 a.m.-5 p.m.

ROSWELL
CHATTAHOOCHEE NATURE CENTER
9135 Willeo Road, Roswell, 770-992-2055; www.chattnaturecenter.com

It's hard to believe that this pristine forest exists just a short drive outside of Atlanta. It's a great place to get away from it all for a hike along an easy trail or for some prime bird-watching—turkey vultures, Cooper's hawks and screech owls are among the feathered creatures that nest in Georgia. To really commune with nature, borrow one of the center's backpacks (free with admission), which include books and field guides, activity sheets and even a kit to make castings of animal tracks. The center also offers overnight camping and workshops.

Admission: adults $5, seniors $4, children 3-12 $2, members and children 2 and under free. Monday-Saturday 9 a.m.-5 p.m., Sunday noon-5 p.m.

STONE MOUNTAIN
STONE MOUNTAIN PARK
U.S. Highway 78 East, Stone Mountain, 770-498-5690; www.stonemountainpark.com

Atlanta's version of Mount Rushmore is carved into this 825-foot-high granite mountain, depicting three Confederate heroes: President Jefferson Davis, General Robert E. Lee and Lieutenant General Thomas J. "Stonewall" Jackson. The mountain and its famous carving (the world's largest relief sculpture) are the centerpiece for a day of fun for folks of all ages. Sporty types can hike up the mountain, but if you're feeling lazy, take the tram for sweeping views of Atlanta's skyline and beyond. The nightly laser show, projected on the side of the mountain and set to music, is a local favorite.

Adventure pass admission (includes more than a dozen attractions in the park): adults $25, seniors and military $22, children 3-11 $20, children under 3 free. Daily 10 a.m.-5 p.m.

WHERE TO STAY

ADAIRSVILLE
★★★BARNSLEY GARDENS RESORT
597 Barnsley Gardens Road, Adairsville, 877-773-2447; www.barnsleyresort.com

You'll impress your sweetie with a romantic getaway to this lovely north Georgia resort. Neatly manicured lawns and tree-lined paths give it the air of an English manor, and you'll love canoodling in your warm, inviting cottage, which has an antique-like appearance with a wood-burning fireplace and pine flooring. It is also an ideal spot for outdoorsmen; you'll find fly and spin fishing in nearby ponds and lakes, quail hunting, an Orvis-run shooting grounds and horseback riding. If you're here for a romantic weekend, bond over a round on the 18-hole championship golf course, a bicycle ride on the grounds, a couples massage at the full-service spa or a romantic dinner at one of the three restaurants. You'll return home feeling like a newlywed.

87 rooms. Restaurant, bar. Fitness center. Tennis. Pool. Spa. Pets accepted. $251-350

ALPHARETTA
★★★MARRIOTT ALPHARETTA
5750 Windward Parkway, Alpharetta, 770-754-9600, 800-228-9290; www.marriott.com

Chandeliers, Oriental rugs and luxurious furnishings accent the lobby of this elegant hotel located in Windward Office Park. Its corporate surroundings, business center services, and upscale décor and amenities make it perfect for business travelers.

318 rooms. Restaurant, bar. $151-250

BRASELTON
★★★CHÂTEAU ÉLAN WINERY & RESORT
100 Rue Charlemagne, Braselton, 800-233-9463; www.chateauelan.com

Drive 30 minutes north of downtown and you'll be transported to a French chateau with a 75-acre vineyard. Popular among locals looking for a quick weekend getaway, this massive resort complex offers cozy rooms full of warm pastel hues and country furnishings, and oversized tubs perfect for soaking away a day's worth of activities, whether you hit the courts for a tennis match or tried your luck on the rock-climbing wall. If you're here for the spa's stress-melting massages and facials, you might want to reserve one of its 14 suites; they're each individually decorated with themes ranging from "Western" to "Hi-Tech." If you really want to live like French royalty, reserve the Presidential Suite, opulently decorated with ornately carved furnishings. And then of course, there's the wine. On a wine tour and tasting you'll learn all about the vineyard's many grape varieties, including the locally famous muscadine; buy a bottle and customize the label with any design—the perfect souvenir for a weekend in the faux-French countryside.

275 rooms. Restaurant, bar. Fitness center. Tennis. Golf. Pool. Spa. Business center. $151-250

COLLEGE PARK
★★★HILTON ATLANTA AIRPORT
1031 Virginia Ave., College Park, 404-767-9000; www.hilton.com

Low-flying planes won't interrupt sleep at this 17-story hotel tower; the guest rooms include triple-paned windows and comfortable mattresses. If you want a few more perks, spring for a room on the executive level, and you'll enjoy gratis continental breakfast and evening hors d'oeuvres daily (you also get an upgraded room, though it will look pretty similar to the white-walled, dark-wood-furniture-filled others). Although downtown is just minutes away (and the free hotel shuttle will deliver you to a nearby MARTA station), you might not want to leave the shadow of the airport—not when there's a basketball court, a swimming pool and whirlpool, video games, a pool table and restaurants to explore.

504 rooms. Restaurant, bar. Fitness center. Pool. Business center. Pets accepted. $61-150

DULUTH
★★★MARRIOTT ATLANTA GWINNETT PLACE
1775 Pleasant Hill Road, Duluth, 770-923-1775, 800-228-9290; www.marriott.com

Located on 11 landscaped acres in Gwinnett County in a northeastern suburb of Atlanta, this hotel offers spacious guest rooms, an indoor and outdoor pool, whirlpool and health club.

426 rooms. Restaurant, bar. Business center. Fitness center. Pool. $151-250

DUNWOODY

★★★W ATLANTA - PERIMETER

111 Perimeter Center West, Dunwoody, 770-396-6800; www.starwoodhotels.com

Located in a suburb north of the city known for its office parks, hospitals and malls, this W is an ideal spot for business travelers who aren't interested in local attractions or the upscale dining found downtown but need to focus on getting the job done. However, this hotel provides a much better setting than a cubicle; the guest rooms are outfitted with balconies, blond-wood furniture, leather upholstered headboards, a sleek all-white color scheme and bathrooms stocked with sweet lemon-scented Bliss spa products.

274 rooms. Restaurant, bar. Fitness center. Pool. Pets accepted. $151-250

★★★WHITWORTH INN

6593 McEver Road, Flowery Branch, 770-967-2386; www.whitworthinn.com

If a quiet, country retreat is what you're looking for, bask in the tranquility of this beautifully landscaped bed and breakfast located 40 miles north of Atlanta. Each lovely room has its own private bath. You'll feel right at home in this cozy space.

10 rooms. Complimentary breakfast. $61-150

GREENSBORO

★★★★THE RITZ-CARLTON LODGE, REYNOLDS PLANTATION

1 Lake Oconee Trail, Greensboro, 706-467-0600, 800-542-8680; www.ritzcarlton.com

Located an hour from Atlanta, this resort on the 8,000-acre Reynolds Plantation overlooks Lake Oconee, Georgia's second-largest lake. Fill your days with fishing, boating or waterskiing on the lake. Golf is a major attraction, with 99 holes designed by legends like Jack Nicklaus, Rees Jones, Tom Fazio and Bob Cupp. Then retire to one of the comfortable guest rooms, designed with a rich blend of American and European fabrics and furniture.

251 rooms. Restaurant, bar. Business center. Fitness center. Spa. Beach. Pool. Golf. Tennis. $251-350

MARIETTA

★★★HYATT REGENCY SUITES ATLANTA NORTHWEST

2999 Windy Hill Road, Marietta, 770-956-1234, 800-233-1234; www.atlantasuites.hyatt.com

Located just 15 minutes from downtown Atlanta, this suburban all-suite property offers an array of amenities for business and leisure travelers. The guest rooms have modern conveniences like flat-screen TVs and wireless Internet access.

202 rooms. Restaurant, bar. Business center. Fitness center. $151-250

★★★HILTON ATLANTA/MARIETTA HOTEL AND CONFERENCE CENTER

500 Powder Springs St., Marietta, 770-427-2500, 888-685-2500; www.mariettaresort.com

Located just a short walk from Marietta Square and overlooking a championship golf course, this resort (the former site of the Georgia Military Institute) works well for business and family vacations, offering comfortable suites and an array of amenities. Along with an outdoor pool, whirlpool, tennis and golf, the resort hosts croquet games on the lawn in the summer.

207 rooms. Restaurant, bar. Pool. Tennis. Golf. $61-150

NORCROSS

★★★HILTON ATLANTA NORTHEAST

5993 Peachtree Industrial Blvd., Norcross, 770-447-4747, 800-445-8667; www.hilton.com

Located a short drive from downtown Atlanta, this hotel has spacious and recently redesigned guest rooms, as well as a warm and friendly staff. Its outer façade is well known locally as it resembles a castle, thus earning the hotel the nickname of "Castle on the Hill."

272 rooms. Restaurant, bar. Fitness center. $61-150

★★★MARRIOTT ATLANTA NORCROSS-PEACHTREE CORNERS

475 Technology Parkway, Norcross, 770-263-8558, 800-228-9290; www.marriott.com

Located in Technology Park, this well-appointed hotel is great for business travelers. The hotel has a well-equipped business center and 4,000 square feet of meeting space.

218 rooms. Restaurant, bar. $61-150

SMYRNA

★★★THE RENAISSANCE WAVERLY HOTEL

2450 Galleria Parkway, Smyrna, 770-953-4500; www.marriott.com

If you're in town for an event at the Cobb Galleria Convention Centre, the adjacent Renaissance Waverly Hotel couldn't be more convenient. Easy access to the trade-show floor isn't all it has to offer: the hotel's airy atrium is a good place to catch your breath after a long day of pressing the flesh, and the recently renovated sage, tawny and white guest rooms are spacious and boast a generous pile of pillows, contemporary wall art and polished-wood furniture. Since you're probably here for work, you'll head to the business center that is even equipped with full secretarial services. To unwind after a long day of meet-and-greet, stop by Tosca Blu Bar to sip one of the signature cocktails before heading over to Medici for some mushroom and butternut squash tortellini or a Tuscan-style rubbed steak.

521 rooms. Restaurant, bar. Fitness center. Pool. Spa. Business center. $151-250

RECOMMENDED

BUFORD

LAKE LANIER RESORT

7000 Holiday Road, Buford, 770-945-8787, 800-840-5253; www.lakelanierislands.com

Best known for its championship golf course, Lake Lanier is set on a hillside surrounded by hardwood trees and Lake Sidney Lanier. The island-like setting has swimming, boating and more. This is a favorite Southern retreat.

224 rooms. Restaurant, bar. Beach. Golf. $61-150

MARIETTA

THE WHITLOCK

57 Whitlock Ave., Marietta, 770-428-1495; www.whitlockinn.com

Located just one block west of Marietta Square on a stately tree-lined street, this fully restored Victorian mansion with distinctively different guest rooms provides all the charm one would expect in the South.

5 rooms. No children under 12. Complimentary breakfast. $61-150

WHERE TO EAT

BRASELTON

★★★CHATEAU ELAN'S LE CLOS

100 Rue Charlemagne Drive, Braselton, 678-425-0900, 800-233-9463; www.chateauelan.com

One of the many elegant restaurants found in the charming Chateau Elan Winery & Resort, Le Clos features contemporary French cuisine. The charming, intimate space seats just 28 diners. Fine, estate-bottled wines from Chateau Elan's vineyards, along with choices from other regions of the world, are expertly paired with the five-course prix fixe menu of haute cuisine.

French. Dinner. Closed Sunday-Thursday. Reservations required. $36-85

GREENSBORO

★★★GEORGIA'S

1 Lake Oconee Trail, Greensboro, 706-467-0600; www.ritzcarlton.com

Located on the lower level of The Ritz-Carlton Lodge Reynolds Plantation, Georgia's offers countryside charm with a fireplace, antler chandeliers and views of Lake Oconee. A menu of inventive regional Southern cuisine featuring local and organic ingredients makes any occasion special.

Southern. Breakfast, lunch, dinner, brunch. Children's menu. Reservations recommended. Outdoor seating. $36-85

ROSWELL

★★★BISTRO VG

70 W. Crossville Road, Roswell, 770-993-1156; www.knowwheretogogh.com

This out-of-the-way restaurant offers a surprisingly lovely dining experience. The food is eclectic American, while the setting is old Southern charm. The dining room combines old world Europe with urban edge and serves New American creations. The wine cellar has more than 500 selections from around the world.

American. Lunch, dinner. Bar. Children's menu. Reservations recommended. $36-85

★★★HI LIFE

3380 Holcomb Bridge Road, Roswell, 770-409-0101; www.hiliferestaurant.com

This American restaurant has a sleek, modern design. The creative food is fresh and flavorful, and so is the cocktail menu. It also features an

---

WHAT IS THE BEST GOLF RESORT IN GREATER ATLANTA?

The Ritz-Carlton Lodge, Reynolds Plantation: Several high-end resorts offer golfers opportunities, but for the true golf lover, the Ritz-Carlton in Greensboro offers 99 holes of golf designed by pros Rees Jones, Jack Nicklaus, Tom Fazio and Bob Cupp. With five courses and professional instruction available, this is where to go to get your golf game on.

extensive wine list.

American. Lunch (Monday-Friday), dinner. Closed Sunday. Bar. Children's menu. Reservations recommended. Outdoor seating. $16-35

VININGS

★★★CANOE

4199 Paces Ferry Road, Vinings, 770-432-2663; www.canoeatl.com

Request a table with a view (or better yet, sit outside) when dining at Canoe. Both the bank of windows and the canopy-shaded patio overlook the restaurant's lovely gardens and the lazily moving Chattahoochee River. Inside is gorgeous, too; the rustic cabin styling somehow manages to be elegant, although diners celebrating a special evening and couples on a date can make the atmosphere pretty noisy. The menu is full of local and artisanal ingredients, thoughtfully prepared: Quail, unexpectedly stuffed with duck, comes garnished with grilled endive, dried cherries and roasted peanuts; and tender braised rabbit is accompanied with ravioli filled with meltingly rich bacon. The kitchen's creativity extends to the dessert menu: A chocolate custard tart is paired with brittled banana and butter rum ice cream.

American. Lunch (Monday-Friday), dinner, Sunday brunch. Bar. Reservations recommended. Outdoor seating. $36-85

RECOMMENDED

VININGS INN

3011 Paces Mill Road, Vinings, 404-438-2202; www.viningsinn.com

The 19th-century house that is now Vinings Inn has been through many incarnations, but it's an eclectic yet effective space for the restaurant it has housed for the past 15 years (prior to that, this building used to contain only the bar, with the restaurant across the street). White-cloth-clad tables fill rambling rooms that retain charming details like fireplaces, wavy vintage-glass windows and creaking wooden floors, not to mention the occasional endearing whiff of musty, old-house smell. The clientele ranges from neighborhood families to business diners to young couples heading upstairs to the friendly bar nestled under the sloping ceiling. The menu changes seasonally, but stalwarts include a generously meaty crab cake and peach barbecue shrimp. With such a comforting atmosphere and solidly satisfying food, here's hoping that it's awhile before this historic building changes identities again.

Southern. Lunch (Saturday-Sunday), dinner. Bar. Reservations recommended. Outdoor seating. $36-85

SPAS

GREENSBORO

★★★★THE RITZ-CARLTON LODGE REYNOLDS PLANTATION SPA

The Ritz-Carlton Lodge, Reynolds Plantation, 1 Lake Oconee Trail, Greensboro, 706-467-0600; www.ritzcarlton.com

The Ritz-Carlton Lodge Spa is a 26,000-square-foot spa offering an array of massages, body treatments, facials and other therapies. Massage techniques include Swedish, deep tissue and reflexology. The resort's wellness center features advanced cardiovascular equipment, an indoor lap pool, health screenings and consultations with counselors who will design an individual exercise program.

COASTAL GEORGIA

Savannah has a wealth of history and architecture that few American cities can match. Residents pride themselves on their Southern charm and hospitality. Famous Southern chef Paula Deen hails from Savannah, and author John Berendt gave the rest of the country a taste of the city's allure in his 1990s novel (and later movie) *Midnight in the Garden of Good and Evil*.

The city's many rich, green parks—it has 16 in the historic district alone—are blooming legacies of the brilliance of its founder, General James E. Oglethorpe. Savannah quickly took its place as a leading city first in the settling of America and later in the wealth and grandeur of the Old South as the leading market and shipping point for tobacco and cotton.

Reconstruction was painful, but 20 years after the Civil War, cotton was king again. By the 20th century, Savannah turned to manufacturing. With more than 200 industries by World War II, the city's prosperity has been measured by the activity of its port, which included ship-building booms during both world wars. Today more than 1,400 historically and architecturally significant buildings have been restored in Savannah's historic district, making it one of the largest urban historic landmark districts in the country. Fountains, small gardens, intricate ironwork and other amazing architectural details decorate this town and add to its beauty. The Victorian district south of the historic district offers some of the best examples of post-Civil War Victorian architecture in the country.

The popular year-round Georgia resort Tybee Island is essentially a V-shaped sandbar fronting the Atlantic for nearly four miles, and the Savannah River for more than two miles. The beach runs the entire length of the island. Its north end is marked by old coastal defenses, a museum and a lighthouse at the tip. Reached by a causeway from Savannah and Highway 80, the beach has a boardwalk, fishing pier, amusements, hotels, motels and vacation cottages.

Sea Island was created in the 1920s by Hudson Motor Company magnate Howard Coffin. The first hotel to open on the island was The Cloisters, which underwent an extensive and impressive multimillion-dollar renovation in 2006. The outstanding golf courses have also been renovated. The small and luxurious Lodge at Sea Island offers an intimate 40-room retreat.

Brunswick, on the southern third of Georgia's seacoast and separated from the Golden Isles by the Marshes of Glynn and the Intracoastal Waterway, is the gateway to St. Simons Island, Jekyll Island and Sea Island. It's also a manufacturing and seafood processing town, known as one of the shrimp capitals of the world. Its harbor is a full oceangoing seaport, as well as a home port to coastal fishing and shrimping fleets. Its natural beauty is enhanced by plantings of palms and flowering shrubs along main avenues, contrasting with moss-covered ancient oaks in spacious parks.

Cumberland Island National Seashore, off the coast of Georgia, is accessible only by a passenger tour boat, which operates year-round. Mainland departures are from Saint Marys. A visit to the island is a walking experience, and there are no restaurants or shops. Salt marshes fringe the island's western side, while white-sand beaches decorate the Atlantic-facing east side. The interior is forested primarily by live oak. Native Americans, Spanish and English have all lived on the island; most structures date from the pre-Civil War plantation era, though there are turn-of-the-century buildings built by the Thomas Carnegie family, who used the island as their 19th-century retreat.

Connected to the mainland by a causeway, Jekyll Island, the smallest of Georgia's coastal islands with 5,600 acres of highlands and 10,000 acres of marshland, was favored by Native Americans for hunting and fishing. Spanish missionaries arrived in the late 16th and early 17th centuries and established a mission. In 1734, during an expedition southward, General James Oglethorpe passed by the island and named it for his friend and financial supporter, Sir Joseph Jekyll. Later William Horton, one of Oglethorpe's officers, established a plantation on the island. Horton's land grant passed to several owners before the island was sold to Christophe du Bignon, a Frenchman who was escaping the French Revolution. It remained in the du Bignon family as a plantation for almost a century. In 1858, the slave ship Wanderer arrived at the island and unloaded the last major cargo of slaves ever to land in the U.S. In 1886, John Eugene du Bignon sold the island to a group of wealthy businessmen from the northeast, who formed the Jekyll Island Club. Club members who wintered at Jekyll in exclusive privacy from early January to early April included J.P. Morgan, William Rockefeller, Edwin Gould, Joseph Pulitzer and R.T. Crane, Jr. Some built fabulous houses they called cottages, many of which are still standing. By World War II, the club had been abandoned for economic and social reasons, and in 1947 the island was sold to the state. The Jekyll Island Authority was created to conserve beaches and manage the island while maintaining it as a year-round resort.

One of Georgia's Golden Isles, St. Simons Island has been under five flags: Spain, France, Britain, the U.S. and the Confederate States of America. Fragments of each culture remain, including Fort Frederica national monument, the fort defending the Georgia colony from the Spaniards. Cotton plantations ruled the island for a time, but today it's a thriving resort community with sandy beaches, golf courses, dolphin watches, shopping and restaurants.

James Oglethorpe recruited Scottish Highlanders to protect Georgia's frontier on the Altamaha River in 1736. Calling their town Darien, they guarded Savannah from Spanish and native attack and carved out large plantations from the South Georgia wilderness. After 1800, Darien thrived as a great timber port until the early 20th century. Today, shrimp boats dock in the river over which Darien Scots once kept watch.

WHAT TO SEE

BRUNSWICK
HOFWYL-BROADFIELD PLANTATION STATE HISTORIC SITE
5556 Highway 17 N., Brunswick, 912-264-7333; www.gastateparks.org

The evolution of this working rice plantation, from 1807 to 1973, is depicted through tours of the plantation house, museum and trails.

Admission: $2.50-$5. Thursday-Saturday 9 a.m.-5 p.m.

DARIEN
FORT KING GEORGE STATE HISTORIC SITE
1600 Wayne St., Darien, 912-437-4770; www.gastateparks.org

South Carolina scouts built this fort in 1721 near an abandoned Native

American village and Spanish mission to block Spanish and French expansion into Georgia, thereby establishing the foundation for the later English Colony of Georgia. The fort and its blockhouse have been reconstructed to original form. The museum interprets the periods of Native American, Spanish and British occupations, the settlement of Darien and Georgia's timber industry.
Tuesday-Sunday 9 a.m.-5 p.m.

JEKYLL ISLAND
JEKYLL ISLAND CLUB NATIONAL HISTORIC LANDMARK DISTRICT
901 Jekyll Island Causeway, Jekyll Island, 912-635-3636; www.jekyllisland.com
Once one of the nation's most exclusive resorts, this restored district is a memorable example of turn-of-the-century wealth. Exhibition buildings and shops are open daily.
Tours are available.

SAVANNAH
ANDREW LOW HOUSE
329 Abercorn St., Savannah, 912-233-6854; www.andrewlowhouse.com
Built for Andrew Low in 1848, this was later the residence of Juliette Gordon Low, founder of Girl Scouts of America. There are period furnishings through-out the residence.
Admission: adults $8, Girl Scouts and children 12 and under $4.50. Monday-Wednesday, Friday-Saturday 10 a.m.-4:30 p.m., Sunday noon-4:30 p.m.

CHRIST CHURCH
28 Bull St., Savannah, 912-234-4131; www.christchurchsavannah.org
The mother church of Georgia, the congregation dates from 1733. Among early rectors were John Wesley and George Whitfield. The present church is the third building erected on this site.
Sunday services: 8 a.m., 10:30 a.m.

CITY HALL
Bull and Bay streets, Savannah, 912-651-6410; www.ci.savannah.ga.us
A gold dome tops the four-story neoclassic façade of this 1905 building, which replaced the original 1799 structure. A tablet outside commemorates the sailing of the *SS Savannah*. A model is displayed in the Council Chamber. Another tablet is dedicated to the *John Randolph*, the first iron-sided vessel launched in American waters.
Monday-Friday.

COLONIAL PARK CEMETERY
E. Oglethorpe Ave. and Abercorn St., Savannah, 912-651-6843; www.savannahga.gov
This was the colony's first and only burial ground for many years. Button Gwinnett, a signer of the Declaration of Independence, is buried in the cemetery, as are other distinguished Georgians. Closed since 1853, it has been a city park since 1896.

DAVENPORT HOUSE
324 E. State St., Savannah, 912-236-8097; www.davenporthousemuseum.org
Constructed by master builder Isaiah Davenport, this is one of the finest examples of Federal architecture in Savannah. Saved from demolition in 1955

HIGHLIGHT

WHAT ARE THE TOP THINGS TO DO IN COASTAL GEORGIA?

STROLL THE SAVANNAH RIVERFRONT
Restoration of the riverfront bluff has worked to preserve and stabilize the historic waterfront, which includes a nine-block brick concourse of parks, studios, museums, shops, restaurants and pubs.

CLIMB LIGHTHOUSES
The Tybee lighthouse is one of the oldest active lighthouses in the U.S. Visitors may climb to the top for a scenic view of Tybee and historic Fort Reven. The St. Simon lighthouse stands at 104 feet high and has been in continuous operation, except during wartime, since 1872. Visitors may climb to the top here also.

VISIT JEKYLL ISLAND
Enjoy seeing dolphins and sea turtles and experiencing salt-water activities on Jekyll Island. Once used as an exclusive retreat, Jekyll Island still gives historians and families a taste of that gilded age.

by the Historic Savannah Foundation, it is now restored and furnished with period antiques.
Admission: adults $8, children ages 6–17 $5. Monday-Saturday 10 a.m.-4 p.m., Sunday 1-4 p.m.

GREEN-MELDRIM HOUSE
1 W. Macon St., Savannah, 912-233-3845; www.stjohnssav.org
The Antebellum house used by General Sherman during the occupation of Savannah from 1864 to 1865 is now the Parish House of St. John's Church.
Tours are available. Suggested donation: $7. Monday, Thursday, Friday, 10 a.m.-4 p.m. Saturday, 10 a.m.-1 p.m.

HISTORIC SAVANNAH WATERFRONT AREA
River Street, Savannah
Savannah's historic district comprises just 2.5 square miles, but they're packed full of historic structures, shops, inns, gardens and culture. After exploring the area, indulge in some Southern cooking and seafood for lunch or dinner.

LAUREL GROVE CEMETERY (SOUTH)
37th St., Ogeechee Road, Savannah; www.savannahga.gov
Laurel Grove was started as a segregated cemetery and today is managed as

two (the north side is the white section). Possibly the oldest black cemetery currently in use, Laurel Grove houses graves of both antebellum slaves and free blacks. Andrew Bryan (1737-1812), a pioneer Baptist preacher, is buried here. *Daily 8 a.m.-5 p.m.*

OWENS-THOMAS HOUSE
124 Abercorn St., Savannah, 912-233-9743; www.telfair.org

This authentically furnished Regency-style house was designed between 1816 and 1819 by William Jay. The walled garden is designed and planted in 1820s style. *Admission: $15. Tuesday-Saturday 10 a.m.-5 p.m., Sunday 1-5 p.m., Monday noon-5 p.m.*

SAVANNAH HISTORY MUSEUM
303 Martin Luther King Jr. Blvd., Savannah, 912-651-6825; www.chsgeorgia.org/shm

This museum traces Savannah's history from its founding in 1733 to present day. It is housed in the Georgia Railway Passenger Shed, a National Historic Landmark. *Admission: adults and children 6-18 $5, children 5 and under free. Monday-Friday 8:30 a.m.-5 p.m., Saturday-Sunday 9 a.m.-5 p.m.*

TRUSTEES' GARDEN SITE
10 E. Broad St., Savannah, 912-443-3277; www.trusteesgarden.com

This is the original site of a 10-acre experimental garden modeled in 1733 after the Chelsea Gardens in London. Peach trees planted in the garden launched Georgia's peach industry. The Pirates' House, a former inn for visiting seamen, has been restored and is now a restaurant. Robert Louis Stevenson referred to the inn in his book, *Treasure Island.*

U.S. CUSTOMS HOUSE
1-5 E. Bay St., Savannah

The U.S. Customs House was erected in 1850 on the site of the colony's first public building. The granite columns' carved capitals were modeled from tobacco leaves. A tablet on Bull Street marks the site where John Wesley preached his first Savannah sermon.

ST. SIMONS ISLAND
ST. SIMONS LIGHTHOUSE
101 12th St., St. Simons Island, 912-638-4666; www.saintsimonslighthouse.org

The original lighthouse, which stood 75 feet high, was destroyed by Confederate troops in 1861 to prevent it from guiding Union invaders onto the island. The present lighthouse, 104 feet high, has been in continuous operation, except during wartime, since 1872. Visitors may climb to the top.

TYBEE ISLAND
TYBEE MUSEUM AND LIGHTHOUSE
30 Meddin Drive, Tybee Island, 912-786-5801; www.tybeelighthouse.org

Climb to the top of one of the oldest active lighthouses in the U.S. A museum tracing the history of Tybee from colonial times to 1845 is housed in a coastal artillery battery built in 1898. Exhibits and a gift shop are located in an 1880s lighthouse keeper's cottage. *Admission: adults $7, seniors, military personnel and children 6-17 $5, children 5 and under free. Wednesday-Monday 9 a.m.-5:30 p.m.*

SPECIAL EVENTS

WHAT ARE THE BEST CULTURAL OFFERINGS?

SAVANNAH SCOTTISH GAMES AND HIGHLAND GATHERING

J.F. Gregory Park, Highway 144, Richmond Hill; www.savannahscottishgames.com
Clans gather for a weekend of Highland games, piping, drumming, dancing and the traditional "Kirkin' o' the Tartans."
Early May.

SAVANNAH TOUR OF HOMES AND GARDENS

18 Abercorn St., Savannah, 912-234-8054; www.savannahtourofhomes.org
Tours are sponsored by Christ Episcopal Church with the Historic Savannah Foundation. They offer day and candlelight tours of more than 30 private houses and gardens.
March.

ST. PATRICK'S DAY PARADE

912-233-4804; www.savannahsaintpatricksday.com
This parade rivals the one in New York City in size and is one of the largest St. Pat's festivals. The route runs north of Jones Street to the river, west of East Broad Street, and east of Boundary Street and the Talmadge Bridge.
March.

WHERE TO STAY

CUMBERLAND ISLAND
★★★GREYFIELD INN
4 N. Second St., Fernandina Beach, Cumberland Island, 904-261-6408, 866-401-8581; www.greyfieldinn.com
Accessible by private ferry from Fernandina Beach, Fla., this inn is a tranquil place to enjoy Cumberland Island's natural beauty and abundant wildlife. Furnished with family heirlooms and antiques, the guest rooms and suites vary widely. Room rates include breakfast, a picnic lunch, cocktail hour, gourmet dinner and snacks throughout the day, as well as unlimited use of the inn's sporting, fishing and beach equipment. Note: There's a two-night minimum stay.
17 rooms. Restaurant, bar. Fitness center. No children under 6. $351 and up

JEKYLL ISLAND
★★★JEKYLL ISLAND CLUB HOTEL
371 Riverview Drive, Jekyll Island, 912-635-2600, 800-535-9547; www.jekyllclub.com
Once a popular and exclusive retreat for the nation's wealthy elite, this gorgeous

hotel on Georgia's historic Jekyll Island pampers guests and entertains with golf, fishing, water sports, shopping and more.

157 rooms. Restaurant, bar. Beach. $151-250

SAVANNAH

★★★17 HUNDRED 90 INN AND RESTAURANT

307 E. President St., Savannah, 912-236-7122, 800-487-1790; www.17hundred90.com

Savannah's oldest inn features 14 rooms furnished with antiques and fireplaces. The inn also has an excellent restaurant.

14 rooms. Restaurant, bar. Complimentary breakfast. $151-250

★★★EAST BAY INN

225 E. Bay St., Savannah, 912-238-1225, 800-500-1225; www.eastbayinn.com

Just steps away from the historic waterfront, this romantic inn has many beautiful rooms filled with period furnishings and antiques. The owners hold a cheese and wine reception every evening for guests.

28 rooms. Restaurant. Complimentary breakfast. $151-250

★★★HILTON SAVANNAH DESOTO

15 E. Liberty St., Savannah, 912-232-9000, 800-774-1500; www.hilton.com

This fully equipped hotel is close to shops, sightseeing and restaurants. The hotel, built in the 1890s, has a rooftop pool and fine dining restaurant.

246 rooms. Restaurant, bar. Fitness center. Business center. $151-250

★★★HYATT REGENCY SAVANNAH

2 W. Bay St., Savannah, 912-238-1234; www.hyatt.com

Perched on the scenic waterfront of the Savannah River, this hotel offers superb accommodations, first-class amenities and an attentive staff.

351 rooms, Restaurant, bar. Business center. $61-150

★★★MARRIOTT SAVANNAH RIVERFRONT

100 General McIntosh Blvd., Savannah, 912-233-7722, 800-228-9200; www.marriott.com

Adjacent to the world-renowned River Street and the historic riverfront, this hotel makes for a truly delightful stay for vacationers. A stroll along the hotel's riverwalk leads to taverns, quaint shops and great restaurants.

341 rooms. Restaurant, bar. $151-250

★★★THE PRESIDENT'S QUARTERS INN

225 E. President St., Savannah, 912-233-1600, 800-233-1776; www.presidentsquarters.com

Once a place where diplomats and generals rested their heads, The President's Quarters now opens its doors to guests of all stripes. Relax in the elegantly appointed parlors or stroll through the renowned gardens.

16 rooms. Restaurant. Complimentary breakfast. $151-250

★★★RIVER STREET INN

124 E. Bay St., Savannah, 912-234-6400, 800-253-4229; www.riverstreetinn.com

Rooms have four-poster beds and French balconies and offer views of the Savannah River. Wine and appetizers are served in the afternoon and homemade chocolates are delivered to rooms in the evening.

86 rooms. Restaurant, bar. $151-250

★★★THE WESTIN SAVANNAH HARBOR GOLF RESORT AND SPA

1 Resort Drive, Savannah, 912-201-2000, 800-937-8461; www.westin.com

Just a water taxi ride away from the historic district, resort features include a PGA-tour quality golf course, full-service spa, waterfront pools, four tennis courts and access to fishing charter boats.

403 rooms. Restaurant, bar. Business center. Tennis. Golf. Spa. Pool. $151-250

SEA ISLAND

★★★★★THE CLOISTER

100 First St., Sea Island, 912-634-3964; www.cloister.com

This 80-year-old resort is an icon of world-class resort luxury. Personal service, children's programs and an array of amenities leave visitors with a regal experience. An impressive $350 million renovation included the addition of a magnificent spa, replete with 23 elaborate treatment rooms and exclusive product lines. The resort features wood-beamed rooms decorated with rich, jewel-toned Turkish rugs and plush, pillow-topped beds. Six dining options abound, including the Forbes Five Star Georgian Room, as well as a casual raw bar and grill, where after-beach oysters and cocktails are the specialty. The five miles of private beachfront is the ideal setting for an afternoon stroll.

212 rooms. Restaurant, bar. Complimentary breakfast. Fitness center. Pool. Spa. Golf. $351 and up

ST. SIMONS ISLAND

★★★KING AND PRINCE RESORT

201 Arnold Road, St. Simons Island, 912-638-3631, 800-342-0212; www.kingandprince.com

Located on the ocean's edge directly on the beach, the resort is within minutes of a quaint shopping village and restaurants. The property offers oceanfront rooms, a one-bedroom house and a five-bedroom house. Outdoor amenities are abundant, including biking, kayak and sailboat rentals, pools, a beach and tennis.

186 rooms. Restaurant, bar. Fitness center. Pool. Golf. Beach. $151-250

★★★★★THE LODGE AT SEA ISLAND GOLF CLUB

100 Retreat Ave., St. Simons Island, 912-638-3611, 888-732-4752; www.seaisland.com

Generations of privileged travelers have made Sea Island their top vacation destination. Created in the spirit of

European sporting estates, this resort features first-rate tennis and equestrian facilities, three championship golf courses and exquisite dining options. Guest rooms are tastefully decorated with hardwood floors, exposed beam ceilings and private balconies overlooking the rolling fairways of the Plantation Golf Course, St. Simons Sound or the Atlantic Ocean. Complimentary bicycles and 24-hour butler service solidify the top-notch customer service.

40 rooms. Complimentary breakfast. Restaurant, bar. Fitness center. Pool. Spa. Beach. Golf. Tennis. Business center. $351 and up

★★★THE LODGE ON LITTLE ST. SIMONS ISLAND

1000 Hampton Point Drive, St. Simons Island, 912-638-7472, 888-733-5774;
www.littlestsimonsisland.com

This small inn is a collection of five cottages and 15 rooms vested in preserving the natural wilderness. The inn offers comfortable lodging and fine restaurants, plus a great view of the surrounding flora and fauna.

15 rooms. Restaurant. $351 and up

RECOMMENDED

SAVANNAH

BALLASTONE INN & TOWNHOUSE

14 E. Oglethorpe Ave., Savannah, 912-236-1484, 800-822-4553; www.ballastone.com

One of Savannah's first bed and breakfasts, the Inn is set in a 160-year-old mansion. It is voted annually by locals as the best romantic getaway in Savannah.

16 rooms. Complimentary breakfast. $151-250

BOHEMIAN HOTEL SAVANNAH RIVERFRONT, SAVANNAH

102 West Bay St., Savannah, 912-721-3800; www.bohemianhotelsavannah.com

Part of the Marriot's growing Autograph Collection of hotels, the Bohemian Hotel Savannah Riverfront is ideally located on the gorgeous Savannah riverfront. Each of the 75 rooms and suites are decorated with unique British campaign furniture that reflects the era when the British first settled in Savannah. The exceptional views are best enjoyed on the roof at the appropriately named Rocks venues.

75 rooms. Restaurant, bar. Fitness center. Spa. $251-350

ELIZA THOMPSON HOUSE

5 W. Jones St., Savannah, 912-236-3620, 800-348-9378; www.elizathompsonhouse.com

Elegantly restored and recently refurbished, rooms offer quiet and comfortable surroundings. The inn is also conveniently located near the historic district.

25 rooms. Complimentary breakfast. $151-250

FOLEY HOUSE INN

14 W. Hull St., Savannah, 912-232-6622, 800-647-3708; www.foleyinn.com

Located in the center of historic Savannah, this inn has been serving guests since the Civil War. It's made up of two restored mansions facing Chippewa Square.

19 rooms. Complimentary breakfast. $151-250

MANSION ON FORSYTH PARK HOTEL AND SPA

700 Drayton St., Savannah, 912-238-5158; www.mansiononforsythpark.com

Another of Marriot's distinctive Autograph Collection of hotels, the Mansion on Forsyth Park is set in a beautifully restored historic Victorian Mansion in the heart of the Historic District. While not exploring the gorgeous Forsyth Park at your doorstep, be sure to check out the hotel's own signature collection of over 400 pieces of unique artwork. The 126 guest rooms are luxuriously appointed. Epicureans can indulge at the 700 Drayton restaurant, as well as at the unusual 700 Cooking school. Those in the need for some relaxation can partake in the aptly named Poseidon Spa.

126 rooms. Restaurant, bar. Business center. Fitness center. Pool. Spa. $251-350

WHERE TO EAT

JEKYLL ISLAND

★★★GRAND DINING ROOM

371 Riverview Drive, Jekyll Island, 912-635-2400; www.jekyllclub.com

The formal dining room of this historic resort is as grand as its name suggests. A dramatic colonnade leads to a large fireplace, lined by plush upholstered chairs. The low country cooking features local seafood.

American. Breakfast, lunch, dinner, Sunday brunch. Children's menu. Jacket required (dinner). Reservations recommended. $36-85

SAVANNAH

★★★ELIZABETH ON 37TH

105 E. 37th St., Savannah, 912-236-5547; www.elizabethon37th.net

Opened in 1981 by chef Elizabeth Terry and her husband, Michael, this charming restaurant is the birthplace of New Southern cuisine. The interior of the 1900 Greek Revival-style mansion has a homey feel with brightly painted walls, antique chairs and warm service. Fresh and authentic cuisine draws admiration from across the country.

American. Dinner. Reservations recommended. $36-85

SEA ISLAND

★★★★★GEORGIAN ROOM

100 First St., Sea Island, 800-732-4752; www.seaisland.com

The magnificent Georgian Room is tucked inside The Cloister. The décor is grand, with bas-relief details, gilded chandeliers and a carved stone fireplace. Tables are set with crisp white linens, hand-painted china and silver flatware. Dishes highlight seasonal, fresh ingredients and might include Wagyu New York Strip with sweetbreads, creamer potatoes and horseradish juice. A chef's tasting menu changes every season and vegetarian dishes are available as well. The staff is polished and attentive, and an extensive wine list rounds out the experience.

Continental. Dinner. Jacket and tie required. Reservations required. $86 and up

ST. SIMONS ISLAND

★★★COLT & ALISON

The Lodge at Sea Island Golf Club, 100 First St., St. Simons Island, 800-732-4752; www.seaisland.com

After working up an appetite on Sea Island Resort's renowned 18 holes, take a seat at the steakhouse named after the golf course's creators: Colt & Alison.

Nestled in the Lodge, the restaurant is a cozy backdrop for a scrumptious meal, enjoyed at the fireside tables and leather chairs. The restaurant is known for its wet- and dry-aged beef. Classic Caesar salad, filet mignon au poivre and bananas foster are all prepared tableside. The wine cellar holds an extensive collection.
American. Dinner, Sunday brunch. $86 and up

SPA

SEA ISLAND
★★★★★THE CLOISTER SPA
The Cloister, 100 First St., Sea Island, 912-638-3611, 888-732-4752; www.seaisland.com

Recently renovated, the Spa at Sea Island focuses on customization, with 23 treatment rooms dedicated to an extensive menu of offerings. Spa guides design an experience for guests that may include anything from nutritional consultations to bodywork, baths, wraps and energy treatments. Turkish and Japanese baths personify the spa's simple approach, with the signature bathing ritual and a seven-step infusion of ginger grass and cherry blossom rice body polishes. A special KidSpa program for spa-goers ages 8-15 promotes healthy skin care and includes kid-friendly massages, sports and nature hikes.

NORTHERN GEORGIA

Northern Georgia is famous for the Blue Ridge Mountains and Native American history as well as mines. Once a part of the Cherokee Nation, the town of Dalton was involved in fierce battles and skirmishes in the Civil War as Union forces advanced on Atlanta. Gold fever struck Dahlonega in 1828, 20 years before the Sutter's Mill discovery in California. Derived from the Cherokee word for the color yellow, the land here yielded so much ore that the federal government established a local mint that produced $6,115,569 in gold coins from 1838-1861. Dahlonega is the seat of Lumpkin County, where tourism, manufacturing, higher education and agribusiness are the major sources of employment.

Forests and natural beauty abound in this area. On the shore of 38,000-acre Lake Sidney Lanier, Gainesville is the headquarters for the Chattahoochee National Forest. Almost a third of the land in Murray County is forest and mountains. Opportunities for fishing, hunting, camping, backpacking and mountain biking abound in the surrounding Cohutta Wilderness and woodlands.

A picturesque mountain town, Hiawassee is on Lake Chatuge, surrounded by the Chattahoochee National Forest. Its backdrop is a range of the Blue Ridge Mountains topped by Brasstown Bald Mountain, Georgia's highest peak. Rock hunting, including hunting for the highly prized amethyst crystal, is a favorite activity in surrounding Towns County. The natural setting of the mountains and the Chattahoochee River helped create the atmosphere for this logging town.

WHAT TO SEE

CHATSWORTH
CHIEF VANN HOUSE STATE HISTORIC SITE
82 Highway 225 N., Chatsworth, 706-695-2598; www.gastateparks.org

This brick house was the showplace of the Cherokee Nation. James Vann

HIGHLIGHT

WHAT ARE THE TOP THINGS TO DO IN NORTHERN GEORGIA?

HIKE THE BLUE RIDGE MOUNTAINS

Head to the Chattahoochee National Forest, which occupies 748,608 acres, and includes Georgia's Blue Ridge Mountains toward the north, which have elevations ranging from 1,000 to nearly 5,000 feet.

SPEND SOME TIME ON THE APPALACHIAN NATIONAL SCENIC TRAIL

Thirteen lean-tos are maintained along 76 miles of the southern portion of the trail. Following the crest of the Blue Ridge divide, the trail begins outside Dahlonega and continues for more than 2,000 miles to Mount Katahdin, Maine.

PAN FOR GOLD

Take an underground mine tour (40-45 minutes) through tunnel network of Consolidated Gold Mines. There are displays of original equipment used and instructors available for gold panning.

was half Scottish, half Cherokee. His chief contribution to the tribe was his help in establishing the nearby Moravian Mission for the education of young Cherokee. The three-story house, with foot-thick brick walls, is modified Georgian in style and partly furnished.

Admission: $3.50-5 Thursday-Saturday 9 a.m.-5 p.m.

DALTON

CROWN GARDEN & ARCHIVES

715 Chattanooga Ave., Dalton, 706-278-0217

This is the headquarters of the Whitfield-Murray Historical Society. There is a genealogical library and changing exhibits include Civil War items.

Tuesday-Friday 10 a.m.-5 p.m., Saturday 9 a.m.-1 p.m.

DAHLONEGA

ANNA RUBY FALLS

Off Highway 356, 6 miles north of Helen, 706-878-3574; www.georgiatrails.com

Approximately 1,600 acres of wilderness surround a double waterfall, with drops of 50 and 153 feet. The scenic area is enhanced by laurel, wild azaleas, dogwood and rhododendron.

Daily 9 a.m.-sunset.

APPALACHIAN NATIONAL SCENIC TRAIL
304-535-6278; www.nps.gov/appa

Thirteen lean-tos are maintained along 76 miles of the southern portion of the trail. Following the crest of the Blue Ridge divide, the trail begins outside Dahlonega and continues for more than 2,000 miles to Mount Katahdin, Maine.

CHATTAHOOCHEE NATIONAL FOREST
1755 Cleveland Highway, Dahlonega, 770-297-3000; www.fs.fed.us/conf

This vast forest, occupying 748,608 acres, includes Georgia's Blue Ridge Mountains toward the north, which have elevations ranging from 1,000 to nearly 5,000 feet. Since the forest ranges from the Piedmont to mountainous areas, the Chattahoochee has a diversity of trees and wildlife.

CONSOLIDATED GOLD MINES
185 Consolidated Gold Mine Road, Dahlonega, 706-864-8473; www.consolidatedgoldmine.com

Take an underground mine tour (40-45 minutes) through a tunnel network. There are displays of original equipment used and instructors available for gold panning. *Monday-Friday 10 a.m.-4 p.m., Saturday-Sunday 10 a.m.-5 p.m.*

DAHLONEGA COURTHOUSE GOLD MUSEUM STATE HISTORIC SITE
1 Public Square, Dahlonega, 706-864-2257; www.gastateparks.org

Located in the old Lumpkin County Courthouse, there are exhibits on the first major gold rush and a display of gold coins minted in Dahlonega. Films are shown every half hour. *Admission: $3.50-5. Monday-Saturday 9 a.m.-5 p.m., Sunday 10 a.m.-5 p.m.*

HIAWASSEE
BRASSTOWN BALD MOUNTAIN-VISITOR INFORMATION CENTER
2941 St., Highway 180, Hiawassee, 706-896-2556; www.fs.fed.us/conf

At 4,784 feet, this is Georgia's highest peak. An observation deck affords a view of four states. The visitor center has interpretive programs presented in a mountaintop theater and exhibit hall. *June-October, daily; late April-May, weekends only, weather permitting.*

WHERE TO STAY

HIAWASSEE
★★★BRASSTOWN VALLEY RESORT
6321 Highway 76, Young Harris, 706-379-9900, 800-201-3205; www.brasstownvalley.com

Guests get lost in the views from this mountain lodge as they take in the beautiful Blue Ridge Mountain countryside. This resort offers a rustic feel with many modern touches. Don't miss the vast stables and riding trails on horseback. *102 rooms. Restaurant, bar. Spa. Golf. Pool. $61-150*

RECOMMENDED

DAHLONEGA
THE SMITH HOUSE
84 S. Chestatee St., Dahlonega, 706-867-7000, 800-852-9577; www.smithhouse.com

This charming inn was originally built in 1899. Rooms include single-serving coffee makers and Bulgari toiletries.

16 rooms. Restaurant. Complimentary breakfast. $61-150

WHERE TO EAT

RECOMMENDED
SMITH HOUSE
84 S. Chestatee St., Dahlonega, 706-867-7000; www.smithhouse.com

Priding itself on being like a "step back in time" into the days of the boarding house, Smith House offers family-style Southern hospitality in a small mountain inn atmosphere. Specialties include fried chicken and sweet baked ham, fried okra and candied yams.

Lunch, dinner. Closed most Mondays. $15 and under.

CENTRAL GEORGIA

The center of the state provides visitors opportunities to connect with its Southern charm and play one of the world's most famous golf courses. One of the larger cities in Georgia, Macon stands out for its musical heritage, its cherry trees and its African-American heritage. Sure, the kazoo was invented here in the 1840s, but more notable is the number of musicians who were born here or have called Macon home over the past century: Lena Horne, The Allman Brothers Band, Otis Redding and Little Richard, to name just a few. Macon is also the birthplace of poet Sidney Lanier. Macon began as a trading post.

Perry is known as the crossroads of Georgia because of its location near the geographic center of the state. The town is full of stately houses and historic churches, while Pine Mountain is a lush area of West Central Georgia that's home to Callaway Gardens, a well-preserved vacation destination. It's less than an hour from Atlanta. Movie buffs might recognize Forsyth, a small town near Macon in the center of the state. The nearby town of Juliette was the setting for the 1991 film *Fried Green Tomatoes*.

Americus was supposedly named for either new world explorer Amerigo Vespucci or for the settlers themselves, who were referred to as "merry cusses" because of their reputed happy-go-lucky ways. The town flourished in the 1890s and many Victorian and Gothic Revival buildings remain from that period. Today the town has the headquarters for International Habitat for Humanity, which has built more than 225,000 homes around the world for those in need.

Best known for its revered National Golf Course and the prestigious Masters tournament held here each April, Augusta lures Northerners every winter for its warmth, fairways and culture. The town of 195,000 supports a symphony and an opera as well as several museums devoted to the role Augusta played in the historical South. Augusta also has numerous boutiques and an array of sites honoring its eclectic collection of famous citizens. Where else can one day of sightseeing bring you President Woodrow Wilson's boyhood home, the only museum in the country dedicated to film comedians Laurel & Hardy and a statue honoring the Godfather of Soul, native Augustan James Brown?

President Franklin D. Roosevelt visited Warm Springs in the 1920s after he was stricken by polio because the area's natural mineral springs were said to heal ailments. He built a house here and is thought to have crafted his plan for the New Deal while staying in Warm Springs. The pools Roosevelt visited are now part of the Roosevelt Warm Springs Institute for Rehabilitation.

WHAT TO SEE

AMERICUS
HABITAT FOR HUMANITY-GLOBAL VILLAGE AND DISCOVERY CENTER
121 Habitat South, Americus, 229-924-6935, 800-422-4828; www.habitat.org

To learn more about Habitat for Humanity and what the organization does around the globe, stop by this site. Exhibits show the living conditions of poor people, as well as examples of the types of homes Habitat constructs in different parts of the world.

AUGUSTA
AUGUSTA SYMPHONY ORCHESTRA
Sacred Heart Cultural Center, 1301 Greene St., Augusta, 706-826-4705; www.augustasymphony.org

The Augusta Symphony's season is packed with concerts and events designed to please all types of audiences. Choose from traditional orchestra concerts, pops performances featuring world famous guest artists, and smaller and more intimate chamber concerts.

Mid-September-mid-May.

THE BOYHOOD HOME OF PRESIDENT WOODROW WILSON
419 Seventh St., Augusta, 706-722-9828; www.wilsonboyhoodhome.org

Recently restored with authentic 1860s décor and artifacts—the era during which the Wilsons lived here—this home-turned-museum celebrates the 28th president's youth.

Tuesday-Saturday 10 a.m.-4 p.m.

FORSYTH
JARRELL PLANTATION STATE HISTORIC SITE
711 Jarrell Plantation Road, Forsyth, 478-986-5172; www.gastateparks.org

This authentic plantation has 20 historic buildings dating from 1847-1940, including a plain-style plantation house, sawmill, gristmill and blacksmith shop.

Tuesday-Saturday 9 a.m.-5 p.m., Sunday 2-5:30 p.m.

HARLEM
LAUREL AND HARDY MUSEUM
250 N. Louisville St., Harlem, 706-556-0401, 888-288-9108; www.laurelandhardymuseum.org

Oliver Hardy was born in nearby Harlem, Georgia, and this museum of memorabilia and movies from the comedy team he formed with Stan Laurel is the only one of its kind in the country.

Daily 10 a.m.-4 p.m.

MACON
GEORGIA MUSIC HALL OF FAME
200 Martin Luther King Jr. Blvd., Macon, 478-751-3334, 888-427-6257; www.georgiamusic.org

Get a taste of Georgia's musical heritage. Exhibits include a soda fountain where you can hear songs from the 1950s; the Jazz Club; Gospel Chapel; Rhythm & Blues Revue and lots more.

Admission: adults $8, seniors $6, children 4-17 $3.50, children 3 and under free. Monday-Saturday 9 a.m.-5 p.m., Sunday 1-5 p.m.

MACON HISTORIC DISTRICT

450 Martin Luther King Jr. Blvd., Macon, 800-768-3401; www.visitmacon.org

The area makes up nearly all of old Macon: 48 buildings and houses have been cited for architectural excellence and listed on the National Register of Historic Places. An additional 575 structures have been noted for architectural significance. Walking and driving tours are noted on Heritage Tour Markers.

OLD CANNONBALL HOUSE & MACON-CONFEDERATE MUSEUM

856 Mulberry St., Macon, 478-745-5982; www.cannonballhouse.org

This Greek Revival house was struck by a Union cannonball in 1864. The museum contains Civil War relics and Macon historical items. Forty-minute guided tours of the home are offered every half hour.

Admission: adults $6, seniors $3, children under 4 free. March-December, Monday-Saturday 10 a.m.-5 p.m.; January-February, Monday-Friday 11 a.m.-5 p.m., Saturday 10 a.m.-5 p.m.

TUBMAN AFRICAN-AMERICAN MUSEUM

340 Walnut St., Macon, 478-743-8544; www.tubmanmuseum.com

Named for Harriet Tubman, this museum features African-American art, African artifacts and traveling exhibits on the history and culture of African-American people. Permanent exhibits look at folk art, black inventors and more.

Admission: adults $6, seniors $5, children 4-17 $4, children 3 and under free. Monday-Friday 9 a.m.-5 p.m., Saturday noon-4 p.m.

PERRY

MASSEE LANE GARDENS

100 Massee Lane, Fort Valley, 478-967-2358; www.camellias-acs.com

The beautiful 10-acre camellia garden reaches its peak blooming season between November and March. The gardens also include a large greenhouse, Japanese garden and rose garden. The Colonial-style headquarters include the Annabelle Lundy Fetterman Educational Museum, and an exhibition hall with rare books and porcelain.

Tuesday-Saturday 10 a.m.-4:30 p.m., Sunday 1-4:30 p.m.

PINE MOUNTAIN

FRANKLIN D. ROOSEVELT STATE PARK

2970 Highway 190, Pine Mountain, 706-663-4858; www.gastateparks.org

One of the largest parks in the state is home to many historic buildings and the King's Gap Indian Trail. Onsite activities include a swimming pool, fishing, hiking, bridle and nature trails, picnicking, camping and cottages.

Daily 7 a.m.-10 p.m.

THE GARDENS AT CALLAWAY

17800 U.S. Highway 27, Pine Mountain, 706-663-2281, 800-225-5292; www.callawaygardens.com

This distinctive public garden and resort, consisting of 14,000 acres of gardens, woodlands, lakes, recreation areas and wildlife, was conceived by textile industrialist Cason J. Callaway to be "the finest garden on earth since Adam was a boy." Originally the family's weekend vacation spot in the 1930s, Callaway and his wife, Virginia, expanded the area and opened it to the public in 1952. Callaway is now home to more than 100 varieties of butterflies, 230 varieties of birds, 400 varieties of fruits and vegetables, and thousands of species of plant life, including the rare

HIGHLIGHT

WHAT ARE THE TOP THINGS TO DO IN CENTRAL GEORGIA?

EXPLORE THE GARDENS AT CALLAWAY
This distinctive public garden and resort consists of 14,000 acres of gardens, woodlands, recreation areas and wildlife. The area also includes 13 lakes.

ENJOY THE AUGUSTA SYMPHONY ORCHESTRA
The symphony's season is packed with concerts and events designed to please all types of audiences. Choose from traditional orchestra concerts, pops performances featuring world famous guest artists, and smaller and more intimate chamber concerts

VISIT THE TUBMAN AFRICAN-AMERICAN MUSEUM
Named for Harriet Tubman, this museum features African-American art, African artifacts and traveling exhibits on the history and culture of African-American people.

planifolia azalea, which is indigenous to the area. The complex offers swimming, boating and other water recreation on its 13 lakes, including 175-acre Mountain Creek Lake and the white sand beach of Robin Lake; 23 miles of roads and paths for hiking or jogging; 63 holes of golf (a 9-hole and three 18-hole courses); 10 lighted tennis courts; two indoor racquetball courts; 10 miles of bike trails, skeet and trapshooting ranges; picnicking, a country store, restaurants and more.

WARM SPRINGS
LITTLE WHITE HOUSE HISTORIC SITE
401 Little White House Road, Warm Springs, 706-655-5870; www.gastateparks.org
President Franklin D. Roosevelt died here on April 12, 1945. Original furniture, memorabilia and the portrait on which Elizabeth Shoumatoff was working on when the president was stricken with a massive cerebral hemorrhage are on display. A film about Roosevelt's life at Warm Springs and in Georgia is shown at the F.D. Roosevelt Museum and Theater.
Admission: adults $6, children 6-18 $5, children 5 and under $1. Daily 9 a.m.-4:45 p.m.

WHERE TO STAY

PINE MOUNTAIN
★★★MOUNTAIN CREEK INN AT CALLAWAY GARDENS
17800 Highway 27, Pine Mountain, 706-663-2281, 800-225-5292; www.callawaygardens.com
Offering plenty of outdoor pursuits, including tennis and a championship golf course, this 14,000-acre property provides a relaxing venue from which to enjoy the Callaway Gardens area. Rooms have views of the gardens and there's

HIGHLIGHT

MASTERS GOLF TOURNAMENT

Augusta National Golf Course, 2604 Washington Road, Augusta, 706-667-6000; www.masters.org
The Masters is one of four major golfing tournaments held each year and one of the world's top golf tournaments. In addition to a cash award, the winner is presented with the famous green sport coat. Augusta is most well-known for the Masters, and at least 10 area clubs offer nonmembers opportunities to play. *First full week in April.*

a large outdoor pool, as well as a children's pool.
323 rooms. Restaurant, bar. Beach. Pool. $61-150

RECOMMENDED

AUGUSTA

AUGUSTA MARRIOTT HOTEL & SUITES
2 10th St., Augusta, 706-722-8900, 800-228-9290; www.marriott.com
Located in the business district downtown along the Savannah River, this Marriott offers spacious rooms with free wireless Internet, comfortable beds with crisp linens and work desks. Dining options include an Italian steakhouse and a coffee house for breakfast that brews Starbucks coffee.
372 rooms. Restaurant, bar. Business center. Fitness center. $61-150

WHERE TO EAT

AUGUSTA

★★★CALVERTS
475 Highland Ave., Augusta, 706-738-4514; www.calvertsrestaurant.com
Established in 1977, this restaurant in the Surrey Center is a local favorite. The menu offers a variety of seafood options, including Chesapeake crab cakes, cedar-planked salmon and sea bass Charleston, served with crabmeat and a lemon caper sauce. Other choices include Calvert's roasted tenderloin and a juicy, thick-cut rib eye stuffed with crab and served with a twice-baked potato.
American. Dinner. Closed Sunday. Bar. Children's menu. Reservations recommended. $36-85

★★★LA MAISON RESTAURANT & VERITAS WINE & TAPAS
404 Telfair St., Augusta, 706-722-4805; www.lamaisontelfair.com
This charming restaurant in a Southern Revival house has been around for more than 20 years and continues to draw crowds. The menu includes delicious starters such as the crab tower, a heap of lump crab with avocado and pink grapefruit, and the ahi tuna nachos with crispy wontons. Entrees include mountain trout, rack of lamb with an apricot teriyaki glaze and buffalo tenderloin. The restaurant features a special menu every year for the Masters.
International. Dinner. Closed Sunday. Bar. Reservations recommended. Outdoor seating. $16-35

WELCOME TO NORTH CAROLINA

NORTH CAROLINA HAS THREE DISTINCTIVE REGIONS: THE COAST, the heartland and the mountains, each with its own regional capital and featured attractions. From bluegrass music and mountain hiking in Asheville to Atlantic beaches a quick drive from Wilmington to the cultural and business centers surrounding the capital city, Raleigh, the state is diverse.

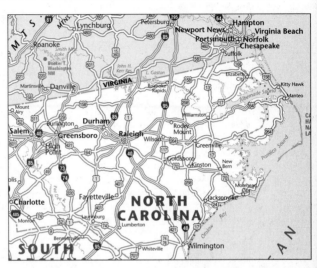

In 1585, the first English settlement was unsuccessfully started on Roanoke Island. Another attempt at settlement was made in 1587, but the colony disappeared, leaving only the crudely scratched word "CROATOAN" on a tree—perhaps referring to the Croatan Native Americans living in the area. To this day historians and archaeologists are still trying to solve the mystery of "The Lost Colony." Eventually English settlers moving south from Virginia founded farms in the North Carolina territory, and even today the state produces two-thirds of the nation's flue-cured tobacco, as well as cotton, peanuts and vegetables. Pine tar and turpentine were other early commodities produced in North Carolina, responsible for the "Tar Heels" moniker given to the people of North Carolina that was later adopted as the mascot for the University of North Carolina. Tales of the exact origins of the nickname are varied (and not always complimentary), but North Carolinians like to say it refers to their ability to persevere. It's said North Carolina troops fighting in the Civil War would stand their ground in battle as though stuck with "tar on their heels."

Individualist and democratic from the beginning, this state refused to ratify the Constitution until the Bill of Rights had been added. In 1860, its Western citizens strongly supported the Union, and North Carolina did not join the Confederate States of America until after Fort Sumter was attacked. Tobacco helped the state recover during Reconstruction and remains a major crop, but mountain communities are also famous for their furniture-making centers. For sports fans, North Carolina delivers with two perennial basketball powerhouses, Duke University and the University of North Carolina at Chapel Hill (Michael Jordan's alma mater). Top-ranking golf courses crisscross the state, and 70 miles of the Appalachian Trail extend along North Carolina's border. For vacationers, this translates into a wealth of things to do.

THE MOUNTAINS

In this region of North Carolina, you'll find hip, fun Asheville. The city has gained a reputation as a charming Blue Ridge Mountains vacation destination. George W. Vanderbilt built his mansion here in the 1890s, and the house and winery attract scores of visitors each year. Asheville is the North Carolina city closest to the Great Smoky Mountains National Park and is also the headquarters for the Uwharrie National Forest, Pisgah National Forest, Nantahala National Forest and Croatan National Forest.

If you're looking for other mountain escapes, there are a number of nearby towns that can accommodate you. Blowing Rock has been a mountain resort area for more than 100 years. Cashiers offers scenic drives on twisting mountain roads, hiking trails, views, waterfalls, lake sports, fishing and other recreational activities. Waynesville provides mountain trails for riding and hiking, and golf and fishing in cool mountain streams. Flat Rock is also home to visit-worthy inns and restaurants.

For a more cultural spot, try Cherokee. It is the capital of the Eastern Band of the Cherokee, who live on the Qualla Reservation at the edge of Great Smoky Mountains National Park and the Blue Ridge Parkway. The reservation, the largest east of the Mississippi, is shared by the descendants of members of the tribe who avoided being driven to Oklahoma on the Trail of Tears.

Home of the Cowee Valley ruby mines, Franklin attracts rock hounds who often find interesting gems in surface mines. Franklin is surrounded by waterfalls, mountain lakes and streams that offer excellent fishing for trout and bass, as well as boating, tubing and swimming. Around the county are 420,000 acres of the Nantahala National Forest, offering hiking trails, camping and fishing.

WHAT TO SEE

ASHEVILLE
ASHEVILLE ART MUSEUM
Two South Pack Square, Asheville, 828-253-3227; www.ashevilleart.org

The museum houses a permanent collection of 20th and 21st century American art, as well as numerous changing exhibits.

Admission: adults $8, seniors, students and children 4-12 $7, children under 4 free. Tuesday-Saturday 10 a.m.-5 p.m., Friday 10 a.m.-8 p.m., Sunday 1-5 p.m.

BILTMORE ESTATE
1 Approach Road, Asheville, 828-255-1333, 800-411-3812; www.biltmore.com

The 8,000-acre country estate includes 75 acres of formal gardens, numerous varieties of azaleas and roses, and the 250-room chateau that is the largest house ever built in the New World. Eighty-five rooms are open for viewing. In the 1890s, George W. Vanderbilt commissioned Richard Morris Hunt to design the house, which took five years to build. Vanderbilt also employed Gifford Pinchot, later governor of Pennsylvania and famous for forestry and conservation achievements, to manage his forests. Tours of the estate include visits to the gardens, conservatory and winery. There are four restaurants on the property; they offer wine tastings.

Admission: Varies. Daily.

BEST ATTRACTIONS

WHAT ARE THE TOP THINGS TO DO?

WALK AROUND THE BILTMORE ESTATE

You'll marvel at this 8,000-acre country estate and its 250-room mansion, which is the largest home ever built in the New World.

SEE LOCAL ART AT THE CHEROKEE HERITAGE MUSEUM AND GALLERY

This museum puts work on display that explores Cherokee culture and history. It also contains the largest collection of contemporary Cherokee arts and crafts.

ENJOY THE GREAT OUTDOORS AT NANTAHALA NATIONAL FOREST

The beautiful national park features a gorge, scenic drives through the Appalachians, waterfalls and the Joyce Kilmer-Slickrock Wilderness area.

VISIT CARL SANDBURG'S HOME

Fans of Pulitzer Prize-winning poet Carl Sandburg will want to visit this national historic site, where he lived until his death in 1967.

BOTANICAL GARDENS AT ASHEVILLE

151 WT Weaver Blvd., Asheville, 828-252-5190; www.ashevillebotanicalgardens.org

This 10-acre tract has thousands of flowers, trees and shrubs native to southern Appalachia. There is also a 125-year-old "dog trot" log cabin.

Admission: free. Daily sunrise-sunset.

CHIMNEY ROCK PARK

Highway 64-74A, Asheville, 828-625-9611, 800-277-9611; www.chimneyrockpark.com

The towering granite monolith Chimney Rock affords a 75-mile view. Four hiking trails lead to the 404-foot Hickory Nut Falls, Moonshiner's Cave, Devil's Head balancing rock and Nature's Showerbath. There are lots of opportunities for fun and relaxation, including trails, stairs and catwalks, picnic areas, a playground, a nature center and an observation lounge. Don't miss the 26-story elevator shaft through granite.

Daily 8:30 a.m.-6 p.m., weather permitting.

FOLK ART CENTER

382 Blue Ridge Parkway, Asheville, 828-298-7928; www.southernhighlandguild.org

The Folk Art Center is home to the Southern Highland Craft Guild. The stone and timber structure and the Blue Ridge Parkway info center include craft exhibits, demonstrations, workshops and related programs.

Admission: free. January-March, daily 9 a.m.-5 p.m.; April-December, daily 9 a.m.-6 p.m.

THOMAS WOLFE MEMORIAL

52 N. Market St., Asheville, 828-253-8304; www.wolfememorial.com

The state maintains the Wolfe boardinghouse as a literary shrine, restored and furnished to appear as it did in 1916. The author wrote about the home in his autobiography, *Look Homeward, Angel.*

Admission: adults $1, students $.50. Tuesday-Saturday 9 a.m.-5 p.m., Sunday 1-5 p.m.

ZEBULON B. VANCE BIRTHPLACE STATE HISTORIC SITE

911 Reems Creek Road, Weaverville, 828-645-6706; www.nchistoricsites.org

Reconstructed in 1961, the log house and outbuildings mark the site where the Civil War governor of North Carolina lived during childhood. It honors the Vance family, who was deeply involved with the early history of the state. There is a visitor center with exhibits, as well as a picnic area.

Admission: free. Tuesday-Friday 9 a.m.-5 p.m.

BLOWING ROCK

APPALACHIAN SKI MOUNTAIN

940 Ski Mountain Road, Blowing Rock, 828-295-7828, 800-322-2373; www.appskimtn.com

The mountain's features include: two quad, and one double chair lift, a rope tow, a handle-pull tow, a patrol, a French-Swiss Ski College, a Ski-Wee children's program, equipment rentals, snowmaking, a restaurant and eight runs. The longest run is 2,700 feet, with a vertical drop of 400 feet.

December-mid-March. Night skiing (all slopes lighted); half-day and twilight rates.

BLOWING ROCK

432 Rock Road, Blowing Rock, 828-295-7111; www.blowingrock.com

The cliff hangs over Johns River Gorge 2,000-3,000 feet below. There are scenic views of Grandfather, Grandmother, Table Rock and Hawksbill mountains.

Daily.

MOSES H. CONE MEMORIAL PARK

Blue Ridge Parkway, Blowing Rock, 828-295-7938; www.nps.gov

This was the former summer estate of a textile magnate. There are bridle paths, two lakes, 25 miles of hiking and cross-country skiing trails.

May-October, daily.

PARKWAY CRAFT CENTER

Blue Ridge Parkway, Blowing Rock, 828-295-7938; www.nps.gov

The center holds demonstrations of weaving, wood carving, pottery, jewelry making and other crafts. Many of the handcrafted items are for sale.

May-October, daily.

TWEETSIE RAILROAD

300 Tweetsie Railroad Lane, Blowing Rock, 828-264-9061, 800-526-5740;
www.tweetsierailroad.com

This is a 3-mile excursion, complete with a mock holdup and raid, on an old narrow-gauge railroad. It also offers a country fair, a petting zoo, amusement park rides, a craft village and a chair lift to Mouse Mountain Picnic Area.

Admission: adults $32, children 3-12 $22, children 2 and under free. May-October, limited hours.

CASHIERS

FAIRFIELD SAPPHIRE VALLEY SKI AREA

4350 Highway 64 W., Sapphire, 828-743-3441, 800-722-3956; www.skisapphire.com

The ski area offerings include: a chair lift, a rope tow, a patrol, a school and snow-making. The longest run is 1,600 feet, with a vertical drop of 200 feet.

Mid-December-mid-March, daily. Night skiing. Evenings, half-day rates.

CHEROKEE

CHEROKEE HERITAGE MUSEUM AND GALLERY

Acquoni Road, Cherokee; www.cherokeeheritagemuseum-gallery.org

This heritage museum in Saunooke Village offers exhibits on Cherokee culture, legends and history with beadwork, sculptures, weaponry, masks and more. It also has the world's largest collection of contemporary Cherokee arts and crafts. There is a gift shop that sells real-deal Cherokee arts and crafts.

Admission: adults $2.50, children 6-10 $1.50, children 5 and under free. Daily 10 a.m.-6 p.m.

MUSEUM OF THE CHEROKEE INDIAN

Highway 441 N., On Cherokee Reservation, Cherokee, 828-497-3481; www.cherokeemuseum.org

The museum houses arts and crafts, audiovisual displays, portraits and prehistoric artifacts depicting the life of the Cherokee.

Admission: adults $10, children 6-12 $6, children 5 and under free. Daily 9 a.m.-5 p.m.

OCONALUFTEE INDIAN VILLAGE

Highway 441 N., Cherokee, 828-497-2111; www.cherokee-nc.com

A replica of a Native American village dating back more than 250 years ago includes a seven-sided council house, an herb garden, craft demonstrations and lectures.

Admission: Varies. Guided tours Mid-May-late October, daily.

FRANKLIN

FRANKLIN GEM AND MINERAL MUSEUM

25 Phillips St., Franklin, 828-369-7831; www.fgmm.org

The museum boasts a nice collection of gems and minerals; Native American artifacts and fossils; and a fluorescent mineral display.

Admission: free. May-October, Monday-Friday noon-4 p.m., Saturday 11 a.m.-3 p.m., 6-9 p.m.; November-April, Saturday 11 a.m.-3 p.m.

NANTAHALA NATIONAL FOREST

90 Sloan Road, Franklin, 828-524-6441

Nantahala, a Native American name meaning "Land of the Noonday Sun," refers to Nantahala Gorge, which is so deep and narrow that the sun reaches the bottom only at noon. In addition to the gorge, the park offers scenic drives through the southern Appalachians, sparkling waterfalls (including the

Whitewater Falls, a series of cascades dropping 411 feet) and the 17,013-acre Joyce Kilmer-Slickrock Wilderness, with more than 100 species of trees native to the region. There is onsite hiking, camping, swimming, boating, fishing for bass and trout as well as hunting for deer, wild boar, turkey and ruffed grouse.

SCOTTISH TARTANS MUSEUM
W.C. Burrell Building, 86 E. Main St., Franklin, 828-524-7472; www.scottishtartans.org

An American extension of the Scottish Tartans Society in Edinburgh, Scotland, the museum's exhibits trace the heritage of Scottish tartans and traditional Scottish dress. If you really like the tartan-patterned kilts on display, you can buy yourself one at the gift shop. There is a research library as well.

Admission: adults $2, children $1. Monday-Saturday 10 a.m.-5 p.m.

HENDERSONVILLE
CARL SANDBURG HOME NATIONAL HISTORIC SITE
81 Carl Sandburg Lane, Flat Rock, 828-693-4178; www.nps.gov

The famous poet's 264-acre farm, Connemara, is maintained as it was when Sandburg and his family lived here from 1945 until his death in 1967. On the grounds are a house and historic barn for the three breeds of goats that Sandburg raised, as well as a visitor center.

Admission: adults $5, seniors $3, children 15 and under free. Tours daily 9 a.m.-5 p.m.

JUMP-OFF ROCK
Fifth Ave., Hendersonville; www.historichendersonville.org

Enjoy panoramic views of the Blue Ridge Mountains from atop Jump-Off Mountain. The lookout point also is the starting point for three hiking trails.

TRYON
FOOTHILLS EQUESTRIAN NATURE CENTER
3381 Hunting Country Road, Tryon, 828-859-9021; www.fence.org

This 300-acre nature preserve has 5 miles of riding and hiking trails, wildlife programs and bird and nature walks. It's host to many equestrian events, including the Block House Steeplechase Race in April, which has happened annually for more than 60 years.

WHERE TO STAY

ASHEVILLE
★★★CUMBERLAND FALLS BED & BREAKFAST
254 Cumberland Ave., Asheville, 828-253-4085, 888-743-2557; www.cumberlandfalls.com

When driving up to the tree- and flower-lined house, you'll think you're returning home. That is, if your home had freshly baked treats, a three-course breakfast and a two-person whirlpool tub always waiting for you. So basically, the Cumberland Falls Bed and Breakfast is like the home sweet home you always dreamed about, with themed rooms and an attentive staff to help plan your day and ensure you feel comfortable when you return. Besides included amenities, the innkeeper can help you set up a special surprise, like chocolate-covered strawberries and champagne to accompany that Jacuzzi.

6 rooms. Complimentary breakfast. No children under 10. $151-250

★★★THE GROVE PARK INN RESORT & SPA
290 Macon Ave., Asheville, 828-252-2711, 800-438-5800;
www.groveparkinn.com

Set in Asheville's Blue Ridge Mountains, guest rooms are decorated in the Arts and Crafts style. Choose from the 18-hole Donald Ross-designed golf course, a superb tennis facility or a 40,000-square-foot spa crafted from natural rock. The Spa offers a range of special services, from hydro bath treatments to flotation body masks.

510 rooms. Restaurant, bar. Spa. Golf. Tennis. $251-350

★★★HAYWOOD PARK HOTEL & PROMENADE
1 Battery Park Ave., Asheville, 828-252-2522, 800-228-2522;
www.haywoodpark.com

This all-suite hotel is decorated with polished brass, warm oak and Spanish marble. Rooms have fine furnishings, a wet bar and bathrooms that features either a garden tub or a Jacuzzi.

33 rooms. Restaurants, bar. $151-250

★★★★INN ON BILTMORE ESTATE
1 Anter Hill Road, Asheville, 828-225-1660, 866-336-1240;
www.biltmore.com

The Inn on Biltmore Estate provides world-class accommodations on the grounds of an American landmark, the historic Vanderbilt Biltmore Estate. The room décor has an English and French manor feel. They come with evening turndown service, complimentary wireless Internet access, terrycloth bathrobes and slippers and 37-inch flat-screen televisions. Carriage rides, horseback rides and river float trips are just a few of the unique recreational activities. The hotel's distinguished character extends to its dining establishments: Bistro, Deerpark, The Dining Room and Stable Café.

213 rooms. Restaurant, bar. Spa. $251-350

★★★RENAISSANCE ASHEVILLE HOTEL
31 Woodfin St., Asheville, 828-252-8211, 800-359-7951;
www.marriott.com

Centrally located around Asheville's main plaza, this comfortable hotel offers visitors shopping in the nearby mall, a farmers market and other complexes in the area. You can also stick to your bright room, which has marble bathrooms and black geometric-patterned headboards against a striped gold and cream wall.

277 rooms. Restaurant, bar. Fitness center. $151-250

WHAT ARE THE BEST OVERALL HOTELS?

Inn on Biltmore Estate:
This historic estate provides top-of-the-line accommodations that make you feel like you're staying in a European manor. The hotel even offers carriage rides.

Old Edwards Inn and Spa:
The inn, which is listed on the National Register of Historic Places, fills its rooms with period antiques. Don't miss the spa, which uses herbs from its own garden.

BLOWING ROCK

★★★CHETOLA RESORT AT BLOWING ROCK

North Main St., Blowing Rock, 828-295-5500, 800-243-8652; www.chetola.com

This Blue Ridge Mountains retreat, bordered on one side by a national forest, houses the Highlands Sports and Recreation Center. A conference center, professional tennis courts and other amenities are within the resort's 78-acre property.

104 rooms. Restaurant, bar. $151-250

★★★CRIPPEN'S COUNTRY INN

239 Sunset Drive, Blowing Rock, 828-295-3487, 877-295-3487; www.crippens.com

This mountain inn offers a lively atmosphere and a good restaurant. The homey rooms come in bright wall shades like pink or blue-green, while the flora bathrooms have 1935 antique claw-footed soaking tubs.

8 rooms. Restaurant. Bar. Complimentary breakfast. No children under 12. $61-150

★★★GLENDALE SPRINGS INN

7414 Highway 16, Glendale Springs, 336-982-2103, 800-287-1206; www.glendalespringsinn.com

Located in a quaint community on the top of the Blue Ridge Mountains, this historic inn is well-known for its dining room and comfortable accommodations. Some of the individually decorated rooms have four-poster beds and claw-foot tubs.

9 rooms. Complimentary breakfast. Restaurant. $61-150

★★★HOUND EARS CLUB

328 Shulls Mills Road, Blowing Rock, 828-963-4321; www.houndears.com

Set atop the Blue Ridge Mountains, this small, secluded resort is a relaxing respite. Try to snag one of the suites, some of which have fireplaces, kitchenettes, sleeper sofas and balconies. The onsite 18-hole golf course was designed by George Cobb, and the views are gorgeous.

28 rooms. Restaurant, bar. $151-250

CASHIERS

★★★THE GREYSTONE

Greystone Lane, Lake Toxaway, 828-966-4700, 800-824-5766; www.greystoneinn.com

The main building of this historic inn was built in 1915 and welcomed the Ford and Rockefeller families. The inn offers extra-fine touches, including individually decorated rooms, a full-service spa and outdoor recreation, such as kayaking, canoeing, tennis and croquet. Rooms have antiques and period reproductions; some come with patios and fireplaces.

33 rooms. Restaurant. Complimentary breakfast. Fitness center. Pool. Beach. $251-350

★★★HIGH HAMPTON INN AND COUNTRY CLUB

1525 Highway 107 S., Cashiers, 828-743-2411, 800-334-2551; www.highhamptoninn.com

Located in the Blue Ridge Mountains, this 1,400-acre property boasts a private lake and a quiet, wooded landscape. Rooms bring the outdoors inn with lots of wood and handmade furniture crafted from tree branches. Guests of the inn, private cottages or colony homes, stay busy with the scenic 18-hole golf course, six clay tennis courts and hiking trails.

120 rooms. Restaurant, bar. Beach. Closed mid-November-April. $151-250

FLAT ROCK

★★★HIGHLAND LAKE INN

86 Lily Pad Lane Highland Lake Road, Flat Rock, 828-693-6812, 800-635-5101; www.hlinn.com

This hotel is just 25 minutes from Asheville, and sits on 26 acres of woods near a lake. Hit the outdoors and play tennis; canoe, kayak or paddleboat in the 40-acre lake; go fishing; or bike around. It's a lovely country getaway in the Blue Ridge Mountains.

63 rooms. Restaurant, bar. Beach. $151-250

HIGHLANDS

★★★★OLD EDWARDS INN AND SPA

445 Main St., Highlands, 828-526-8008; www.oldedwardsinn.com

Nestled in the charming mountain town of Highlands, this historic inn is on the National Register of Historic Places. Each guest room, suite and cottage is filled with period antiques and modern amenities. Plus, you'll get 24-hour access to the butler's pantry, which is stocked with fresh fruit, beverages and Dove bars, in case you need a midnight snack. The luxurious 25,000-square-foot full-service spa uses herbs and botanicals from its garden.

28 rooms. Restaurant, bar. Complimentary breakfast. Fitness center. No children under 11. $351 and up

TRYON

★★★PINE CREST INN

85 Pine Crest Lane, Tryon, 828-859-9135, 800-633-3001; www.pinecrestinn.com

Located in the foothills of the Blue Ridge Mountains, near the Foothills Equestrian Nature Center, this lovely inn evokes an English country manor. The innkeepers have restored the hardwood floors, stone fireplaces and other historic fixtures to make it authentic.

39 rooms. Complimentary breakfast. Restaurant. $251-350

WAYNESVILLE

★★★BALSAM MOUNTAIN INN

68 Seven Springs Drive, Balsam, 828-456-9498, 800-224-9498; www.balsaminn.com

This 100-year-old-inn sits in the Blue Ridge Mountains and features a popular restaurant as well as a library and access to great hiking trails. The rooms are all different, but they have beadboard walls, vintage furnishings and artwork. They also don't come with TVs, radios, telephones or alarm clocks, so that you'll get a real get-away-from-it-all experience.

50 rooms. Restaurant. Complimentary breakfast. $61-150

★★★THE SWAG COUNTRY INN

2300 Swag Road, Waynesville, 828-926-0430, 800-789-7672; www.theswag.com

The Swag Country Inn sits atop a 5,000-foot mountain with a private entrance to the Great Smoky Mountains National Park. The rooms and suites feature handmade quilts, woven rugs and original artwork. Nature trails cover the property, and picnic baskets and brown-bag lunches are available for hikers.

15 rooms. Closed mid-November-April. Restaurant (public by reservation). Complimentary breakfast. Children over 7 only in main building. $351 and up

RECOMMENDED

ASHEVILLE
ALBEMARLE INN
86 Edgemont Road, Asheville, 828-255-0027, 800-621-7435; www.albemarleinn.com

This dramatic, majestic home, with enormous white pillars and manicured gardens, offers guests luxurious rooms, a complimentary breakfast, and afternoon wine and hors d'oeuvres. The rooms have their own décor; the steel-blue-colored Sunrise Suite has an elaborate canopy bed made of wood and lots of fabric.

11 rooms. Complimentary breakfast. No children under 12. $151-250

APPLEWOOD MANOR INN
62 Cumberland Circle, Asheville, 828-254-2244, 800-442-2197; www.applewoodmanor.com

This Colonial turn-of-the-century home was built in 1910. Rooms are filled with antiques and personal touches like fresh flowers and chocolates on your pillow.

4 rooms. Complimentary breakfast. No children under 12. $61-150

THE BEAUFORT HOUSE VICTORIAN INN
61 N. Liberty St., Asheville, 828-254-8334, 800-261-2221; www.beauforthouse.com

Experience Victorian afternoon tea, gourmet breakfasts and elegant guest rooms in the former home of Charleton Heston. The mansion is surrounded by 2 acres of landscaped grounds complete with 5,000 flowers.

11 rooms. Complimentary breakfast. No children under 10. $61-150

CEDAR CREST VICTORIAN INN
674 Biltmore Ave., Asheville, 828-252-1389, 877-251-1389; www.cedarcrestinn.com

Dating from 1891, this luxurious mansion has been transformed into a romantic inn that is listed on the National Register of Historic Places. Of particular note is the ornate woodwork on the first floor and the Victorian gardens filled with dogwood and rhododendrons.

12 rooms. Complimentary breakfast. No children under 10. $151-250

GRAND BOHEMIAN HOTEL, ASHEVILLE
11 Boston Way, Asheville, 828-505-2949, 888-717-8756; www.bohemianhotelasheville.com

Part of Marriot's growing collection of snazzy Autograph Hotels, the Grand Bohemian is ideally located for those visiting the famous Biltmore Estate. The resort has rustic touches such as antler chandeliers, dark woods and a large four-sided fireplace in the lobby, and is swathed in rich fabrics and beautiful artwork. Rooms have plush beds with large upholstered headboards and luxurious bathrooms with carved vanities. Be sure to visit the Grand Bohemian Galley, which houses more than 100 works of art by local and national artists. When you return from exploring the nearby Smoky Mountains or the local boutiques, stop in at Red Stag Grill for a well-prepared cocktail and one of their signature cuts of meat. The Poseidon Spa is a peaceful respite for a facial or massage while the fitness center is open round-the-clock for workout buffs.

104 rooms. Restaurant, bar. Fitness Center. Spa. $151-250

LION AND THE ROSE
276 Montford Ave., Asheville, 828-255-7673, 800-546-6988; www.lion-rose.com

This elegantly restored Georgian mansion is nestled in beautifully landscaped gardens in one of Asheville's historic districts and within walking distance of downtown. Decadent complimentary breakfasts are a delightful perk.

5 rooms. Complimentary breakfast. No children under 12. $151-250

THE OLD REYNOLDS MANSION
100 Reynolds Heights, Asheville, 828-254-0496, 800-709-0496; www.oldreynoldsmansion.com

This antebellum mansion sits on a hill overlooking the mountains. There are verandas throughout the home to enjoy the views.

10 rooms. Complimentary breakfast. Closed November-June, Sunday-Thursday. $61-150

OWL'S NEST
2630 Smokey Park Highway, Candler, 828-665-8325, 800-665-8868, www.engadineinn.com

Located just outside of Asheville, this inn was built in 1885 and has been restored to its original Victorian grandeur. The mountain views from the wraparound porches are exquisite. Enjoy a cozy, romantic dinner by the fireplace.

5 rooms. Complimentary breakfast. No children under 12. $61-150

INN AT RAGGED GARDENS
203 Sunset Drive, Blowing Rock, 877-972-4433; www.ragged-gardens.com

The 19th-century inn has original stone pillars and floors, period furnishings, individually decorated rooms and a full acre of beautifully landscaped property.

11 rooms. Complimentary breakfast. No children under 12. $151-250

BOONE
LOVILL HOUSE INN
404 Old Bristol Road, Boone, 828-264-4204, 800-849-9466; www.lovillhouseinn.com

Captain E.F. Lovill, a Civil War hero and state senator, built this traditional farmhouse in 1875. The 11-acre, wooded property has a charming wraparound porch with plenty of rocking chairs.

6 rooms. No children under 12. Complimentary breakfast. Closed March. $151-250

HENDERSONVILLE
LODGE ON LAKE LURE BED & BREAKFAST
361 Charlotte Drive, Lake Lure, 828-625-2789, 800-733-2785; www.lodgeonlakelure.com

This is an elegant bed and breakfast in the countryside. The beauty of the lake adds a wonderful backdrop to this scenic property. Many of the individually decorated rooms have balconies so that you can enjoy the view.

16 rooms. Complimentary breakfast. No children under 8. $151-250

WAYNESVILLE
YELLOW HOUSE ON PLOT CREEK ROAD
89 Oakview Drive, Waynesville, 828-452-0991, 800-563-1236; www.theyellowhouse.com

A fabulous yellow house tucked into the hills at a 3,000-foot elevation, this property has rooms with rustic décor that complements the remarkable landscape. The romantic, cozy rooms have fireplaces, terry cloth-lined bathrobes, herbal bath salts, piped-in music, and many come with a patio or balcony.

6 rooms. Complimentary breakfast. $61-150

WHERE TO EAT

ASHEVILLE

★★★FLYING FROG CAFÉ
Haywood Park Hotel, 1 Battery Park Ave., Asheville, 828-254-9411; www.flyingfrogcafe.com

Located in the first floor of the Haywood Park Hotel, the Flying Frog Restaurant is in the center of downtown Asheville, surrounded by shopping, lodging and entertainment venues. Decorated in a modern Indian theme, the restaurant has booths draped with sheer curtains, a display kitchen and private wine room. The variety of menu options changes seasonally. Expect starters like samosa tikki, spicy fried cutlets with peas, raisins, onions and ginger served with date-tamarind and cilantro-ginger chutneys, as well as entrées like filet mignon slathered in a Brie and gorgonzola sauce.

Continental, Indian. Dinner. Closed Monday-Tuesday. Bar. $36-85

★★★HORIZONS
Grove Park Inn, 290 Macon Ave., Asheville, 828-252-2711, 800-438-5800; www.groveparkinn.com

Located in the Grove Park Inn, this restaurant has elegant décor and innovative classic cuisine. Enjoy views of the mountains and the groomed golf course through large windows while listening to live piano music. House specialties include wild-striped bass and an extensive wine list. A special nine-course meal at the chef's table in the kitchen and wine dinners organized around specific tastes and interests are available.

International. Dinner. Closed Sunday-Monday. Reservations recommended. Jacket required. Bar. $86 and up

★★★THE MARKET PLACE
20 Wall St., Asheville, 828-252-4162; www.marketplace-restaurant.com

Located in the center of downtown on a side street with quaint shops, this restaurant offers organic cheeses and salads, free-range chicken and local trout. Meat is smoked over hickory and oak.

American, French. Dinner. Closed Sunday. Outdoor seating. Bar. $36-85

★★★REZAZ
28 Hendersonville Road, Asheville, 828-277-1510; www.rezaz.com

Rezaz is two restaurants in one: the main dining room has sleek, modern décor and an upscale Mediterranean menu; wine bar Enoteca, the informal side of the restaurant, has display cases of meat, cheeses and decadent desserts. The restaurant is in the historic Biltmore Village, opposite the entrance to the Biltmore Estate.

Mediterranean. Breakfast, lunch, dinner. Closed Sunday. Reservations recommended. Bar. $16-35

BLOWING ROCK

★★★CRIPPEN'S
Crippen's Country Inn, 239 Sunset Drive, Blowing Rock, 828-295-3487, 877-295-3487; www.crippens.com

This spacious, cozy dining room is located in Crippen's Country Inn. Chef James Welch's seasonal menu features many organic meats, seafood and homemade breads and desserts. If you see the chocolate steak on the menu—espresso-encrusted grilled tenderloin infused with bittersweet chocolate—be sure to order it.

American. Dinner. Reservations recommended. Outdoor seating. Children's menu. Bar. $36-85

HIGHLANDS
★★★MADISON'S RESTAURANT & WINE GARDEN
Old Edwards Inn and Spa, 445 Main St., Highlands, 828-526-5477; www.oldedwardsinn.com

There's something old, something new, something Southern and everything delicious at Madison's Restaurant and Wine Garden at Old Edwards Inn and Spa. The chef uses local ingredients to cook Madison's contemporary cuisine, serving up Southern with a twist to locals and visitors for breakfast, dinner or just dessert and drinks. Weather permitting, pop the cork on a bottle in the Wine Garden and take in views of the lush North Carolina scenery. Mountains and countryside not your thing? Dine inside on Carolina mountain trout, with a side of white truffle macaroni and cheese. Definitely save room for the plantation chocolate soufflé.

American, Southern. Breakfast, lunch, dinner. $36-85

TRYON
★★★PINE CREST INN RESTAURANT
85 Pine Crest Lane, Tryon, 828-859-9135, 800-633-3001; www.pinecrestinn.com

This rustic restaurant serves fusion cuisine and features beamed ceilings, a stone fireplace and heavy pine tables. The menu changes often, but you can anticipate dishes like lamb chops with red jalapeño jelly and Vermont goat cheese or local trout amandine with beurre blanc. There's also an award-winning wine list.

American. Breakfast, dinner, Sunday brunch. Bar. Children's menu. Reservations recommended. Outdoor seating. $16-35

SPAS

HIGHLANDS
★★★★THE SPA AT OLD EDWARDS INN
Old Edwards Inn and Spa, 445 Main St., Highlands, 828-526-8008; www.oldedwardsinn.com

Tucked into the mountains of the North Carolina Highlands, the Old Edwards Inn and Spa offers luxury rooms, suites and cottages for those looking to be one with nature, or one with a pedicure. Chilling out is the only task at hand at

---

WHAT ARE THE BEST WINE BARS?

Madison's Restaurant & Wine Garden:
Madison's provides the perfect setting for wine sipping: a lovely alfresco garden with a waterfall and live music in the summer, plus truffle popcorn for munching.

Rezaz:
Inside this formal restaurant is Enoteca, a laidback wine bar that specializes in Italian vintages with antipasti and small plates for pairing.

this 25,000-square-foot spa, which boasts treatments that use native North Carolina herbs and botanicals (some grown in the spa's own garden) for the signature Carolina Cocoon treatments. Or try one of the rubdowns—go exotic with the Balinese massage or bliss out with hot-spring stone massage—for a knot-kneading experience. For the ultimate in relaxation, just book a Spa Suite and let the royal treatments come to you.

PIEDMONT

The hilly, plains-filled Piedmont region offers plenty of beautiful scenery, especially in the fall. Piedmont is also a thriving arts and entertainment hub, not least because of the many universities in the area. Chapel Hill is the quintessential college town, as it's home to the University of North Carolina, the oldest state university in the country. Most notorious for its basketball fandom and renowned athletic alumni such as Michael Jordan, UNC is also a leading academic institution and part of the "Research Triangle" with Duke University in Durham and North Carolina State University in Raleigh, the state capital.

The Carolinas' largest metropolis, and one of the country's fastest-growing areas, Charlotte is a top banking center. Charlotte offers much to see and do, whether it's history (the birthplace of the 11th president, James K. Polk), sports (professional football, baseball, basketball, and NASCAR) or the arts (try the free and fabulous public art walking tour).

If you feel the need for speed, go to Concord in the heart of NASCAR country. The town boasts several NASCAR teams, Lowe's Motor Speedway, and a NASCAR research and development office. For those who need a break from car racing, hit more than 200 stores at Concord Mills outlet mall. Or visit nearby Cornelius, which is steeped in NASCAR culture, or Mooresville, home of the North Carolina Auto Racing Hall of Fame.

For more entertainment, try the state's third largest city, Greensboro. It offers a unique science museum, numerous high-quality golf courses and the biggest water park in the Carolinas. Shoppers will want to spend their vacation money in Hickory, the country's center of furniture making. In a 200-mile radius of the town, 60 percent of the nation's furniture is produced and visitors often come looking for unique and interesting pieces. Golf, car racing and baseball add to the entertainment, along with a number of historical sites and museums.

Those seeking a more get-away-from-it-all respite, head to famous year-round resort village Pinehurst, which has been named the site of the 2014 U.S. Open. The New England-style resort was designed more than 100 years ago by Frederick Law Olmsted, who also designed New York's Central Park and landscaped Asheville's Biltmore Estate. Handsome estates and other residences, mostly Georgian Colonial, dot the village. The Pinehurst Resort and Country Club has a 200-acre lake, 24 tennis courts and other recreational facilities that are open to members as well as to guests staying there.

HIGHLIGHT

WHAT ARE THE BEST PLACES FOR FAMILY FUN IN PIEDMONT?

DISCOVERY PLACE
Bring your curious kids to this science museum, where they can visit the aquarium, science circus and rain forest and learn from hands-on displays.

NASCAR SPEEDPARK, CONCORD MILLS
Aspiring race car drivers will want to hit the five racetracks at this NASCAR-themed amusement park. It also provides kiddie rides, laser tag and mini-golf.

PARAMOUNT'S CAROWINDS
Children who love stomach-turning rides will get their adrenalin pumping at this theme park, which offers roller coasters and a 12-acre water park.

WHAT TO SEE

CHAPEL HILL
HORACE WILLIAMS HOUSE
610 E. Rosemary St., Chapel Hill, 919-942-7818; www.chapelhillpreservation.com
This historic house is home to the Chapel Hill Preservation Society. It hosts changing art exhibits and chamber music concerts.
Tuesday-Friday, also Sunday afternoons; closed the first two weeks in August.

MOREHEAD-PATTERSON MEMORIAL BELL TOWER
Stadium Drive and South Road, Chapel Hill
The 172-foot Italian Renaissance campanile concert chimes have 12 bells ranging in weight from 300 pounds to nearly two tons. Popular tunes ring daily.

NORTH CAROLINA BOTANICAL GARDEN
15501 Old Mason Farm Road, Chapel Hill, 919-962-0522; www.ncbg.unc.edu
The garden is approximately 600 acres with a variety of trees and plants of the southeastern U.S. There are wildflower areas, herb gardens and nature trails.
Admission: free. Monday-Friday 8 a.m.-5 p.m., Saturday 9 a.m.-6 p.m., Sunday 1-6 p.m.

OLD WELL
Cameron Avenue, Chapel Hill
Long the unofficial symbol of the university, this well was the only source of water here for nearly a century. The present Greek temple structure dates from 1897.

SOUTH (MAIN) BUILDING

Cameron Avenue, and Raleigh Street, Chapel Hill

The cornerstone was laid in 1798, but the building was not completed until 1814, during which time students lived inside the roofless walls in little huts. Future President James K. Polk lived here from 1814 to 1818.

UNIVERSITY OF NORTH CAROLINA AT CHAPEL HILL

250 E. Franklin St., Chapel Hill, 919-962-1630; www.unc.edu

Approximately 27,000 students attend the institution, founded in 1795. The 720-acre campus has more than 200 buildings and is packed with Southern charm.

CHARLOTTE

THE CHARLOTTE MUSEUM OF HISTORY AND HEZEKIAH ALEXANDER HOMESITE

3500 Shamrock Drive, Charlotte, 704-568-1774; www.charlottemuseum.org

This museum includes the Hezekiah Alexander House, the oldest dwelling still standing in Mecklenburg County. There is also a two-story springhouse with a working log kitchen. Tours are included with entry.

Admission: adults $6, seniors and students $5, children 6-12 $3, children 5 and under free. Tuesday-Saturday 10 a.m.-5 p.m., Sunday 1-5 p.m.; open Monday in summer.

DISCOVERY PLACE

301 N. Tryon St., Charlotte, 704-372-6261, 800-935-0553; www.discoveryplace.org

The hands-on science museum gives kids a chance to learn about electricity, weather, rocks, minerals and other scientific wonders. Check out the aquarium, science circus, life center, rain forest, collections gallery, OMNIMAX theater and major traveling exhibits.

Admission: adults $12, seniors $10, children $9. Monday-Friday 9 a.m.-4 p.m., Saturday 10 a.m.-6 p.m., Sunday noon-5 p.m.

JAMES K. POLK MEMORIAL STATE HISTORIC SITE

308 S. Polk St., Pineville, 704-889-7145; www.nchistoricsites.org

This historic site is the birthplace of the 11th president of the United States. On the property, you'll find a replica of a log cabin and outbuildings with authentic furnishings. There is also a visitor center with exhibits and films.

Admission: free. Tuesday-Saturday 9 a.m.-5 p.m.

LEVINE MUSEUM OF THE NEW SOUTH

200 E. Seventh St., Charlotte, 704-333-1887; www.museumofthenewsouth.org

This museum chronicles the history of the post-Civil War South with an ever-changing series of exhibits featuring industry, ideas, people and historical eras such as the civil-rights movement.

Admission: adults $6, seniors, students and children 6-18 $5, children 5 and under free. Monday-Saturday10 a.m.-5 p.m., Sunday noon-5 p.m.

PARAMOUNT'S CAROWINDS

14523 Carowinds Blvd., Charlotte, 704-588-2600, 800-888-4386; www.carowinds.com

This 100-acre family theme park has more than 40 rides, shows and attractions including 12-acre water entertainment complex WaterWorks, the Nickelodeon Central children's area, Drop Zone stunt tower and roller coasters. The

13,000-seat Paladium amphitheater hosts special events.

Admission: adults and children 48" or taller $39.99, seniors and children under 48" $22.99 (online prices). June-late August, daily; March-May and September-October, weekends.

U.S. NATIONAL WHITEWATER CENTER

820 Hawfield Road, Charlotte, 704-391-3900; www.usnwc.org

An official Olympic training site and site for World Cup whitewater rafting since 2006, this 307-acre park on the Catawba River was modeled after Olympic rafting courses. Four thousand linear feet of whitewater rafting as well as biking, canoeing, wall climbing, kayaking and more are offered at this playground for serious sports enthusiasts. Mountain bikes are available to rent.

CONCORD

CONCORD MOTORSPORT PARK

7940 Highway 601 S., Concord, 704-782-4221; www.concordmotorsportpark.com

The NASCAR weekly series runs Saturday nights from April through October at this asphalt tri-oval 30 miles northeast of Charlotte in the heart of NASCAR country. The grandstands seat 8,000, and there are spots for 28 RVs at Turn 3.

DALE EARNHARDT TRIBUTE

3003 Dale Earnhardt Plaza, Kannapolis, 800-848-3740; www.visitcabarrus.com

The people of Kannapolis have preserved the memory of their favorite son, Dale Earnhardt, in 900 pounds of bronze. Nearby are murals depicting Earnhardt's race-car-driving career.

NASCAR SPEEDPARK, CONCORD MILLS

8461 Concord Mills Blvd., Concord, 704-979-6770; www.nascarspeedpark.com

When the kids need to burn off some energy, bring them to this 7-acre race-themed amusement park. It offers five racetracks, a state-of-the-art interactive arcade, an 18-hole miniature golf course, kiddie rides and laser tag.

Admission: adults and children over 54" $27.99, children under 4" $24.99. Daily.

REED GOLD MINE STATE HISTORIC SITE

9621 Reed Mine Road, Midland, 704-721-4653; www.reedmine.com

The Reed Gold Mine State Historic Site boasts the first documented discovery of gold in the United States in 1799. Stop and check out the underground mine tours, history trail, working machinery, demonstrations and exhibits, or enjoy the panning area and see what you find.

Admission: free. Panning: $2 per pan. Tuesday-Saturday 9 a.m.-5 p.m. Panning area: April-October, daily; fee.

RICHARD PETTY DRIVING EXPERIENCE

Lowe's Motor Speedway, 5555 Concord Parkway S., Concord, 800-237-3889; www.1800bepetty.com

Always wanted to rip a stock car around the curves at a NASCAR racetrack? This is the largest of the driving schools that takes fans right onto the track at Lowe's Motor Speedway. For anywhere between $99 for a ride-along to almost $3,000 for an advanced racing experience, you can live your racing dream.

CORNELIUS
LAKE NORMAN
www.visitlakenorman.org

Lake Norman is the state's largest freshwater lake at 32,510 acres. It was created by the Cowans Ford Dam, a Duke Power project on the Catawba River. There are nine public access areas, with fishing areas and boating access.

MEMORY LANE MOTORSPORTS & HISTORIC AUTOMOTIVE MUSEUM
769 River Highway, Mooresville, 704-662-3673; www.memorylaneautomuseum.com

One-of-a-kind vehicles from race cars to vintage cars and motorcycles are on display at the museum, as well as toys, memorabilia and more.

Admission: adults $10, children 6-12 $6, children 5 and under free. Monday-Saturday 10 a.m.-5 p.m.

NORTH CAROLINA AUTO RACING HALL OF FAME
119 Knob Hill Road, Mooresville, 704-663-5331; www.ncarhof.com

As Mooresville's official visitor's center, the museum offers a large display of more than 35 cars dedicated to all types of auto racing. The gift shop is also the official Race City, USA merchandise headquarters and carries a wide selection of racing memorabilia.

Admission: adults $6, seniors and children 6-12 $4. Monday-Friday 10 a.m.-5 p.m., Saturday-Sunday 10 a.m.-3 p.m.

DURHAM
BENNETT PLACE STATE HISTORIC SITE
4409 Bennett Memorial Road, Durham, 919-383-4345; www.nchistoricsites.org

This was the site of the April 26, 1865, surrender of Confederate General Johnston to Union General Sherman. There is a reconstructed Bennett homestead and picnicking onsite, as well as an informative audiovisual display.

Admission: free. Tuesday-Saturday 9 a.m.-5 p.m.

DUKE HOMESTEAD STATE HISTORIC SITE
2828 Duke Homestead Road, Durham, 919-477-5498; www.nchistoricsites.org

This was the ancestral home of the Duke family. The estate houses the first Duke tobacco factory, a curing barn, outbuildings and farm crops. There is a tobacco museum, exhibits and a film. Tours are available.

Admission: free. Tuesday-Saturday 9 a.m.-5 p.m.

DUKE UNIVERSITY
2138 Campus Drive, Durham, 919-684-3214; www.duke.edu

Duke University is one of the nation's top private universities, situated on 8,000 acres. It includes the original Trinity College. The West Campus, occupied since 1930, is the showplace of the university.

DUKE'S WALLACE WADE STADIUM
290 Frank Bassett Road, Durham, 919-681-2583; www.goduke.com

Home of the Duke Blue Devils, the stadium packs in the crowds during college basketball season. Tickets are hard to come by, so plan ahead if you want to catch a game.

DURHAM BULL ATHLETIC PARK
409 Blackwell St., Durham, 919-687-6500; www.durhambulls.com

This 10,000-seat stadium is home to the Durham Bulls Triple A baseball team, affiliated with the Tampa Bay Devil Rays.

NORTH CAROLINA MUSEUM OF LIFE AND SCIENCE
433 W. Murray Ave., Durham, 919-220-5429; www.ncmls.org

The museum highlights North Carolina wildlife. Hands-on science exhibits; aerospace, weather and geology collections; a train ride; a farmyard; a science park; discovery rooms; and the Butterfly House round out the offerings.

Admission: adults $12.95, seniors and military personnel $10.95, children 3-12 $9.95, children 2 and under free. Tuesday-Saturday 10 a.m.-5 p.m., Sunday noon-5 p.m.

SARAH P. DUKE GARDENS
426 Anderson St., Durham, 919-684-3698; www.hr.duke.edu

There are 55 acres of landscaped gardens and pine forest, with regional plants on display.

Admission: free. Monday-Saturday 9 a.m.-6 p.m., Sunday noon-5 p.m.

GREENSBORO

CHARLOTTE HAWKINS BROWN MEMORIAL STATE HISTORIC SITE
6136 Burlington Road, Sedalia, 336-449-4846; www.nchistoricsites.org

In 1902 C.H. Brown, granddaughter of a former slave, founded Palmer Memorial Institute, which became one of the finest preparatory schools for blacks in the nation. The campus later became the state's first historic site honoring education for African-Americans. There are guided tours of the historic campus, a visitor center and an audiovisual program. Picnicking is allowed.

Admission: free. Monday-Saturday 9 a.m.-5 p.m.

FIRST HORIZON PARK
408 Bellemeade St., Greensboro, 336-268-2255; www.gsohoppers.com

The Greensboro Grasshoppers, minor league affiliates of the Florida Marlins, play in this 8,000-seat brick stadium.

GREENSBORO HISTORICAL MUSEUM
130 Summit Ave., Greensboro, 336-373-2043; www.greensborohistory.org

Housed in an 1892 building in the downtown area, the museum features displays on the Revolutionary War, First Lady Dolley Madison and writer O. Henry, among others.

Admission: free. Tuesday-Saturday 10 a.m.-5 p.m., Sunday 2-5 p.m.

GUILFORD COURTHOUSE NATIONAL MILITARY PARK
2332 New Garden Road, Greensboro, 336-288-1776; www.nps.gov

On March 15, 1781, Lord Cornwallis won a costly victory that was one link in a series of events that led to his surrender at Yorktown in October of the same year. After destroying a quarter of the enemy troops, General Nathanael Greene (for whom the city is named) made a successful retreat and then severely hampered the British plan of subduing the Southern colonies. The 220-acre park, established in 1917, has monuments marking important locations and honoring those who fought here. There is a self-guided auto tour and walking trails. The visitor center has a museum housing Revolutionary War weapons and shows a 20-minute film.

Daily 8:30 a.m.-5 p.m.

NATURAL SCIENCE CENTER OF GREENSBORO

4301 Lawndale Drive, Greensboro, 336-288-3769; www.natsci.org

This natural science museum includes a zoo and indoor exhibits on geology and paleontology. Check out the 36-foot-tall Tyrannosaurus Rex model and inquire about the schedule of planetarium shows.

Admission: adults $8, seniors and children 3-13 $7, children 2 and under free. Monday-Saturday 9 a.m.-5 p.m., Sunday 12:30-5 p.m.

HICKORY

HICKORY MUSEUM OF ART

234 Third Ave., Hickory, 828-327-8576; www.hickorymuseumofart.org

American realist 19th- and 20th-century art, including works by Gilbert Stuart, are on display here. European, Oriental and pre-Columbian pieces often rotate in through the changing exhibits.

Admission: free. Tuesday-Sunday 10 a.m.-4 p.m., Sunday 1-4 p.m.

NEWTON

CATAWBA COUNTY MUSEUM OF HISTORY

21 E. First St., Newton, 828-465-0383; www.catawbahistory.org

Exhibits include a fire engine, a country doctor's office, Waugh Cabin, Bar-ringer Cabin, a blacksmith shop and an agriculture exhibit.

Admission: free. Wednesday-Saturday 9 a.m.-4 p.m., Sunday 1:30-4:30 p.m.

PINEHURST

SANDHILLS HORTICULTURAL GARDENS

Sandhills Community College, 3395 Airport Road, Pinehurst, 910-695-3882; www.sandhills.edu

The 25 acres include the Ebersole Holly Garden, Rose Garden, Conifer Garden, Hillside Garden (with bridges, waterfalls and gazebo), Desmond Native Wetland Trail Garden, a nature conservancy, and a bird sanctuary and the Sir Walter Raleigh Garden (a formal English garden).

Admission: free. Daily.

RALEIGH

MORDECAI HISTORIC PARK

1 Mimosa St., Raleigh, 919-857-4364; www.raleigh-nc.org

This preserved plantation home has many original furnishings and is noted for its neoclassical architecture. Also here is the house in which Andrew Johnson, 17th president of the U.S., was born. Guided tours are on offer.

Tuesday-Saturday.

NORTH CAROLINA MUSEUM OF HISTORY

5 E. Edenton St., Raleigh, 919-807-7900; www.ncmuseumofhistory.org

Several innovative exhibits convey the state's history. There is a particularly good exhibit on the role Native Americans played in North Carolina's past.

Admission: free. Monday-Saturday 9 a.m.-5 p.m., Sunday noon-5 p.m.

PULLEN PARK
408 Ashe Ave., Raleigh, 919-831-6468; www.raleigh-nc.org
The scenic 72-acre park in the center of downtown features a 1911 carousel, a train ride, paddle boats, an indoor aquatic center, ball fields, tennis courts, a playground and picnic shelters.

STATE CAPITOL
1 E. Edenton St., Raleigh, 919-733-4994; www.ncstatecapitol.com
A simple, stately Greek Revival-style building, the State Capitol is brimming with history. The old legislative chambers, in use until 1963, have been restored to their 1840s appearance, as have the old state library room and the state geologist's office. Self-guided tours are available.
Daily.

WILLIAM B. UMSTEAD STATE PARK
8801 Glenwood Ave., Raleigh, 919-571-4170; www.ncparks.gov
On 5,480 acres with a 55-acre lake, this park is great for fishing, boating, hiking, riding, picnicking and camping.

WINSTON-SALEM
BOWMAN GRAY STADIUM
1250 S. Martin Luther King Jr. Drive, Winston-Salem, 336-727-2748;
www.bowmangrayracing.com
Bowman Gray Stadium is a multiuse public arena that hosts Winston-Salem State Rams college football games as well as a NASCAR short track. Part of the city's Lawrence Joel Veterans Memorial Coliseum Complex, Bowman Gray has hosted races for more than 50 years, making it the longest-operating NASCAR short track in the country.

HISTORIC OLD SALEM
900 Old Salem Road, Winston-Salem, 336-721-7300, 888-653-7253; www.oldsalem.org
Old Salem is a restoration of a planned community that Moravians, with their Old World skills, turned into the 18th-century trade and cultural center of North Carolina's Piedmont region. Many of the sturdy structures built for practical living have been restored and furnished with original or period pieces. Early crafts are demonstrated throughout the town. A number of houses are privately occupied, but nine houses and the outbuildings are open to the public. Self-guided tours start at the visitor center on Old Salem Road. Special events are held during the year.
Tuesday-Sunday.

REYNOLDA HOUSE, MUSEUM OF AMERICAN ART
2250 Reynolda Road, Winston-Salem, 336-758-5150; www.reynoldahouse.org
On the estate of the late R. J. Reynolds of the tobacco dynasty, the museum houses American paintings, original furniture, art objects and elaborate costume collections. Adjacent is Reynolda Gardens, with 125 acres of open fields, naturalized woodlands, formal gardens and a greenhouse.
Admission: adults $10, seniors $9, students and children 18 and under free. Tuesday-Saturday 9:30 a.m.-4:30 p.m., Sunday 1:30-4:30 p.m.

WAKE FOREST UNIVERSITY
1834 Wake Forest Road, Winston-Salem, 336-758-5000; www.wfu.edu

Established in 1834, Wake Forest has 5,600 students. Sites to visit on campus include the Fine Arts Center, the Museum of Anthropology and Reynolda Village, a complex of shops, offices and restaurants.

WHERE TO STAY

CARY

★★★★★THE UMSTEAD HOTEL AND SPA
100 Woodland Pond, Cary, 919-447-4000, 866-877-4141; www.theumstead.com

Located in wooded suburban Cary, just outside of Raleigh in the Research Triangle area, this contemporary, elegant hotel offers a stylish stay. Rooms are decorated in muted neutrals and feature luxury linens, fully stocked bars and plenty of room to spread out. Enjoy the full-service Umstead Spa or its state-of-the-art fitness center. Herons restaurant, which serves creative contemporary American cuisine, is a local favorite.

150 rooms. Restaurant, bar. Spa. Pool. $351 and up

CHAPEL HILL

★★★THE CAROLINA INN
211 Pittsboro St., Chapel Hill, 919-933-2001, 800-962-8519; www.carolinainn.com

This historic 1924 inn is set in the middle of the University of North Carolina campus and around the corner from the Chapel Hill Medical Center. The entrance, with a high portico and pillars, and its red-brick building echo a Georgian Revival theme. Inside, hardwood floors, Oriental rugs, mahogany tables, palms and fresh flowers add to the beautiful setting. Guest rooms continue the theme and include mahogany two-poster beds and furnishings. Art galleries, museums, charming shops and fine restaurants are all just a short distance away.

184 rooms. Restaurant, bar. $151-250

★★★FRANKLIN HOTEL
311 W. Franklin St., Chapel Hill, 919-442-9000, 866-831-5999; www.franklinhotelnc.com

The Franklin Hotel combines the intimacy and charm of a bed and breakfast with the services and amenities of a larger hotel. The guest rooms are beautifully done in chocolate brown and celadon, while the seven VIP penthouse suites are the definition of luxury. Breakfast is an elegant affair at Windows Restaurant, while guests and locals mingle over drinks and light fare at Roberts, the lobby and patio bar.

67 rooms. Restaurant, bar. $251-350

★★★SHERATON HOTEL
1 Europa Drive, Chapel Hill, 919-968-4900, 800-325-3535; www.sheraton.com

This modern hotel is on the main road and connects the UNC-Chapel Hill campus and the Duke University campus, just a short distance to Interstate 85 and the Research Triangle. The wraparound open lobby features marble floors and floor-to-ceiling windows looking out to the pool and water fountain. Guest rooms are spacious with desks and sofas.

168 rooms. Restaurant, bar. $151-250

★★★SIENA HOTEL

1505 E. Franklin St., Chapel Hill, 919-929-4000, 800-223-7379;
www.sienahotel.com

Southern hospitality and grand European styling make the Siena Hotel a favorite in Chapel Hill. The guest rooms and suites are tastefully decorated with fine Italian furnishings and rich fabrics, while modern amenities ensure the highest levels of comfort. Guests receive privileges at the UNC golf course and nearby fitness center. Il Palio Ristorante charms visitors throughout the day with a delicious Northern Italian-influenced menu.

79 rooms. Restaurant, bar. Complimentary breakfast. $151-250

CHARLOTTE

★★★★THE BALLANTYNE HOTEL & LODGE, A LUXURY COLLECTION HOTEL

10000 Ballantyne Commons Parkway, Charlotte, 704-248-4000,
866-248-4824; www.theballantynehotel.com

This elegant resort within the city limits of Charlotte is a paradise for golf enthusiasts, with one of the state's best 18-hole courses and the renowned Dana Rader Golf school. Rooms are crisply and classically decorated and have lavish finishes, such as marble entrances and bathrooms. The Gallery Restaurant offers creative selections and seasonal ingredients. For a less formal affair, try the Gallery bar, which serves a tapas menu and a lengthy selection of cocktails, whiskeys and after-dinner drinks.

249 rooms. Restaurant, bar. Spa. $151-250

★★★THE DUKE MANSION

400 Hermitage Road, Charlotte, 704-714-4400, 888-202-1009;
www.dukemansion.com

This 1915 Southern estate is a lovely setting for a weekend getaway, and the mansion also serves as a facility for meetings and retreats. The charming Colonial Revival house was once owned by James Buchanan Duke, founder of Duke University. Acres of gardens surround the well-maintained house. Treetop rooms as well as standard guest rooms—some with sleeping porches—are decorated with traditional and antique furniture.

20 rooms. Complimentary breakfast. $151-250

★★★THE DUNHILL HOTEL

237 N. Tryon St., Charlotte, 704-332-4141, 800-354-4141;
www.dunhillhotel.com

This was one of the city's first luxury hotels when

WHAT ARE THE BEST HOTELS FOR GOLFERS?

The Ballantyne Hotel and Lodge: Duffers will be itching to hit the resort's 18-hole course, hailed as one of the state's best. Those who need help with their swing can get lessons at the great golf school.

The Carolina Hotel: The hotel offers 31 miles of golfing, making it the largest number of golf holes in the world at a single resort. Try to conquer its eight 18-hole courses.

it opened as the Mayfair Manor in 1929. Guest rooms feature 18th-century furniture, antiques and four-poster beds. The Dunhill's onsite restaurant, the Monticello, is an elegant spot for a special night out.

60 rooms. Restaurant, bar. Business center. $151-250

★★★HILTON CHARLOTTE CENTER CITY
222 E. Third St., Charlotte, 704-377-1500, 800-445-8667; www.charlotte.hilton.com

Perfect for business or pleasure, this hotel in the financial district is near shops and restaurants. Also nearby are beaches, golf courses and the Carolina Mountains. Rooms have oversized desks, 42-inch flat-screen TVs and black marble bathrooms.

400 rooms. Restaurant, bar. Business center. Fitness center. Pool. $151-250

★★★HILTON UNIVERSITY PLACE
8629 J. M. Keynes Drive, Charlotte, 704-547-7444, 800-445-8667;
www.charlotteuniversity.hilton.com

A beautiful sunlit atrium lobby anchors the Hilton. Guest rooms and suites sport a sleek contemporary style and afford great views of the university area. The Lakefront Restaurant offers a menu of steak- and seafood-focused fare.

393 rooms. Restaurant, bar. Business center. Fitness center. Pool. $151-250

★★★MARRIOTT CITY CENTER
100 W. Trade St., Charlotte, 704-333-9000, 800-228-9290; www.marriottcitycenter.com

Located in the central uptown business district, this hotel is only blocks from the Charlotte Convention Center and Bank of America Stadium. When you need to relax, try the bright-yellow rooms with flat-screen televisions and iPod docking stations, or do a few laps in the indoor pool.

438 rooms. Restaurant, bar. Fitness center. Pool. $151-250

★★★THE MOREHEAD INN
1122 E. Morehead St., Charlotte, 704-376-3357, 888-667-3432; www.moreheadinn.com

Meticulously kept gardens can be found at this charming Southern inn, which is listed on the National Register of Historic Places. Hardwood floors, Oriental rugs, antiques and beautiful tapestries are placed throughout, while four-poster beds and fireplaces provide cozy touches in guest rooms.

12 rooms. Complimentary breakfast. $151-250

★★★OMNI HOTEL
132 E. Trade St., Charlotte, 704-377-0400, 800-843-6664; www.omnihotels.com

The ultramodern Omni Hotel is within walking distance of the Charlotte Convention Center and the Overstreet Mall, which offers shopping and dining. The Charlotte-Douglas Airport is only 15 minutes away. Comfortable earth-toned guest rooms have robes, triple sheets and views of the city.

374 rooms. Restaurant, bar. Business center. Fitness center. $151-250

★★★THE RITZ-CARLTON, CHARLOTTE
201 East Trade Street, Charlotte, 704-547-2244; www.ritzcarlton.com

Open since late 2009, this environmentally friendly Ritz-Carlton is a choice place to stay while visiting Charlotte. Rooms feature flat-screen televisions built into bathroom mirrors, floor-to-ceiling windows and Frette linens. Best of all, the two-story penthouse spa is a pampering retreat; enjoy an evening swim surrounding by the twinkling city lights in the Aqua Lounge. For lunch or dinner, head to BLT Steak for a modern steakhouse experience. The hotel's environmental commitment includes a green, vegetated roof and hotel uniforms made of recycled materials.

146 rooms. Restaurant, bar. Spa. Pool. $251-350

★★★THE WESTIN CHARLOTTE
601 S. College St., Charlotte, 704-375-2600, 800-937-8461; www.westin.com

Rooms and suites are modern and comfortable and feature countless amenities, from in-room video games to the hotel's signature luxury bedding. Spa services are also available. The Ember Grille serves American cuisine for breakfast, lunch and dinner, while Charlotte's Treats and Eats offers light fare during the day.

700 rooms. Restaurant, bar. Business center. Spa. $151-250

DURHAM

★★★MARRIOTT DURHAM CIVIC CENTER
201 Foster St., Durham, 919-768-6000, 800-909-8375; www.marriott.com

This hotel is near the theater district, Durham Athletic Park and Duke University. Fountains that flow through the atrium lobby give it an elegant charm. Try to get a room on the concierge level, which entitles you to free continental breakfast, evening hors d'oeuvres and desserts, and drinks all day.

187 rooms. Restaurant, bar. $151-250

★★★MARRIOTT RESEARCH TRIANGLE PARK
4700 Guardian Drive, Durham, 919-941-6200, 800-228-9290; www.marriott.com

This ultramodern hotel is only five minutes from Research Triangle Park and the Raleigh-Durham Airport. North Carolina State, University of North Carolina and Duke University campuses are all close by. The sunny rooms come with pillow-top mattresses, featherbeds and duvets.

223 rooms. Restaurant, bar. $151-250

★★★MILLENNIUM HOTEL
2800 Campus Walk Ave., Durham, 919-383-8575, 866-866-8086; www.millennium-hotels.com

Conveniently located near Duke University and Medical Center, this hotel caters to business travelers with amenities such as wireless Internet access and a business center. Relax in the lounge, where mahogany bookshelves, overstuffed sofas and wing-backed chairs provide the atmosphere of a private club.

313 rooms. Restaurant, bar. Business center. $61-150

★★★WASHINGTON DUKE INN & GOLF CLUB
3001 Cameron Blvd., Durham, 919-490-0999, 800-443-3853; www.washingtondukeinn.com

Campus living never looked this elegant, yet the Washington Duke Inn & Golf Club calls Duke University campus home. Rooms and suites reflect English country influences, as does the daily afternoon tea. With four restaurants—none of which are unappetizing cafeteria food—dining choices here are terrific. A leading golf course just outside the door and privileges at the university's fitness facilities means there's always plenty to do.

271 rooms. Restaurant, bar. Fitness center. $251-350

GREENSBORO

★★★GRANDOVER RESORT & CONFERENCE CENTER

1000 Club Road, Greensboro, 336-294-1800, 800-472-6301; www.grandover.com

The Grandover Resort & Conference Center features exceptional award-winning golf, fine dining, stylish accommodations and Southern hospitality. The Ken Venturi Golf school is here along with 36 holes. A full-service spa, four clay tennis courts, a state-of-the-art fitness center, an indoor-outdoor pool, two racquetball courts and a volleyball court also provide fun diversions.

247 rooms. Restaurant, bar. Fitness center. Pool. Spa. Golf. Tennis. $151-250

★★★MARRIOTT GREENSBORO AIRPORT

1 Marriott Drive, Greensboro, 336-852-6450, 800-228-9290; www.marriott.com

This hotel is located at the Piedmont Triad International Airport but offers 17 acres of its own landscaped grounds with a lake and a pavilion, so you won't feel like you're in the middle of all the hubbub. The comfortable guest rooms feature the Marriott Revive bedding. Try dinner at JW's Steakhouse or a nightcap at Pitchers Bar and Grill.

299 rooms. Restaurant, bar. $151-250

★★★O. HENRY HOTEL

624 Green Valley Road, Greensboro, 336-854-2000; 877-854-2100; www.ohenryhotel.com

This locally owned boutique hotel, named for writer William Sydney Porter (better known by his pen name, O. Henry), who was born and raised in Greensboro, is decorated with North Carolina pine walls and ceilings, marble floors, Oriental rugs, leather and brocade furniture and large windows that overlook a cloistered courtyard. Spacious guest rooms include separate dressing rooms and soaking tubs.

131 rooms. Restaurant, bar. Complimentary breakfast. Fitness center. Pool. $151-250

PINEHURST

★★★★THE CAROLINA HOTEL

1 Carolina Vista Drive, Pinehurst, 910-295-6811, 800-487-4653; www.pinehurst.com

With eight 18-hole courses designed by the sport's leading names, including Fazio, Jones, Maples and Ross, the 31 miles of greens at this property contain 780 bunkers and the largest number of golf holes in the world at a single resort. This Victorian-era hotel provides guests with handsomely furnished accommodations and first-class service. Two of the Pinehurst resort's nine restaurants as well as a luxurious spa are located here.

220 rooms. Restaurant, bar. Spa. Beach. Golf. Tennis. $251-350

★★★HOLLY INN

155 Cherokee Road, Pinehurst, 910-295-6811, 800-487-4653; www.pinehurst.com

The Holly Inn was the first hotel built in Pinehurst (dating to 1895) and is part of the Pinehurst Resort. The inn has dark wood paneling, fireplaces and antique furniture. The onsite 1895 restaurant features an American-Continental menu with Carolina influences. The Tavern is more casual and serves lunch and dinner. Guests at the Holly Inn have access to all the activities of the Carolina Hotel.

82 rooms. Restaurant, bar. $151-250

★★★MAGNOLIA
65 Magnolia Road, Pinehurst, 910-295-6900, 800-526-5562; www.themagnoliainn.com

This historical 1896 inn is nestled in the quaint New England-style village of Pinehurst and is within walking distance of the Carolina Hotel, golf courses, tennis, dining and shopping. The rooms feature private baths with claw-foot tubs, four-poster beds and air conditioning. Two guest rooms also offer fireplaces, perfect for a romantic getaway.

11 rooms. Restaurant, bar. Complimentary breakfast. $61-150

PITTSBORO

★★★★★THE FEARRINGTON HOUSE COUNTRY INN
2000 Fearrington Village Center, Pittsboro, 919-542-2121; www.fearrington.com

The Fearrington House offers just the right mix of country style and worldly sophistication. Part of a charming village of shops, this country house hotel is on Colonial-era farmland. The inn's former incarnation as a dairy barn is evident today in the striped Galloway cows that graze the grounds. The rooms and suites feature a country theme with authentic details like salvaged church doors used as headboards. Canopied beds and original art create a stylish look.

33 rooms. Restaurant, bar. Complimentary breakfast. Business center. Fitness center. Pool. Spa. Tennis. No children under 6. $251-350

RALEIGH

★★★MARRIOTT RALEIGH CRABTREE VALLEY
4500 Marriott Drive, Raleigh, 919-781-7000, 800-909-8289; www.marriott.com

Guests will enjoy comfortable accommodations at the Marriott Raleigh Crabtree Valley, and will appreciate ultramodern features like marble floors, an atrium lobby and a lush indoor tropical garden. Accessible to Interstate 440 and Highway 70, the hotel is 15 minutes from Research Triangle Park and the airport, and across the street from Crabtree Valley Mall. Nearby activities include tennis, and museums of art, history and natural science.

375 rooms. Restaurant, bar. Fitness center. Pool. $151-250

★★★SHERATON RALEIGH HOTEL
421 S. Salisbury St., Raleigh, 919-834-9900, 800-325-3535; www.sheraton.com

The Sheraton Raleigh has a convenient location adjacent to the convention center and near the state capitol, dining, museums and entertainment. Marble floors, high ceilings and a balcony overlooking the lobby give the hotel a polished look. Guest rooms offer beds with fluffy duvets and pillows.

355 rooms. Restaurant, bar. $151-250

RECOMMENDED

CHAPEL HILL

HOLIDAY INN CHAPEL HILL
1301 N. Fordham Blvd., Chapel Hill, 919-929-2171, 888-452-5765; www.hichapelhill.com

For the truly school-spirited, the hotel lobby is painted in UNC colors, the front desk staff dresses in referee uniforms, all types of sports equipment are displayed on the outside walls leading to the rooms and the floors have blue footprints with tar on the heel.

134 rooms. Restaurant, bar. $61-150

WINSTON-SALEM

BROOKSTOWN INN

200 Brookstown Ave., Winston-Salem, 336-725-1120, 800-845-4262; www.brookstowninn.com

This historic inn was built in 1837 as a textile mill. The conversion preserved the original handmade brick and exposed-beam construction. The romantic rooms include European-style breakfast.

70 rooms. Complimentary breakfast. $151-250

WHERE TO EAT

CARY

★★★★HERONS

The Umstead Hotel and Spa, 100 Woodland Pond, Cary, 919-447-4200; www.theumstead.com

Gourmet dining in a suburban hotel seems like an oxymoron, but Herons at the Umstead Hotel is an exception. Herons puts a Southern spin on American cuisine in a fashionable setting complete with a 2,500-bottle wine cellar. A special menu designed for those getting a massage or other treatment in the hotel's spa is available. Of course, decadence is too, beginning with the restaurant's homemade cinnamon bun French toast with brown sugar streusel at breakfast and ending with the luscious brownie sundae baked Alaska.

Southern, American. Dinner. $36-85

CHAPEL HILL

★★★BONNE SOIRÉE

431 W. Franklin St., Chapel Hill, 919-928-8388

Smack-dab in the middle of Chapel Hill's vibrant Franklin Street, Bonne Soirée is a hit with locals and visitors alike. This intimate restaurant is sophisticated without being stuffy. The menu is handwritten and the wines are handpicked. The chef crafts his country French cooking with precision and pride, at times making it difficult to believe you're in North Carolina rather than the French countryside.

French. Dinner. $16-35

★★★★CAROLINA CROSSROADS

The Carolina Inn, 211 Pittsboro St., Chapel Hill, 919-933-9277, 800-962-8519; www.carolinainn.com

Set in the historic Carolina Inn, the Carolina Crossroads dining room is elegantly classic and delivers a picture-perfect example of Southern hospitality and charm. The menu features regional dishes, from a classic North Carolina pulled pork sandwich to salmon with grilled acorn squash in white-wine butter sauce. Local, seasonal ingredients are incorporated into many of the dishes.

Southern. Breakfast, lunch, dinner, Sunday brunch. Reservations recommended. Outdoor seating. Children's menu. Bar. $36-85

★★★ELAINE'S ON FRANKLIN

454 W. Franklin St., Chapel Hill, 919-960-2770; www.elainesonfranklin.com

Elaine's on Franklin promises that each meal is made up of "food for the soul, prepared for the heart." Among a menu of fresh greens and local meat and seafood, you'll see some unique dishes, such as tuna ceviche and even something for the herbivores: white lasagna with housemade wheat pasta. Your palate will continue the love affair with a selection of organic wines and the definition of soul food: a dessert menu with bread pudding and warm chocolate cake.

American, Southern. Dinner. Closed Sunday-Monday. $36-85

★★★IL PALIO

Siena Hotel, 1505 E. Franklin St., Chapel Hill, 919-929-4000, 800-223-7379; www.sienahotel.com

Located in the Siena Hotel, this Italian restaurant gives guests a fine-dining experience with tasteful interpretations of Italian-Mediterranean classics. A prix fixe Market Tasting Menu offers a chef's choice selection of food made from all local and seasonal ingredients. The restaurant features nightly live piano or guitar music and an impressive wine and martini list.

Northern Italian. Breakfast, lunch, dinner, Sunday brunch. Reservations recommended. Bar. $36-85

★★★JUJUBE RESTAURANT

Glen Lennox Shopping Center, 1201-L Raleigh Road, Chapel Hill, 919-960-0555; www.jujuberestaurant.com

Jujube proclaims it's "almost Asian," but that doesn't mean it's a copout or a fake. Southern stomachs will delight as they ease their way into exotic cuisine, with North Carolina shrimp lo mein and wontons made of beef short rib and goat cheese. Dates can cuddle at secluded tables along the brightly colored wall while adventurous types can sit chef-side at the open-kitchen bar. Each week the restaurant hosts special dinners and events where food and drink are the main guests. On Wednesdays, the kitchen goes Italian with its specials, and an advanced reservation will get you the Tuesday 20-course chef's table.

Asian. Lunch, dinner. $16-35

★★★LANTERN

423 W. Franklin St., Chapel Hill, 919-969-8846; www.lanternrestaurant.com

Lantern's head chef and owner Andrea Reusing wanted to create authentic Asian food using local, seasonal ingredients in a simply chic setting. Restaurant-goers' taste buds are treated with entrées tickled by curries and ginger, tamarind and lemongrass, mingling American cooking with Thai and Vietnamese flavors. Save room for spirits; Lantern's exhaustive wine selection is only to be outdone by the über-cosmopolitan cocktail list, which features The Red Geisha (muddled fresh organic strawberries with lime, ginger and vodka) and a Saketini worth raising a glass for.

Asian. Dinner. Closed Sunday. $36-85

WHAT ARE THE BEST RESTAURANTS FOR SOUTHERN CUISINE?

Carolina Crossroads: Get Southern hospitality and charm as well as regional dishes like classic pulled pork sandwiches and cioppino brimming with local seafood and collard greens.

Elaine's on Franklin: The restaurant touts its "food for the soul," like the unusual tuna ceviche. But the real soul food comes in the form of desserts like lemon-buttermilk pudding cake.

Herons: Upscale American cuisine gets the Southern treatment at Herons, with dishes like poached lobster with potato-beet hash, clementine and toasted sabayon.

Magnolia Grill: Magnolia pushes Southern fare beyond its borders in dishes like sea bass carpaccio with Thai crab vinaigrette. Don't miss sinful sweets like shaker pie.

CHARLOTTE

★★★BONTERRA

1829 Cleveland Ave., Charlotte, 704-333-9463; www.bonterradining.com

Bonterra is close to Uptown Charlotte in the historic Southend District. Choose from an extensive wine list featuring 100 selections by the glass and 300 bottles; wine tastings can be booked for groups of 15 to 50 people. Pair your wine with hunger-inducing dishes like deep-fried lobster tails, braised veal osso bucco, fire-roasted filet mignon and Sonoma County duck breast.

American, California. Dinner. Closed Sunday. Reservations recommended. Outdoor seating. Bar. $36-85

★★★★GALLERY RESTAURANT

Ballantyne Resort, 10000 Ballantyne Commons Parkway, Charlotte, 704-248-4000, 866-248-4824; www.gallery-restaurant.com

The setting is relaxing and welcoming at Gallery Restaurant & Bar, located on the ground level of the Ballantyne Resort. Enjoy artfully presented dishes such as cedar plank-roasted sea bass with blue crab, shallots and English pea risotto, or rosemary and citrus-roasted free-range chicken. Fine service makes dining here a delight.

American. Breakfast, lunch, dinner. Reservations recommended. Outdoor seating. Bar. $36-85

★★★LAVECCHIA'S SEAFOOD GRILLE

225 E. Sixth St., Charlotte, 704-370-6776; www.lavecchias.com

LaVecchia's features seafood entrées, such as Chilean sea bass and seared yellowfin tuna, as well as prime steaks. To complement the menu, the restaurant is decked out in a modern, urban, marine-themed design. A live jazz band spices things up on Friday and Saturday nights.

Seafood, steak. Dinner. Closed Sunday. Reservations recommended. Outdoor seating. Children's menu. Bar. $36-85

★★★MCNINCH HOUSE

511 N. Church St., Charlotte, 704-332-6159; www.mcninchhouserestaurant.com

This restaurant's unique setting, attention to detail and ever-changing but consistently strong French menu are well-suited for special-occasion dinners. Expect sophisticated dishes such as pistachio-crusted pork over andouille grits, toasted spinach and shiitake-green peppercorn ragout. Situated in a historic building, McNinch House is in a residential area on the west side of Church Street and within walking distance of downtown hotels and businesses.

French. Dinner. Closed Sunday-Monday. Reservations recommended. Jacket required. Bar. $86 and up

★★★TAVERNA 100

100 N. Tryon St., Charlotte, 704-344-0515; www.taverna100.com

Located in uptown Charlotte, Taverna 100 is housed in Founders Hall in the Bank of America's Corporate Center. Fresh herbs and olive oils accent the flavorful Mediterranean dishes, many of which are prepared on the wood-burning grill or the rotisserie.

Mediterranean. Lunch, dinner. Closed Sunday. Reservations recommended. Outdoor seating. Children's menu. Bar. $36-85

★★★UPSTREAM
6902 Phillips Place, Charlotte, 704-556-7730; www.upstreamit.com

With a wide selection of fresh seafood, a sushi and oyster bar, and an extensive wine list, this Charlotte dining spot (near SouthPark Mall) is a local favorite. Start with the lobster bisque or the jumbo lump crab cakes before trying an entrée such as the mushroom-crusted mahi mahi, sake-marinated South American sea bass or the pan-roasted Idaho trout.

Seafood. Lunch, dinner, brunch. Bar. Reservations recommended. Outdoor seating. $36-85

DURHAM

★★★FAIRVIEW
Washington Duke Inn & Golf Club, 3001 Cameron Blvd., Durham, 919-490-0999, 800-443-3853; www.washingtondukeinn.com

Located in the Washington Duke Inn & Golf Club, this Southern-influenced restaurant has traditional décor and nightly piano music. Try for a seat by one of the many windows for a beautiful view of the golf course. Weather permitting, the terrace is the perfect spot for outdoor dining. Nibble on dishes like pan-roasted dayboat North Carolina grouper with shrimp jambalaya or fennel-pepper-rubbed ahi tuna with a blue crab and olive oil-cured tomato risotto.

American. Breakfast, lunch, dinner, Sunday brunch. Reservations recommended. Outdoor seating. Children's menu. Bar. $36-85

★★★FOUR SQUARE RESTAURANT
2701 Chapel Hill Road, Durham, 919-401-9877; www.foursquarerestaurant.com

The location might throw you off, but once you sidle up to the elegant converted Victorian that houses Four Square, you'll be in the right place for a romantic meal. Past the wraparound porch await seven dining rooms—easily converted to party space if you're in need of a venue—with fireplaces and a screened porch for warmer weather use. Dining here will never get old, as the menu changes monthly to make sure the kitchen is always cooking up the freshest tastes, using local produce, cheese and meat each season in dishes like ras el hanout-spiced Virginia scallops with watercress and panisse or buckwheat and butternut squash maki rolls with smoked tofu custard, bourbon ponzu and fried cashews.

American. Dinner. Closed Sunday. $36-85

★★★MAGNOLIA GRILL
1002 Ninth St., Durham, 919-286-3609; www.magnoliagrill.net

At Magnolia Grill, husband-and-wife chefs and co-owners Ben and Karen Barker exhibit an independent streak in Southern cooking. He handles the savories, taking Southern ingredients beyond regional confines in dishes such as smoked trout with avocado and red pepper slaw and sea bass carpaccio with Thai crab vinaigrette; she creates the sweets taking Southern comforts upscale with the likes of lemony shaker pie and upside-down caramel banana cake with bourbon-praline ice cream.

American, Southern. Dinner. Closed Sunday-Monday. Bar. Reservations recommended. $36-85

★★★NANA'S RESTAURANT
2514 University Drive, Durham, 919-493-8545; www.nanasdurham.com

Locals like to frequent the bar for a quick bite and a glass or two off the wine

list, but first-timers will want to treat their taste buds to all three courses: pâté or peekytoe crab chowder to start, fish or fowl next, and a local cheese plate or Nana's crème brûlée for dessert. All of your special-occasion needs are covered here: There's space to host big parties or plan a more intimate outing with a tasting menu and wine pairings. The restaurant offers cooking classes with the chef.
American. Dinner. Closed Sunday. $36-85

★★★PAPA'S GRILLE
1821 Hillandale Road, Durham, 919-383-8502; www.papasgrille.com
Watch the chefs work in the open display kitchen of this restaurant in a little strip mall near Route 70 and Interstate 85. Bistro tables surround the outside of the room, while dining room tables are set with crisp white tablecloths, dark blue glasses and candles. Executive chef Sam Papanikas is known for his cast-iron pan-seared graviera cheese flambé and lavender-glazed lamb tenderloin.
Mediterranean. Lunch, dinner. Closed Sunday. Reservations recommended. Children's menu. Bar. $36-85

GREENSBORO
★★★BISTRO SOFIA
616 Dolley Madison Road, Greensboro, 336-855-1313; www.bistrosofia.com
This restaurant, northwest of downtown Greensboro, serves dishes using homegrown organic vegetables, berries and herbs. The early-evening prix fixe menu is $25 for three courses, with bistro favorites such as steak frites making appearances on the ever-changing menu.
American. Dinner. Closed Monday. Reservations recommended. Outdoor seating. Children's menu. Bar. $36-85

★★★RESTAURANT MUSE
3124 Kathleen Ave., Greensboro, 336-323-1428; www.restaurantmuse.net
Exquisite French cuisine prepared with fresh local ingredients draws diners back to Restaurant Muse time and time again. Chef and owner Mitchell Nicks offers creative plates that include roasted rack of lamb brushed with bergamot and mustard as well as his "untraditional Brutus salad" with pancetta, spicy chile dressing, fried artichoke hearts and a manchego cheese crisp. An à la carte menu is available, as is a chef's tasting menu.
French. Lunch, dinner, brunch. Reservations recommended. Outdoor seating. Bar. $36-85

HICKORY
★★★1859 CAFÉ
443 Second Ave. S.W., Hickory, 828-322-1859; www.hickoryonline.com
The international cuisine at this restaurant includes options such as pesto-crusted scallops with mushroom risotto, sautéed duck breast with strawberry rhubarb sauce, and pork tenderloin stuffed with spiced fruit and walnuts.
International. Dinner. Closed Sunday. Reservations recommended. Outdoor seating. Bar. $16-35

★★★VINTAGE HOUSE
271 Third Ave. N.W., Hickory, 828-324-1210
This restaurant is a converted 100-year-old Victorian home located two blocks

from the downtown center of Hickory. Dine in one of five dining rooms, two of which are enclosed porches with large windows overlooking the gardens.

American. Dinner. Closed Sunday. Bar. Reservations recommended. $36-85

PINEHURST

★★★THE 1895 GRILLE

The Holly Inn, 155 Cherokee Road, Pinehurst, 910-235-8434, 800-487-4653; www.pinehurst.com

This charming restaurant is in the historic Holly Inn and is part of the famous Pinehurst Resort. The restaurant features a Continental menu with a Carolina influence and plenty of original preparations for seafood and steak, like shrimp and grits with gorgonzola or pancetta-wrapped filet mignon.

American, Continental. Breakfast, dinner. Closed Monday-Tuesday. Bar. Reservations recommended. $36-85

PITTSBORO

★★★★THE FEARRINGTON HOUSE RESTAURANT

The Fearrington House Inn, 2000 Fearrington Village Center, Pittsboro, 919-542-2121; www.fearrington.com

This charming Victorian-style country restaurant is on several rolling acres near Chapel Hill. The property is dotted with flower gardens and lush landscapes, and the restaurant is accented with elegant antique furnishings. The upscale menu is American, with techniques borrowed from France and robust flavors taken from the surrounding region. The thoughtful, seasonal menu is complemented by a deep international wine list that features close to 500 selections with a focus on California varietals.

American, French. Dinner. Reservations recommended. Outdoor seating. Jacket required. Bar. $36-85

RALEIGH

★★★ANGUS BARN

9401 Glenwood Ave., Raleigh, 919-787-2444, 800-277-2270; www.angusbarn.com

This steakhouse is one of the few restaurants in the country to age its own beef before it is hand cut and grilled. Also on the menu are steakhouse classics like oysters Rockefeller and chateaubriand. Two cozy, basement-level wine cellars can be reserved for private dining and hold extensive collection of bottles from around the world. A collection of antiques adds charm.

Seafood, steak. Dinner. Reservations recommended. Children's menu. Bar. $36-85

★★★J. BETSKI'S

10 W. Franklin St., Raleigh, 919-833-7999; www.jbetskis.com

You'll see some schnitzel and spaetzle at this unique addition to the Raleigh restaurant scene—not to mention a 'wurst or two. Owner John F. Korzekwinski injects his German and Polish heritage into Southern cuisine, offering up traditional Old World dishes that North Carolina natives can relish. And what better than to pair the seasonal menu's pretzel dumplings and duck confit with than a hefty lager or other bubbly brew off of the beer menu? A glass of wine won't take away from your experience, as the list offers selections from Germany and Austria.

German, Polish. Dinner, late-night. Closed Sunday. $36-85

★★★SECOND EMPIRE

330 Hillsborough St., Raleigh, 919-829-3663; www.second-empire.com

This restaurant is housed in a renovated Second Empire Victorian home, which was built in 1879. The original heartwood pine floors, masonry walls and windows add to the elegant atmosphere in the upstairs dining room, which offers fine dining. For a more casual dinner, head downstairs to the Tavern or the Atrium Room, both of which offer seasonal, organic and fresh ingredients with original presentations.

Contemporary American. Dinner. Closed Sunday. Reservations recommended. Bar. $36-85

★★★SIMPSON'S

5625 Creedmoor Road, Raleigh, 919-783-8818; www.simpsonsrestaurant.com

Enjoy the romantic atmosphere as you dine by candlelight and listen to the pianist who plays here Friday and Saturday evenings. The restaurant, styled after an old English pub, serves an impressive steak and seafood menu.

Steak, seafood Dinner. Closed Sunday. Reservations recommended. Bar. $36-85

WINSTON-SALEM
★★★RYAN'S RESTAURANT

719 Coliseum Drive, Winston-Salem, 336-724-6132; www.ryansrestaurant.com

An inviting brick pathway surrounded by philodendrons along with a cascading waterfall leads guests to Ryan's. The décor here is simple yet elegant, and tables offer a view of the woods and brook below. The menu features steakhouse standards, along with a wide selection of seafood dishes, such as pepper-seared tuna with red cabbage slaw.

Seafood, steak. Dinner. Closed Sunday. Reservations recommended. Outdoor seating. Bar. $36-85

RECOMMENDED

GREENSBORO
GATE CITY CHOP HOUSE

106 S. Holden St., Greensboro, 336-294-9977; www.gatecitychophouse.com

The main dining room at this steakhouse features a display kitchen and walls adorned with pictures of Greensboro. Menu selections include grilled peppered salmon, Carolina crab cakes, roasted prime rib and filet mignon.

Seafood, steak. Lunch, dinner. Closed Sunday. Reservations recommended. Outdoor seating. Children's menu. Bar. $36-85

SPAS

CARY
★★★★THE UMSTEAD SPA

The Umstead Hotel and Spa, 100 Woodland Pond, Cary, 919-447-4170; www.theumsteadspa.com

A tranquil, Asian-inspired space, the spa at the Umstead Hotel offers 14,000 square feet devoted to pampering treatments that range from hot-stone massage to milk hydrotherapy baths. Private spa suites, which accommodate four to six people, are perfect for parties and include access to a massage room, a color therapy tub and more. To keep you full and hydrated during your spa day, you'll receive fruit, Evian water and a bottle of champagne. The spa also has a fitness studio and salon services.

CHARLOTTE
★★★★THE SPA AT BALLANTYNE
Ballantyne Hotel & Lodge, 1000 Ballantyne Commons Parkway, Charlotte, 704-248-4141; www.theballantynehotel.com

Tucked inside Charlotte's luxurious Ballantyne Hotel & Lodge, this spa offers a classic pampering experience delivered by an amiable, well-trained staff. With 16 treatment rooms, there's ample space for sampling Swedish massages, rejuvenating facials or moisturizing body wraps. The spa also provides a full range of nail and salon services. Lovebirds can opt for side-by-side massages in the privacy of a couples' suite.

PINEHURST
★★★★THE SPA AT PINEHURST
1 Carolina Vista Drive, Pinehurst, 910-235-8320, 800-487-4653; www.pinehurst.com

Featuring more than 40 different treatments, this spa is influenced by its Southern location. Pine-inspired treatments dominate the menu, from the pine salt body rub to the exfoliating pine cream of the Pinehurst deluxe body treatment. If your body is in knots, try one of the spa's eight different massage therapies, including a special rubdown designed for golfers.

WHERE TO SHOP

CONCORD
CONCORD MILLS
8111 Concord Mills Blvd., Concord, 704-979-3000; www.concordmills.com

This outlet mall has more than 200 stores, including factory outlets for popular chains such as Banana Republic and Saks Fifth Avenue. It also houses a movie theater.

HICKORY
20 MILES OF FURNITURE
Hickory, 800-737-0782; www.20milesoffurniture.com

This area offers golf, shopping and dining, but is best known for its nearly 40 furniture stores. Plant tours are available.

HICKORY FURNITURE MART
2220 Highway 70 S.E., Hickory, 800-462-6278; www.hickoryfurniture.com

More than 1,000 home-furnishing lines are displayed in this 1 million-square-foot complex, which includes 100 factory outlets, stores and galleries, a museum, a café, shipping service, a visitor center, and a motel.

THE COAST

North Carolina's Coast boasts 300 miles of barrier island beaches. You might recognize them as the setting of '90s teen drama *Dawson's Creek*. Wilmington played a key role in the popular show, with its small-town beach atmosphere in a historic area. As the major city on North Carolina's Cape Fear coast, the town offers a steady mix of industry and tourism, with historic sites, a vibrant and historic downtown, and access to Cape Fear beaches.

Edenton is one of the oldest communities in North Carolina and was the capital of the colony for more than 22 years. It's known as the South's prettiest small town because of the large number of original historic homes dating back to the 1700s.

Fayetteville is the state's farthest inland port, at the head of navigation on the Cape Fear River with an eight-foot-deep channel connecting it to the Intracoastal Waterway. The town is a center for retail, manufacturing and conventions, and the home of Fort Bragg and Pope Air Force Base.

Found on the eastern side of Roanoke Island, the quaint town of Manteo has more bed and breakfasts than any other Outer Banks village. Fishing in the waters off Manteo is excellent. A large sport fishing fleet is available for booking at Oregon Inlet as well as on Roanoke Island.

New Bern, originally settled by Swiss and German immigrants, is famous for being the birthplace of Pepsi-Cola, which was first sold at a local drugstore. Many Georgian-style and Federal-style buildings give New Bern an architectural look unique in North Carolina. The Neuse and Trent rivers are ideal for swimming, boating, and freshwater and saltwater fishing.

WHAT TO SEE

BEAUFORT
BEAUFORT HISTORIC SITE
138 Turner St., Beaufort, 252-728-5225; www.historicbeaufort.com

The site includes an old burial ground, a restored old jail, restored houses, a courthouse dating back to 1796, an apothecary, an art gallery and a gift shop. Get a self-guided walking tour map from the historical center (138 Turner St.).

Admission (tours): adults $8, children $4. Tours: Monday-Saturday 10 a.m., 11:30 a.m., 1 p.m., 3 p.m. Shop: Monday-Saturday 9:30 a.m.-5 p.m.

CAPE LOOKOUT NATIONAL SEASHORE
131 Charles St., Harkers Island, 252-728-2250; www.nps.gov

Part of the National Park System on the outer banks of North Carolina, the Cape Seashore extends 55 miles south from Ocracoke Inlet and includes unspoiled barrier islands. There are no roads or bridges; it's accessible by boat only. Catch a ferry from Beaufort, Harkers Island, Davis, Atlantic or Ocracoke (April-November). It offers excellent fishing and shell collecting, primitive camping; and interpretive programs (seasonal). The lighthouse, at Cape Lookout is still operational.

Visitor center: daily 8:30 a.m.-4:30 p.m.

EDENTON
HISTORIC EDENTON
108 N. Broad St., Edenton, 252-482-2637; www.nchistoricsites.org

Take a tour of historic properties, which may be seen individually or as a group. Allow 2½ to 3 hours for the complete tour.

April-October, Monday-Saturday 9 a.m.-5 p.m., Sunday 1-5 p.m.; November-March, Monday-Saturday 10 a.m.-4 p.m., Sunday 1-4 p.m.

HIGHLIGHT

WHAT ARE THE TOP THINGS TO DO ON THE COAST?

VISIT THE WRIGHT BROTHERS NATIONAL MEMORIAL
See the field where the first powered flight took place in 1903. The hangar buildings in which the Wrights lived have been re-created as well.

RELAX ON THE SANDS OF CAPE HATTERAS NATIONAL SEASHORE
This Outer Banks beach is considered to be one of the country's best. Its crystal-blue waters and sandy shores make it a top spot to swim or just lay out in the sun.

TAKE A STROLL THROUGH THE ELIZABETHAN GARDENS
You'll be transported to another time and place on these grounds, which include a Sunken Garden, the Queen's Rose Garden and a 16th-century gazebo.

DRINK UP AT THE PEPSI STORE
Pepsi drinkers will want to stop in this store, which is where the brand's first soda was invented. Pick up some Pepsi memorabilia and quench your thirst with a drink.

JAMES IREDELL HOUSE
108 N. Broad St., Edenton, 252-482-2637; www.nchistoricsites.org
Tour the home of early Attorney General of North Carolina James Iredell, who was appointed by George Washington to the first U.S. Supreme Court.
Admission: free. April-October, Monday-Saturday 9 a.m.-5 p.m., Sunday 1-5 p.m.; November-March, Tuesday-Saturday 10 a.m.-4 p.m., Sunday 1-4 p.m.

SOMERSET PLACE STATE HISTORIC SITE
2572 Lake Shore Road, Creswell, 252-797-4560; www.albemarle-nc.com
Located on Lake Phelps in Pettigrew State Park, the original plantation encompassed more than 100,000 acres. It was one of the largest in North Carolina. The first primary crop was rice, which gave way to corn and wheat. The mansion and outbuildings date back to the 1830s.
Admission: free. April-October, Monday-Saturday 9 a.m.-5 p.m., Sunday 1-5 p.m.; November-March, Monday-Saturday 10 a.m.-4 p.m., Sunday 1-4 p.m.

FAYETTEVILLE
CAPE FEAR BOTANICAL GARDEN
536 N. Eastern Blvd., Fayetteville, 910-486-0221; www.capefearbg.org

This garden is on 85 acres overlooking Cross Creek and the Cape Fear River. The grounds feature wildflowers, oaks and native plants.

Admission: adults $6, children 6-12 $1, children 5 and under free. Mid-December-mid-February, Monday-Saturday 10 a.m.-5 p.m.; March-mid-December, Monday-Saturday 10 a.m.-5 p.m., Sunday noon-5 p.m.

FIRST PRESBYTERIAN CHURCH
102 Ann St., Fayetteville, 910-483-0121; www.firstprez.com

Classic Southern colonial-style architecture and whale-oil chandeliers are on display here. Among contributors to the original building (destroyed by fire in 1831) were James Monroe and John Quincy Adams.

FORT BRAGG AND POPE AIR FORCE BASE—82ND AIRBORNE DIVISION WAR MEMORIAL MUSEUM
Gela and Ardennes streets, Fort Bragg, 910-432-3443; www.bragg.army.mil

The military museum houses weapons and other relics of World War I and II, Vietnam, Korea and Desert Storm. There are also exhibits on the history of the 82nd airborne division and a gift shop.

Admission: free. Tuesday-Saturday 10 a.m.-4:30 p.m.

GOLDSBORO
CLIFFS OF THE NEUSE STATE PARK
345 Park Entrance Road, Seven Springs, 919-778-6234; www.ncparks.gov

With more than 700 acres on the Neuse River, this state park provides swimming, a bathhouse, fishing and boating (rowboat rentals). There are nature trails, picnicking, a museum and an interpretive center.

GOVERNOR CHARLES B. AYCOCK BIRTHPLACE STATE HISTORIC SITE
264 Governor Aycock Road, Fremont, 919-242-5581; www.nchistoricsites.org

The site has a mid-1800s farmhouse and outbuildings. There is an audio-visual presentation in an 1893 one-room school that is worth seeing as well. Picnicking is allowed, so pack your lunch.

Admission: free. Monday-Saturday 9 a.m.-5 p.m.

GREENVILLE
GREENVILLE MUSEUM OF ART
802 Evans St., Greenville, 252-758-1946; www.gmoa.org

Collections emphasize North Carolina contemporary fine arts and drawings as well as paintings and prints of the period from 1900-1945.

Admission: free. Tuesday-Friday 10 a.m.-4.30 p.m., Saturday 1-4 p.m.

RIVER PARK NORTH SCIENCE AND NATURE CENTER
1000 Mumford Road, Greenville, 252-329-4560; www.greenvillenc.gov

This 309-acre park has four lakes and a mile of Tar River water frontage. The science center near the park entrance offers hands-on exhibits. Fishing, pedal boats and picnicking are all allowed onsite.

Admission: free, Tuesday-Saturday 9:30 a.m.-5 p.m., Sunday 1-5 p.m.

KILL DEVIL HILLS
WRIGHT BROTHERS NATIONAL MEMORIAL
1401 National Park Drive, Kill Devil Hills, 252-441-7430; www.nps.gov

The field where the first powered flight took place on December 17, 1903, is marked, showing the takeoff point and landing place. The living quarters and hangar buildings used by the Wrights during their experiments have been replicated. The visitor center has reproductions of a 1902 glider and a 1903 flyer, with exhibits on the story of their invention.

Summer, daily 9 a.m.-6 p.m.; September-May, daily 9 a.m.-5 p.m.

MANTEO
CAPE HATTERAS NATIONAL SEASHORE
1401 National Park Drive, Manteo, 252-473-2111; www.nps.gov

This free 75-mile-long beach in the Outer Banks is ranked among the top in the country. It's hailed for being one of the best places to surf along the East Coast. Cape Hatteras is also great for fishing, windsurfing, kayaking and camping. The black-and-white-striped lighthouse, the clean blue water and the sand dunes make it a picturesque spot.

ELIZABETHAN GARDENS
1411 National Park Drive, Manteo, 252-473-3234; www.elizabethangardens.org

These 10½ acres include the Great Lawn, the Sunken Garden, the Queen's Rose Garden, an herb garden, a 16th-century gazebo with thatched roof and ancient garden statuary. Plants bloom all year, so you can see some greenery even in the winter months. The Gate House Reception Center displays period furniture, English portraits and coat of arms.

Admission: adults $8, children 6-17 $5, children 5 and under free. Daily.

ROANOKE ISLAND FESTIVAL PARK
Manteo waterfront, 252-475-1500; www.roanokeisland.com

This park boasts a representative 16th-century sailing vessel similar to those that brought the first English colonists to the New World more than 400 years ago. In summer, there is a living history interpretation. There's also a visitor center with exhibits and an audiovisual program.

February-December, daily.

MOREHEAD CITY
FORT MACON STATE PARK
E. Fort Macon Road, Atlantic Beach, 252-726-3775

This restored fort, built in 1834, was originally used as a harbor defense. The beach has lifeguards in summer as well as a bathhouse, surf fishing, and hiking and nature trails. The museum features interpretive programs and battle re-enactments.

NEW BERN
ATTMORE-OLIVER HOUSE
512 Pollock St., New Bern, 252-638-8558

This house, headquarters for the New Bern Historical Society, exhibits 18th- and 19th-century furnishings and historical objects, including Civil War artifacts.

Early April-mid-December, Tuesday, Thursday, Saturday; also by appointment.

TRYON PALACE HISTORIC SITES AND GARDENS

610 Pollock St., New Bern, 800-767-1560; www.tryonpalace.org

Built from 1767 to 1770 by Royal Gov. William Tryon, this colonial building burned in 1798 and lay in ruins until it was rebuilt between 1952 and 1959. It served as the colonial and first state capitol. Reconstruction furnishings and 18th-century English gardens are beautiful and authentic. Guided tours are available.

Admission: adults $20, students $10. Monday-Saturday 9 a.m.-5 p.m., Sunday 1-5 p.m.

PEPSI STORE

256 Middle St., New Bern, 252-636-5898; www.pepsistore.com

This is the site of the pharmacy in which Caleb Bradham first served his invention, "Brad's Drink," in 1858. When orders for the concoction took off, he renamed it Pepsi-Cola. Now the site is a store full of Pepsi memorabilia. Of course, don't leave without having a fountain soda.

SOUTHPORT

BRUNSWICK TOWN-FORT ANDERSON STATE HISTORIC SITE

8884 St. Philips Road S.E., Southport, 910-371-6613; www.southport-oakisland.com

Brunswick, founded in 1726, thrived as a major port exporting tar and lumber. Fearing a British attack, its citizens fled when the Revolution began. In 1776, the town was burned down by British sailors. Twenty-three foundations have been excavated. Built across part of the town are the Civil War earthworks of Fort Anderson, which held out for 30 days after the fall of Fort Fisher in 1865.

Tuesday-Saturday 10 a.m.-4 p.m.

FORT FISHER STATE HISTORIC SITE

1610 Fort Fisher Blvd. S., Kure Beach, 910-458-5538; www.nchistoricsites.org

This was the largest earthworks fort in the Confederacy. Until the last few months of the Civil War, it kept Wilmington open to blockade-runners. Some of the heaviest naval bombardment of land fortifications took place here December 24-25, 1864, and January 13-15, 1865. The visitor center has exhibits and audiovisual shows.

October-March, Tuesday-Saturday 10 a.m.-4 p.m.

WILMINGTON

BATTLESHIP NORTH CAROLINA

Battleship Road, Wilmington, 910-251-5797; www.battleshipnc.com

All aboard this World War II vessel moored on the west bank of Cape Fear River. Tour the museum, gun turrets, galley, bridge, sick bay, engine room and wheelhouse.

Admission: adults $12, seniors and military personnel $10, children 6-11 $6, children 5 and under free. Memorial Day-Labor Day, daily 8 a.m.-8 p.m.; Labor Day-Memorial Day, daily 8 a.m.-5 p.m.

BURGWIN-WRIGHT HOUSE

224 Market St., Wilmington, 910-762-0570; www.burgwinwrighthouse.com

British General Cornwallis had his headquarters at this restored colonial town house built on the foundation of an abandoned town jail. Enjoy the 18th-century furnishings and gardens.

Admission: adults $10, children 5-12 $4, children 4 and under free. Tuesday-Saturday.

MOORES CREEK NATIONAL BATTLEFIELD

40 Patriot Paul Drive, Currie, 910-283-5591; www.nps.gov

In 1776, the loosely knit colonists took sides against each other—patriots versus loyalists. Cols. Moore, Lillington and Caswell, with the blessing of the Continental Congress, broke up the loyalist forces, captured the leaders and seized gold and weapons. The action defeated British hopes of an early invasion through the South and encouraged North Carolina to be the first colony to instruct its delegates to vote for independence in Philadelphia.

Daily.

CAPTAIN J. N. MAFFITT RIVER CRUISES

Wilmington, 910-343-1611, 800-676-0162; www.cfrboats.com

Located at the foot of Market Street, this five-mile narrated sightseeing cruise covers Wilmington's harbor life and points of interest. There is also a river taxi service (additional fee) from battleship *North Carolina*.

Admission: varies. May-September, daily.

POPLAR GROVE PLANTATION

10200 Highway, 17, Wilmington, 910-686-9989; www.poplargrove.com

The restored Greek Revival-style plantation incorporates a manor house, smokehouse, tenant house, blacksmith, loom weaver and basket weaver.

Admission: adults $10, seniors and military personnel $9, students 6-15 $5. Monday-Saturday 9 a.m.-5 p.m., Sunday noon-5 p.m.

WHERE TO STAY

KILL DEVIL HILLS

★★★THE SANDERLING

1461 Duck Road, Duck, 252-261-4111, 877-650-4812; www.sanderlinginn.com

Nestled on the northern reaches of the Outer Banks, the Sanderling is designed to complement the natural setting and includes an eco-center and low-rise, cedar-shingled buildings. Composed of three inns and oceanside villas, the Sanderling offers secluded beaches, conference centers and a full-service spa. The restaurant is housed in a historic U.S. lifesaving station.

88 rooms. Restaurant, bar. Spa. Beach. $151-250

MANTEO

★★★TRANQUIL HOUSE INN

405 Queen Elizabeth St., Manteo, 252-473-1404, 800-458-7069; www.tranquilinn.com

Built in 1988 in the style of a 19th-century Outer Banks resort, this waterfront property offers a continental breakfast and evening wine and cheese with each of its rooms. Elegant dockside dining overlooking Shallowbag Bay can be found at 1587 Restaurant.

25 rooms. Restaurant. Complimentary breakfast. $151-250

MOREHEAD CITY

★★★SHERATON ATLANTIC BEACH OCEANFRONT HOTEL

2717 W. Fort Macon Road, Atlantic Beach, 252-240-1155, 800-624-8875; www.sheratonatlanticbeach.com

Each room at this beachfront hotel features a private balcony. There are two

WHAT ARE THE BEST OCEANFRONT HOTELS?

The Sanderling:
The Outer Banks hotel offers secluded beaches and beautiful views of the ocean. The spa does water-inspired treatments like the Sea of Life facial, which uses seashells.

Tranquil House Inn:
This Outer Banks resort puts you right on the water. You can also gaze at the lovely vista while dining dockside at the elegant 1587 Restaurant.

restaurants, two lounges and two pools, as well as nearby golf and tennis courts.

200 rooms. Restaurant, bar. Complimentary breakfast. Pool. $151-250

WILMINGTON

★★★HILTON WILMINGTON RIVERSIDE

301 N. Water St., Wilmington, 910-763-5900, 800-445-8667; www.wilmingtonhilton.com

This hotel is a short walk from shops, restaurants, cultural attractions and the city's riverwalk. Guest rooms are comfortable and offer magnificent views of Cape Fear River.

274 rooms. Restaurant, bar. $61-150

★★★THE WILMINGTONIAN

101 S. Second St., Wilmington, 910-343-1800, 800-525-0909; www.thewilmingtonian.com

Located in downtown Wilmington, just two blocks from Cape Fear River and a 40-minute drive from the beaches on the Atlantic Coast, this renovated inn caters to both leisure and business travelers with roomy suites and plentiful amenities.

40 rooms. Restaurant, bar. Complimentary breakfast. $61-150

RECOMMENDED

EDENTON
LORDS PROPRIETORS INN

300 N. Broad St., Edenton, 252-482-3641, 888-394-6622; www.edentoninn.com

This inn is actually three separate homes set on two acres. All rooms are decorated with period antiques and reproductions. The New American dining room is for inn guests only and offers an impressive seasonal menu.

20 rooms. $151-250

THE GRAYSTONE INN

100 S. Third St., Wilmington, 910-763-2000, 888-763-4773; www.graystoneinn.com

The antique-filled inn includes a music room with a grand piano, a mahogany-paneled library and a chandelier-lit dining room. Rooms are decorated in period furnishings, some with claw-foot tubs.

9 rooms. Complimentary breakfast. No children under 12. $151-250

ROSEHILL INN

114 S. Third St., Wilmington, 910-815-0250, 800-815-0250; www.rosehill.com

This elegant Victorian home was built in 1848. Each of the large, luxurious guest rooms has its own individual charm and is perfect for a romantic retreat.

6 rooms. Complimentary breakfast. No children under 14.
$151-250

THE VERANDAS

202 Nun St., Wilmington, 910-251-2212; www.verandas.com

This 8,500-square-foot Victorian-Italianate mansion sits two blocks from the Cape Fear River. Climb the spiral staircase to the enclosed cupola for a spectacular sunset view.

8 rooms. Complimentary breakfast. No children under 12.
$151-250

WHERE TO EAT

RECOMMENDED
KILL DEVIL HILLS
FLYING FISH CAFÉ

2003 S. Croatan Highway, Kill Devil Hills, 252-441-6894; www.flyingfishcafeobx.com

With a name like Flying Fish, the restaurant must specialize in seafood, and it delivers with entrées like pan-friend Carolina crab cakes with housemade corn pudding. But the Flying Fish also proudly calls itself the home of the Chocolate Hurricane, chocolate done five ways and wrapped in a white and dark chocolate cylinder.

Mediterranean. Dinner. Reservations recommended.
Children's menu. Bar. $16-35

PORT O' CALL

504 Virginia Dare Trail, Kill Devil Hills, 252-441-7484; www.outerbanksportocall.com

Victorian décor, antiques and brass accents lend the old-fashioned Port O' Call a warm, cozy atmosphere. You have your choice of land- or sea-based dishes; there's a meat menu with everything from filet mignon to baby-back ribs, and seafood entrées include oysters and crabmeat-stuffed flounder. Come in on Thursday to Saturday nights and you'll get live music to go with your meal.

Seafood, steak. Dinner. Closed January-March. Children's
menu. Bar. $16-35

WILMINGTON
EDDIE ROMANELLI'S

5400 Oleander Drive, Wilmington, 910-799-7000; www.romanellisrestaurant.com

Eddie Romanelli's offers straightforward fare but also puts an Italian twist on favorite American dishes;

WHICH RESTAURANTS SERVE THE BEST SEAFOOD?

Elijah's:
Locals crowd the Cape Fear Riverwalk restaurant to indulge in comfort seafood like the favorite hot crab dip or the creamy Carolina chowder with clams and shrimp.

Pilot House:
This restaurant puts a Southern slant on seafood with dishes like crab fritters, maple-glazed salmon and sweet potato grouper.

calamari comes with pepperoncini and diced tomatoes and potato skins are stuffed with prosciutto, tomatoes and mozzarella. For the main course, try crabmeat-filled cannelloni topped with shrimp and Alfredo sauce, or the meat-happy lasagna, with layers of Italian sausage, ground beef and meatballs.

Italian, American. Lunch, dinner, late-night. Children's menu. Bar. $16-35

ELIJAH'S

2 Ann St., Wilmington, 910-343-1448; www.elijahs.com

The restaurant's prime spot on the Cape Fear Riverwalk may lure you in, especially so you can dine alfresco. But what will keep you coming back is the fresh seafood. Don't miss the popular hot crab dip starter. Entrées like soft-shell crab or shrimp and scallops broiled in Parmesan cream sauce are good picks. But you can have a little bit of everything with the Carolina Bucket, which is filled with steamed clams, crab legs, oysters, mussels, shrimp, sausage, new potatoes and corn on the cob.

American. Lunch, dinner, Sunday brunch. Reservations recommended. Outdoor seating. Children's menu. Bar. $16-35

FREDDIE'S

111 K Ave., Kure Beach, 910-458-5979; www.freddieskurebeach.com

Freddie's, an Italian joint in an Irish pub atmosphere, has a bit of an identity crisis. Most of the menu is decidedly Italian, with standards like chicken Florentine and lasagna. But the pork chops are the stars of the entrées. The pork possibilities seem endless: you can get your chop with cherry peppers and balsamic; with sliced peaches sautéed in butter, brown sugar, pecans and peach liquor; or sautéed apples, walnuts and amaretto sauce. Like the décor, it somehow all works.

Italian, American. Dinner. Children's menu. Reservations recommended. $16-35

PILOT HOUSE

2 Ann St., Wilmington, 910-343-0200; www.pilothouserest.com

You might not realize the sunny-looking yellow house is a restaurant, but the river-front deck filled with diners noshing on seafood and Southern-inspired cuisine gives it away. Follow suit by sitting under one of the bright blue umbrellas and order dishes like baked flounder with lump crab and asparagus over grits swimming in hollandaise, or grouper with fried sweet potato crisps and mushroom ravioli.

American, Southern. Lunch, dinner, Sunday brunch. Outdoor seating. Children's menu. Bar. $36-85

PORT CITY CHOP HOUSE

1981 Eastwood Road, Wilmington, 910-256-4955; www.chophousesofnc.com

When you crave a simple but nicely done steak, come to this chophouse. The meaty menu features all of the classics, including New York strip, porterhouse, bone-in rib-eye and chateaubriand for two. It also serves seafood like lobster. But be careful not to go overboard with all the carnivorous goodness. You won't want to miss the rich six-layer Mile High chocolate cake with a scoop of housemade chocolate ice cream rolled in pecans.

Seafood, steak. Lunch, dinner. Closed Sunday. Reservations recommended. Outdoor seating. Children's menu. Bar. $36-85

WELCOME TO SOUTH CAROLINA

LOVELY BEACHES, A TEMPERATE YEAR-ROUND CLIMATE AND golf courses to rival the world's best have made tourism one of South Carolina's most important industries. Hilton Head resorts are packed with families when the weather is warm, while Myrtle Beach is the town of choice for golf lovers. The surrounding area has more than 100 courses.

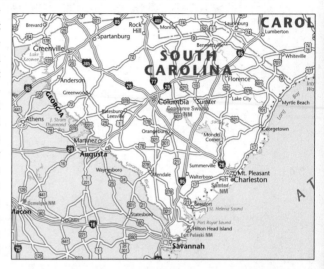

This state's turbulent and romantic history tells a story that is deeply rooted in its people and the history of the U.S. During the American Revolution, almost 200 battles and skirmishes were fought in South Carolina. The initial overt act of revolution occurred at Fort Charlotte on July 12, 1775, making it the first British property seized by American Revolutionary forces. Less than 100 years later on December 20, 1860, South Carolina became the first state to secede from the Union. The clash that started the Civil War also began on South Carolina soil when Confederate soldiers bombed and seized Fort Sumter in 1861, holding onto the fort until the evacuation of Charleston in 1865. Impoverished and blackened by the fires of General Sherman's "March to the Sea," South Carolina emerged from the difficult Reconstruction days and was readmitted to the Union in 1868.

Today, South Carolina has a diversified economy, with tourism playing a big role. The state is known for its water sports, deep-sea fishing, car racing and, of course, golf.

BEST ATTRACTIONS

SOUTH CAROLINA'S BEST ATTRACTIONS

MIDLANDS
If you seek entertainment, the Midlands has it, especially anything racing related. Horse racing and NASCAR contests are found in this region.

CHARLESTON
This historic city is full of charm. Check out the stately antebellum mansions, pristine beaches, museums and excellent restaurants.

LOW COUNTRY
Low Country is known for several things: fantastic cuisine, top-notch golf courses and some of the nation's top resort areas, including Hilton Head and Myrtle Beach.

MIDLANDS

Smack-dab in the middle of the state, the Midlands region offers a little something for everyone. Camden, the oldest inland town in the state, is famous for its horseback riding, horse shows, hunt meets, polo and steeplechase races. There are 200 miles of bridle paths in the area and three race tracks. Springdale Course is an extremely difficult and exciting steeplechase run. If you are more into racing cars than horses, Darlington is your city. It is the state's stock car racing center and home to the Stock Car Hall of Fame, as well as what is said to be the nation's largest automobile auction market.

Located within three miles of the geographic center of the state, Columbia was laid out as the capital in a compromise between the contending up-country and low-country farmers. One of the nation's first planned cities, Columbia rarely departs from a checkerboard pattern. Historical sites abound, as Columbia has a rich revolutionary and Civil War history. In 1865, General William T. Sherman's troops reduced Columbia to ashes, destroying 84 blocks and 1,386 buildings. Today, a city of stately buildings, a rejuvenated downtown and a thriving economy based on government, higher education and a mix of industries make South Carolina's biggest city a popular place to visit and a great town in which to live.

Located at the junction of highways and railways, Greenwood is best known for its sports and recreation. Rolling hills, year-round temperate climate and lots of undeveloped wooded land have made this a haven for golfers.

Both a college and an industrial town, Rock Hill takes its name from the flint rock that had to be cut when a railroad was built through town. Today it is home to Winthrop University and flanked by state parks.

Once the center of a prosperous agricultural area, Sumter has in recent years become an industrial center. As a tourism spot, Sumter offers a unique contrast of antebellum mansions and modern facilities. Shaw Air Force Base, headquarters of the 9th Air Force and the 363rd Tactical Fighter Wing, is nearby.

WHAT TO SEE

AIKEN

AIKEN COUNTY HISTORICAL MUSEUM

433 Newberry St., Southwest, Aiken, 803-642-2015; www.aikencountysc.gov

The museum is packed with period room scenes and displays of a late-1800s home. A log cabin and one-room schoolhouse are on the grounds. Special features include an archaeology exhibit and a 1950s drug store. There is also a museum store here.

Admission: free. Tuesday-Friday 9:30 a.m.-4:30 p.m., Saturday-Sunday 2-5 p.m.

REDCLIFFE

181 Redcliffe Road, Beech Island, 803-827-1473; www.southcarolinaparks.com

Built in the 1850s, this Greek Revival-style mansion is furnished with Southern antiques, art collections, historic documents and books.

Admission: free. Tours: adults $4, seniors $2.50, children 6-15 $3. Thursday-Monday 9 a.m.-5 p.m. Tours: Thursday-Monday 1 p.m., 2 p.m., 3 p.m.

CAMDEN

BETHESDA PRESBYTERIAN CHURCH

502 DeKalb St., Camden, 803-432-4593; www.bethesdapresbyterianchurch.org

Designed by the architect of the Washington Monument, Robert Mills, the church is considered a masterpiece.

Monday-Friday 9 a.m.-4 p.m.

HISTORIC CAMDEN REVOLUTIONARY WAR SITE

222 S. Broad St., Camden, 803-432-9841; www.historic-camden.net

At this archaeological site of South Carolina's oldest inland town, there is a visitor area with two early 19th-century log cabins and a restored 18th-century townhouse. Trails lead to the reconstructed foundation of a pre-Revolutionary War powder magazine, the Kershaw-Cornwallis House and two reconstructed British fortifications. The site of the Battle of Camden, a National Historic Landmark, is five miles north of town.

Admission: free. Tours: adults $5, seniors $4, children 6-18 $3, children 5 and under free. Tuesday-Saturday 10 a.m.-5 p.m., Sunday 2-5 p.m. Tours: Tuesday-Friday 10:30 a.m., 3 p.m., Saturday 10:30 a.m.-noon and 1:30-4 p.m., Sunday 2:30-4 p.m.

COLUMBIA

COLUMBIA MUSEUM OF ART

Main and Hampton streets, Columbia, 803-799-2810; www.columbiamuseum.org

Galleries house Renaissance paintings as well as 19th- and 20th-century

BEST ATTRACTIONS

WHAT ARE THE TOP THINGS TO DO IN THE MIDLANDS?

GET YOUR MOTOR RUNNING AT DARLINGTON RACEWAY

Race fans will want to try to see a race at this unusual egg-shaped track, the oldest super-speedway in the country.

RACE OVER TO THE STOCK CAR MUSEUM AND HALL OF FAME

In the museum, several rooms are filled with stock cars that raced on the Darlington Raceway, including Richard Petty's winning blue Plymouth.

EXPLORE NINTEY SIX NATIONAL HISTORIC SITE

History buffs will want to check out this site, an early village that was the site of the first land battle of the American Revolution.

TAKE A LOAD OFF AT THE SWAN LAKE IRIS GARDENS

Let your stresses melt away while strolling through these lovely 150-acre gardens. You'll see Japanese irises and a lake inhabited by all eight swan species.

American works, with an emphasis on Southeast and European paintings. There are concerts, films, lectures and special events accenting the exhibitions.

Admission: adults $10, seniors $8, students $5, children 5 and under free. Wednesday-Thursday, Saturday 10 a.m.-5 p.m.; -Friday 10 a.m.-5 p.m. in December; Sunday 1-5 p.m.

CONFEDERATE RELIC ROOM AND MUSEUM

Columbia Mills Building, 301 Gervais St., Columbia, 803-737-8095; www.crr.sc.gov

This relic collection from the Colonial period through the space age gives special emphasis on South Carolina's Confederate period.

Admission: adults $5, seniors and military personnel $4, children 13-17 $2, children 12 and under free. Tuesday-Saturday 10 a.m-5 p.m. First Sunday of the month 1-5 p.m.

FIRST BAPTIST CHURCH

1306 Hampton St., Columbia, 803-256-4251; www.fbccola.com

The church is the site of the first Secession Convention, which marked the beginning of the Civil War, on December 17, 1860.

Monday-Friday, Sunday.

FORT JACKSON

Fort Jackson, 4394 Strom Thurmond Blvd., Columbia, 803-751-1742; www.jackson.army.mil

Fort Jackson is the most active initial entry training center for the U.S. Army, with 16,000 soldiers assigned. The museum on Jackson Boulevard has displays on the history of the fort and today's army.

Monday-Friday 8:30 a.m.-4:30 p.m.

GOVERNOR'S MANSION

800 Richland St., Columbia, 803-737-1710; www.scgovernorsmansion.org

This impressive edifice was built in 1855 as the officers' quarters for the Arsenal Academy. Tours run every half-hour; reservations are required.

Admission: free. Tours: Tuesday-Wednesday 10 a.m., 10:30 a.m., 11 a.m.

HAMPTON-PRESTON MANSION

1615 Blanding St., Columbia, 803-252-7742; www.historiccolumbia.org

Purchased by Wade Hampton I, the mansion was occupied by the Hamptons and the family of his daughter, Mrs. John Preston. In February 1865, the house served as headquarters for Union General J. A. Logan. Many surviving Hampton family furnishings and decorative arts are on display. Tours are available on the hour.

Admission: adults $6, seniors, military personnel, students $5, children 6-17 $3, children 5 and under free. Tuesday-Sunday.

RIVERBANKS ZOO AND GARDEN

500 Wildlife Parkway, Columbia, 803-779-8717; www.riverbanks.org

Exhibits of animals in natural habitat areas will entice the whole family. The aquarium-reptile complex has diving demonstrations. Check the schedule for penguin and sea lion feeding times.

Admission: adults $11.75, seniors and military personnel $10.75, children 3-12 $9.25, children 2 and under free. Daily 9 a.m.-5 p.m.; April-September, Saturday-Sunday 9 a.m.-6 p.m.

ROBERT MILLS HISTORIC HOUSE AND PARK

1616 Blanding St., Columbia, 803-252-7442; www.historiccolumbia.org

One of a few residences designed by Robert Mills, Federal architect and designer of the Washington Monument, the house contains art and furnishings from the Regency period. Tours leave on the hour.

Admission: adults $6, seniors, military personnel, students $5, children 6-17 $3, children 5 and under free. Tuesday-Saturday 10 a.m.-4 p.m., Sunday 1-5 p.m.

TRINITY CATHEDRAL

1100 Sumter St., Columbia, 803-771-7300; www.trinityepiscopalcathedral.org

A reproduction of a church in Yorkminster, England, Trinity is the oldest church building in Columbia and one of the largest Episcopal congregations in the U.S. A Hiram Powers baptismal font, box pews and English stained glass are highlights. Three Wade Hamptons (a politically prominent South Carolina family) are buried in the churchyard; the graves of seven governors and six bishops are also here.

Daily.

DARLINGTON
DARLINGTON RACEWAY
1301 Harry Byrd Highway, Darlington, 866-459-7223; www.darlingtonraceway.com

Remembered as the original "Super Speedway," the track first opened in 1950 and is famous for its unique egg shape. Hundreds of miles raced, millions of fans and numerous legends have left their mark here. Major races go down in May; check for ongoing events and racing schools on the website.

Monday-Friday 9 a.m.-5 p.m.

JOE WEATHERLY STOCK CAR MUSEUM AND NATIONAL MOTORSPORTS PRESS ASSOCIATION STOCK CAR HALL OF FAME
1301 Harry Byrd Highway, Darlington, 843-395-8499; www.darlingtonraceway.com

Darlington Raceway, the oldest super-speedway in the country, also houses the sport's hall of fame. The museum details the history of NASCAR's storied Darlington and features everyone from NASCAR's first champion, Red Byron, to David Pearson and Dale Earnhardt. Several rooms are filled with stock cars that once sped across the raceway, including the blue Plymouth that Richard Petty drove to victory in 10 races back in 1967.

Admission: adults $5, children 12 and under free. Daily 10 a.m.-5 p.m., Saturday 10 a.m.-4 p.m.

FLORENCE
FLORENCE STOCKADE
Stockade and National Cemetery roads, Florence

The stockade was a Civil War prison that housed Union soldiers transferred from the notorious Andersonville prison. Roughly 2,800 soldiers died there, including Florena Budwin, whom Friends of the Florence Stockade say is the only female Civil War prisoner to die in captivity. The stockade is a Civil War Heritage Site.

Daily.

WAR BETWEEN THE STATES MUSEUM
107 S. Guerry St., Florence, 843-669-1266; www.florenceweb.com

Explore artifacts, pictures and stories from the Civil War.

Admission: adults $2, children $1. Wednesday, Saturday 10 a.m.-5 p.m.

GAFFNEY
COWPENS NATIONAL BATTLEFIELD
4001 Chesnee Highway, Gaffney, 864-461-2828; www.nps.gov

This was the scene of the victory of General Daniel Morgan's American Army over superior British forces on January 17, 1781. The battle wounded the British Army substantially enough to help set the stage for Cornwallis' surrender. It features an 843-acre tract with exhibits, an information and visitor center, a self-guided road tour, a walking trail with audio stations and a restored 1830 historic house.

Daily 9 a.m.-5 p.m.

GREENWOOD
BAKER CREEK STATE PARK
863 Baker Creek Road, McCormick, 864-443-2457; www.discoversouthcarolina.com

This state park occupies approximately 1,300 acres and is ideal for lake

swimming, boating and fishing. There are also multiple bridle trails.
Daily 6 a.m.-6 p.m.

NINETY SIX NATIONAL HISTORIC SITE
1103 Highway 248 S., Ninety Six, 864-543-4068; www.nps.gov

This is the site of old Ninety Six, an early village in South Carolina backcountry, so named because it is 96 miles away from the Cherokee Village of Keowee on the Cherokee Path. The South's first land battle of the American Revolution in 1775 and the 28-day siege of Ninety Six in 1781 occurred here. The earthworks of the British-built Star Fort remain, along with reconstructed siege works and other fortifications of the period. Also here are subsurface remains of two village complexes, a trading post-plantation complex and a network of 18th-century roads.
Daily 8 a.m.-5 p.m.

ROCK HILL
ANDREW JACKSON STATE PARK
196 Andrew Jackson Park Road, Lancaster, 803-285-3344; www.southcarolinaparks.com

This 360-acre park is sprinkled with nature trails, camp sites and boat docks. The log house museum contains documents and exhibits of Jackson lore.

CATAWBA CULTURAL CENTER
1536 Tom Steven Road, Rock Hill, 803-328-2427; www.ccppcrafts.com

Located on the Catawba Reservation, this center strives to preserve the heritage of the Catawbas' culture. Tours and programs are available by appointment.
Monday-Saturday 9 a.m.-5 p.m.

HISTORIC BRATTONSVILLE
1444 Brattonsville Road, McConnells, 803-684-2327; www.chmuseums.org

Learn about local history in this restored village of more than two dozen structures, including a Backwoodsman Cabin, the Colonel Bratton Home, the Homestead House and the Brick Kitchen. A gift shop is also on the premises. Guided tours are on offer by appointment, or opt to take a self-guided audio tour.
Monday-Saturday 10 a.m.-5 p.m., Sunday 1-5 p.m.

MUSEUM OF YORK COUNTY
4621 Mount Gallant Road, Rock Hill, 803-329-2121; www.chmuseums.org

This intimate museum contains a large collection of mounted African hoofed mammals and a large African artifacts collection. The Hall of Western Hemisphere has mounted animals from North and South America. If you're looking for a souvenir, the gift shop sells Catawba pottery.
Admission: adults $5, seniors $4, children 4-17 $3, children 3 and under free. Monday-Saturday 10 a.m.-5 p.m., Sunday 1-5 p.m.

SANTEE
EUTAW SPRINGS BATTLEFIELD SITE
Santee, 12 miles Southeast off Highway 6

The site marks the spot where ragged colonials fought the British on September 8, 1781, in what is considered to be the last major engagement in South Carolina. Both sides claimed victory.

FORT WATSON BATTLE SITE AND INDIAN MOUND
Santee, 803-478-2217; www.discoversouthcarolina.com

Climb this 48-foot-high mound that is the site of an American Revolution battle on April 15-23, 1781, during which General Francis Marion attacked and captured a British fortification, its garrison, supplies and ammunition. The summit awards you with a view of the Santee-Cooper waters.

SANTEE NATIONAL WILDLIFE REFUGE
Secondary State Road, Summerton, 803-478-2217; www.discoversouthcarolina.com

A great destination for birds (and bird-watchers) in winter, the refuge has an observation tower and nature trails.

Tuesday-Sunday 8 a.m.-4 p.m.

SUMTER
CHURCH OF THE HOLY CROSS
335 N. Kings Highway, Stateburg, 803-494-8101, 800-688-4748;
www.discoversouthcarolina.com

Boasting unusual architectural design and construction, the church is built from pise de terre (rammed earth). The structure is also noted for stained-glass windows set to catch the rays of the rising sun. Many notable South Carolinians from the 1700s are buried in the old church cemetery, including U.S. statesman Joel R. Poinsett.

OPERA HOUSE
21 N. Main St., Sumter, 803-436-2500, 888-688-4748; www.sumter-sc.com

Today the 1893 Opera House stands not only as a symbol of the past but also as an active sign of the ongoing progressive spirit of the people of Sumter. The 600-seat auditorium is used for concerts, school events and other local happenings.

Many performances are free.

POINSETT STATE PARK
6660 Poinsett Park Road, Wedgefield, 803-494-8177; www.southcarolinaparks.com

Visit the approximately 1,000 acres of mountains and swamps named for Joel R. Poinsett, who introduced the poinsettia (which originated in Mexico) to the U.S. Though you won't find that holiday plant here, you will see Spanish moss, mountain laurel and rhododendron. Enjoy fishing, boating and the onsite nature center.

SUMTER COUNTY MUSEUM
122 N. Washington St., Sumter, 803-775-0908;
www.sumtercountymuseum.org

This two-story Edwardian house depicts Victorian lifestyle with period rooms, historical exhibits, war memorabilia, economic and cultural artifacts, artwork and archives (for genealogical research). It's surrounded by formal gardens designed by Robert Marvin.

Admission: adults $3, children 6-17 $1. Tuesday-Saturday 10 a.m.-5 p.m.

SUMTER GALLERY OF ART
200 Hasel St., Sumter, 803-775-0543; www.sumtergallery.org

Located in the 24,000-square-foot facility at the Sumter County Cultural Center, regional artwork on display includes paintings, drawings, sculpture,

SPECIAL EVENTS

CAROLINA CUP STEEPLECHASE

Springdale Race Course, 200 Knights Hill Road, Camden, 803-432-6513, 800-780¬8117; www.carolina-cup.org
This annual rite of spring draws more than 70,000 fans every year to enjoy the sport of steeplechase horse racing alongside spring fashions and elaborate tailgate parties.
Early April.

COLONIAL CUP INTERNATIONAL STEEPLECHASE

Springdale Race Course, 200 Knights Hill Road, Camden, 803-432-6513, 800-780¬8117; www.carolina-cup.org
The Colonial Cup draws more than 15,000 fans and horsemen from around the world and provides the season's grand finale—often deciding all the national titles, including jockey of the year, trainer of the year and horse of the year.
Mid-November.

photography and pottery. There is a permanent collection of touchable works for the blind as well.
Admission: free. Tuesday-Saturday 11 a.m.-5 p.m., Sunday 1:30-5 p.m.

SWAN LAKE IRIS GARDENS
822 W. Liberty St., Sumter, 803-436-2640; www.sumter-sc.com
Hosting one of the country's premier Iris festivals, held every May, the 150-acre garden is home to Kaempferi and Japanese irises, seasonal plantings, nature trails and ancient cypress, oak and pine trees. There is a 45-acre lake with all eight species of swan.

WHERE TO STAY

AIKEN
★★★THE WILLCOX
100 Colleton Ave. S.E., Aiken, 803-648-1898, 877-648-2200; www.thewillcox.com
This distinguished mansion set on 2,000 acres of the Hitchcock Woods offers some of the best of South Carolina's horse country. Guest rooms and suites are decorated with antiques, Oriental rugs and feather-topped four-poster beds. Most accommodations have working fireplaces. The onsite spa offers everything from massages to rejuvenating facials.
22 rooms. Complimentary breakfast. Restaurant. Spa. $251-350

FLORENCE
★★★ABINGDON MANOR
307 Church St., Latta, 843-752-5090, 888-752-5090; www.abingdonmanor.com
This opulent Greek Revival-style building is listed on the National Register of

Historic Places. The grand entry hall and comfortable guest rooms are only part of the charm. An excellent restaurant, full breakfast and nightly cocktails make this hotel a nice retreat.

7 rooms. Restaurant, bar. Complimentary breakfast. No children under 11. $151-250

RECOMMENDED

COLUMBIA

HILTON COLUMBIA CENTER

924 Senate St., Columbia, 803-744-7777, 800-445-8667; www.hiltoncolumbia.com

This stately looking brick hotel is in the center of Columbia's financial, entertainment and historic district. There's plenty going on in the hotel to keep you there, including a heated outdoor saltwater pool, a whirlpool and an outpost of the mouth-watering Ruth's Chris Steak House. The classic rooms have two-poster beds, dark wood furnishings and a taupe and black color scheme. Damask-pattered carpeting gives the rooms a contemporary spin.

222 rooms. Restaurant, bar. Business center. Fitness center. Pool. $151-250

INN AT CLAUSSEN'S

2003 Greene St., Columbia, 803-765-0440; www.theinnatclaussens.com

The sign on this big brick building says "Claussen's Bakery," but the only baked goods you'll get will be in the free continental breakfast delivered to your hotel room each morning on a tray. This former bakery has been converted into a hotel, but some touches of its older self still show, like the hardwood floors. The individually decorated rooms range from traditional furnishings with four-poster beds and deep, rich colors to contemporary spaces with color schemes of black, gray and white. Be sure to stop by the nightly wine reception for a drink and some cheese and crackers.

28 rooms. Restaurant, bar. Complimentary breakfast. Business center. $61-150

COLUMBIA MARRIOTT

1200 Hampton St., Columbia, 803-771-7000, 800-593-6465; www.marriott.com

Set in downtown Columbia, the hotel is only eight miles from the airport, but no need to cab it; the Marriott offers a complimentary airport shuttle service. The navy and yellow rooms come with down comforters, pillow-top beds, complimentary wireless Internet and 42-inch flat-screen televisions. Snag a room on the concierge level to get free morning and evening snacks and beverages.

300 rooms. Restaurant, bar. Business center. Pool. $61-150

WHERE TO EAT

COLUMBIA

★★★RISTORANTE DIVINO

803 Gervais St., Columbia, 803-799-4550; www.ristorantedivino.com

Ristorante Divino is in Columbia's historic downtown district. The wine cellar features more than 3,000 bottles of wine and includes 400 varieties to complement the classic Italian dishes on the menu, like gnocchi with gorgonzola-cream sauce or veal marsala.

Northern Italian. Dinner. Closed Sunday. Reservations recommended. Bar. $36-85

FLORENCE

★★★ABINGDON MANOR RESTAURANT

Abingdon Manor, 307 Church St., Latta, 843-752-5090, 888-752-5090;
www.abingdonmanor.com

This elegant restaurant, located inside a charming inn of the same name, offers a creative menu of American fare using fresh ingredients from the onsite garden. Expect dishes like lobster Thermidor in a sherry-infused cream sauce or scallops swimming in an orange-tequila cream sauce.

American. Dinner. Closed Sunday. Bar. Reservations recommended. $36-85

RECOMMENDED

COLUMBIA

HAMPTON STREET VINEYARD

1201 Hampton St., Columbia, 803-252-0850; www.hamptonstreetvineyard.com

Wine drinkers will want to imbibe at this restaurant, which offers a lengthy wine list of more than 650 bottles as well as a menu of 35 by-the-glass options. While the wine takes center stage, the food isn't merely a supporting player. Southern-tinged fare goes upscale with pan-roasted pheasant breast atop collard greens, black-eyed peas with a bacon-red wine vinaigrette, and short ribs are slathered with hoisin barbecue sauce and come with chipotle whipped potatoes and haricots vert.

American. Lunch, dinner. Closed Sunday. Reservations recommended. Outdoor seating. Bar. $36-85

HENNESSY'S

1649 Main St., Columbia, 803-799-8280; www.hennessyssc.com

You'll find a classic steakhouse atmosphere at this white tablecloth restaurant. On the menu, you will find steaks like the cinnamon-red chile beef filet with cabernet reduction and Vidalia onion rings. But it also offers grilled Atlantic salmon with lemon beurre blanc, and shrimp with grits and andouille sausage. Check out the nice-sized wine list for a glass to pair with your meal.

Steak. Lunch, dinner. Closed Sunday. Reservations recommended. Bar. $16-35

MOTOR SUPPLY COMPANY

920 Gervais St., Columbia, 803-256-6687; www.motorsupplycobistro.com

With a name like "Motor Supply Company," it would be easy to mistake this local favorite for a car parts shop. But instead of spark plugs, it sells pan-seared foie gras with pea shoots and honey-glazed apples. The restaurant is all about fresh ingredients, so the menu changes daily depending on what's available. You can expect dishes like seared Charleston red drum topped with marinated eggplant, or sautéed white shrimp in a sesame soy emulsion with wilted bok choy.

International. Lunch, dinner, Sunday brunch. Closed Monday. Reservations recommended. Outdoor seating. Bar. $36-85

RUTH'S CHRIS STEAK HOUSE

Hilton Columbia, 924 Senate St., Columbia, 803-744-7777, 800-445-8667; www.hiltoncolumbia.com

This branch of the national steak-house chain resides in the lobby of the Hilton Columbia hotel. It's famous for its succulent steaks in its various forms, including thick-cut filets, rib-eyes, porterhouses and New York strips. Not in the mood for red meat? The menu also includes plenty of grilled seafood, chicken, pork and salads.

Steak. Breakfast, lunch, dinner. Bar. $36-85

WHERE TO SHOP

GAFFNEY

PRIME OUTLETS GAFFNEY

1 Factory Shops Blvd., Gaffney, 864-902-9900, 888-545-7194; www.primeoutlets.com

This open-air, village-style mall features 65 outlet shops including Tommy Hilfiger, J.Crew, Gap Outlet, BCBG Max Azria, Banana Republic Factory Store and more.

Monday-Saturday 10 a.m.-9 p.m., Sunday 1:30-7 p.m.

CHARLESTON

Charleston has been called one of the most mannerly cities. Indeed, this is what Southern hospitality is all about. The place has all the genteel charm you'd expect, and then some.

The city manages to strike the perfect mix of old and new. It has the second largest historical district in North America (behind Savannah). Preservation is serious business around here: Many of the houses look the same as they did in the early 1800s, but this is a living, breathing city. The dollhouse-pretty homes with large verandas that catch the breeze off the harbor are just as lived in today as they were back then.

Take plenty of time to stroll the residential lanes ("downtown" Charleston is on a peninsula that is less than two miles long) to observe all the different types of architecture, including Georgian, Adamesque, Victorian, Italianate and Greek Revival. Most homes have tiny plaques that explain the architecture (residents are used to people stopping and looking). One of the most famous parts of the city is Rainbow Row, named for the burst of pastel colors from the homes that line the streets. These candy-colored homes mostly represent an 18th-century Georgian style, with arched doorways and gambrel roofs. On East Battery, you'll see magnificent waterfront mansions with "widows" windows where the women used to sit and wait for the ships to come into the harbor. You'll also see more of the colonial-style single (just one room wide) and double homes Charleston is known for on Church and Meeting streets.

For a bit of a rest, duck into one of the churches—you certainly won't have trouble finding one. Charleston is also called the Holy City, thanks to its 187 churches (this divides up into three per block). That's because the city was founded purely as a financial endeavor, not a religious refuge, so there was always a lot of religious freedom. You'll notice that one church, St. Philip's (142 Church St., 843-722-7734; www.stphilipschurchsc.org), has a large steeple that is leaning slightly to the left— that's from cannonballs that were fired during the Civil War. Another church, St. John the Baptist (120 Broad St., 843-724-8395; www.catholic-doc.org/cathedral) is covered in gold stars, representing the man-hours it took to build it.

One of the most popular activities is a carriage ride, which is a nice introduction to the city. Guides (usually students from the College of South Carolina) take you on a leisurely hoof, casually filling you in on historical facts and points of interest.

HIGHLIGHT

WHAT ARE THE TOP THINGS TO DO IN CHARLESTON?

SEE SOME ART AT THE CHARLESTON MUSEUM

Opened in 1824, the Charleston is the nation's oldest museum. Its diverse collection includes George Washington's silver christening cup and a whale skeleton.

VISIT THE LOVELY DRAYTON HALL

Charleston is known for its amazing antebellum mansions and estates like Drayton Hall, which is one of the oldest plantation houses in the area.

WALK THROUGH MAGNOLIA PLANTATION AND GARDENS

The world-famous gardens date back to 1676, making them America's oldest. Stop to sniff the magnolias, azaleas and other blossoms throughout the 50 acres.

WHAT TO SEE

AIKEN-RHETT HOUSE

48 Elizabeth St., Charleston, 843-723-1159; www.historiccharleston.org

Built around 1818, this palatial residence was added onto and redecorated by Governor and Mrs. William Aiken Jr. in the mid-1800s. The house remained in the family until 1975, and many original pieces of furniture are still in the rooms for which they were purchased.

Admission: $10; $16 combination ticket for Aiken-Rhett and Nathaniel Russell House. Monday-Saturday 10 a.m.-5 p.m., Sunday 2-5 p.m.

BOONE HALL PLANTATION

1235 Long Point Road, Mount Pleasant, 843-884-4371; www.boonehallplantation.com

This 738-acre estate includes a 1935 Georgian-style house similar to the original plantation house that fell into ruin, a cotton-gin house, a pecan grove, nine slave cabins and gardens of antique roses. The property has been used to film many TV shows and movies. Battle reenactments are held during the summer and draw Civil War buffs.

Admission: adults $17.50, children 6-12 $7.50, children 5 and under free. April-Labor Day, Monday-Saturday 8:30 a.m.-6:30 p.m., Sunday 1-5 p.m.; Labor Day-March, Monday-Saturday 9 a.m.-5 p.m., Sunday 1-4 p.m.

CALHOUN MANSION

14-16 Meeting St., Charleston, 843-722-8205; www.calhoumansion.net

It may not be the oldest or the most historic, but it certainly is the most over-the-top; and unlike all the other homes you'll tour in Charleston, this one is still lived in. The current owner, a Washington patent attorney, resides here amidst his huge collection of stuff, hosting dinner parties during which music pours onto the street from the veranda, and opening up the doors to tourists who gape at all the loot. You'll find icons, Buddha statues, Tiffany hardware, a collection of taxidermy and everything in between. There is no rhyme or reason to it all; it simply must be seen to be believed. Guides who give the tours with a wink make it even more fun.

Admission: $15. Tours:11 a.m.-5 p.m.

CHARLESTON MUSEUM

360 Meeting St., Charleston, 843-722-2996; www.charlestonmuseum.org

Founded in 1773 and first opened to the public in 1824, the Charleston Museum claims status as America's first museum. Key artifacts in the collection include an impressive early silver display (George Washington's christening cup is among the pieces), South Carolina ceramics, the chairs that delegates sat in to sign South Carolina's Ordinance of Secession and firearms used in the Civil War. Children will enjoy the museum's hands-on exhibits.

Admission: Adults $10, kids 3-12 $5. Monday-Saturday 9 a.m.-5 p.m., Sunday 1-5 p.m.

CHARLES TOWNE LANDING

1500 Old Town Road, Charleston, 843-852-4200; www.southcarolinaparks.com

In 1670, colonists established the first permanent English settlement in the Carolinas at this location. Today, visitors find archaeological investigations, reconstructed fortifications, formal gardens, as well as nature trails, a colonial village and a replica of *Adventure*, a 17th-century trading ketch. Tram tours are available, and there also is a natural habitat zoo of indigenous animals onsite.

Admission: adults $7.50, seniors $3.75, students 6-15 $3.50, children 5 and under free. Daily 8:30 a.m.-5 p.m.

THE CITADEL, MILITARY COLLEGE OF SOUTH CAROLINA

171 Moultrie St., Charleston, 843-225-3294; www.citadel.edu

Established in 1842 by an act of the South Carolina General Assembly, the college of nearly 2,000 students enjoys a picturesque setting on the bank of the Ashley River. Stroll the campus and get a sense of the life of a cadet. During the school year, try to come on Friday afternoon at 3:45 to see the military dress parade—widely considered one of the best free shows in Charleston. A small museum portrays cadet life.

Admission: free. Museum: Sunday-Friday 2-5 p.m., Saturday noon-5 p.m. Tours of the campus can be arranged for groups of eight or more; call 843-953-6779 Monday through Friday.

DOCK STREET THEATRE

135 Church St., Charleston, 843-577-7183, 800-454-7093; www.charlestonstage.com

In 1736, a building on this site opened as the very first in America constructed specifically for theatrical productions. Later, the street name changed to Queen, but the Dock Street Theatre name stuck. Today's theater is on the site of the original and presents productions of the Charleston Stage Company during the spring and fall. Dock Street Theatre is also a performance venue for Charleston's Spoleto Festival.

DRAYTON HALL

3380 Ashley River Road, Charleston, 843-769-2600; www.draytonhall.org

One of the oldest-surviving pre-American Revolution plantation houses in the area, this Georgian Palladian home is surrounded by live oaks and is on the Ashley River. Held in the Drayton family for seven generations before its donation to the National Trust, the mansion has been maintained in near original condition.

Admission: adults $17, children 12-18 $8, children 6-11 $6, children 5 and under free. November-February, daily 8:30 a.m.-4 p.m.; March-October, daily 8:30 a.m.-5 p.m. Tours: every hour on the hour.

EDMONDSTON-ALSTON HOUSE

4300 Ashley River Road, Charleston, 843-556-6020, 800-782-3608; www.middletonplace.org

This Greek Revival-style house has an uninterrupted view across the harbor. Guided tours are offered daily.

Tuesday-Saturday 10 a.m.-4:30 p.m., Sunday-Monday 1:30-4:30 p.m.

FORT SUMTER

See where the Civil War began, when Confederacy troops fired onto Fort Sumter on April 12, 1861, after Union forces occupied it. The ferry ride over provides a good history lesson before you arrive. Boats to the fort depart daily at 9:30 a.m., noon and 2:30 p.m. The whole trip is a little over 2 hours; adult tickets cost $15, children 6 to 11 cost $9, and children under 5 are free. Ticket offices open at 8:30 a.m. (Liberty Square) or 9 a.m. (Patriots Point). April-Labor Day. Call for hours for the rest of the year. Ferries leave from Patriots Point or the Fort Sumter Visitor Education Center at Liberty Square. Visit www.fortsumtertours.com for more information.

FRENCH HUGUENOT CHURCH

44 Queen St., Charleston, 843-722-4385; www.frenchhuguenotchurch.org

As early as 1687, French Huguenots were worshipping in a church on this site. The current church is a National Historic Landmark. Completed in 1845, it was the first Gothic Revival-style building in Charleston. The church features distinctive windows, buttresses and unusual ironwork.

Daily.

GIBBES MUSEUM OF ART

135 Meeting St., Charleston, 843-722-2706; www.gibbesmuseum.org

The more than 100-year-old museum houses an eclectic collection that includes Japanese woodblock prints as well as miniature rooms depicting traditional American and French architecture, decorative arts and design. This museum is known for its portraits of famous South Carolinians by notable artists, including Thomas Sully, Benjamin West and Rembrandt Peale. Don't miss the Charleston Renaissance Gallery, which showcases works by Charleston artists responsible for the city's cultural renaissance in the 1920s and 1930s. Tours are available.

Admission: adults $9, seniors, students and military personnel $7, children 6-12 $5, children 5 and under free. Tuesday-Saturday 10 a.m.-5 p.m., Sunday 1-5 p.m.

HEYWARD-WASHINGTON HOUSE

360 Meeting St., Charleston, 843-722-2996; www.charlestonmuseum.org

This brick double house, noteworthy for its collection of Charleston-made furniture, was built in 1772 during the Revolutionary era. Rice planter Daniel Heyward gave the house to his son Thomas Heyward, Jr., a signer of the Declaration of Independence. George Washington stayed here during his weeklong visit to the city in 1791. Dubose Heyward used the neighborhood in which the house stands as the setting for *Porgy and Bess*.

Admission: adults $10, children 3-12 $4, children 2 and under free. Monday-Saturday 10 a.m.-5 p.m., Sunday 1-5 p.m.

JOSEPH MANIGAULT HOUSE

360 Meeting St., Charleston, 843-722-2996; www.charlestonmuseum.org

This home was designed by Gabriel Manigault for his brother Joseph. The siblings were descendants of a French Huguenot family. This elegant neoclassical three-story brick town house, a National Historic Landmark, reflects the wealthy lifestyle of the Manigault family, as well as living conditions of the slaves who worked here.

Admission: adults $10, children 3-12 $4, children 2 and under free Monday-Saturday 10 a.m.-5 p.m., Sunday 1-5 p.m.

MAGNOLIA PLANTATION AND GARDENS

3550 Ashley River Road, Charleston, 843-571-1266, 800-367-3517; www.magnolia¬plantation.com

These internationally famous gardens are America's oldest (circa 1676). Eleven generations of Draytons have lovingly attended to this magical place. The gardens cover 50 acres with camellias, azaleas, magnolias and hundreds of other flowering species. Tour the classic Southern home, which has a great collection of early American antiques; hike the nature trail (where you're likely to spot alligators, turtles, herons and more) or take a boat ride through the canals of the former rice fields and the Ashley River. The plantation itself includes more than 500 acres. Canoe and bicycle rentals are available.

Admission: adults $15, children 6-12 $10, children 5 and under free. March-October, 8 a.m.-dusk; November-February, call for hours.

MIDDLETON PLACE PLANTATION

4300 Ashley River Road, Charleston, 843-556-6020, 800-782-3608; www.middletonplace.org

Once the home of Arthur Middleton, a signer of the Declaration of Independence, Middleton Place has America's oldest landscaped gardens and a restored House Museum. Laid out in 1741, the gardens feature ornamental butterfly lakes, sweeping terraces, and a wide variety of flora and fauna.

Admission: adults $25, children 7-15 $5, children 6 and under free. Daily 9 a.m.-5 p.m.

NATHANIEL RUSSELL HOUSE

51 Meeting St., Charleston, 843-724-8481; www.historiccharleston.org

This Federal-style brick mansion is like a time capsule. Built by export/import trade merchant Nathaniel Russell in 1808, the home has only had four owners and is exactly as it was back then—the residence has been restored, but never renovated. The "floating" three-story spiral staircase is a wonder.

Admission: $10. Monday-Saturday 10 a.m.-5 p.m., Sunday 2-5 p.m.

SPECIAL EVENTS

SPOLETO FESTIVAL USA

Gaillard Municipal Auditorium, 77 Calhoun St., Charleston, 843-579-3100; www.spoletousa.org
One of the best arts festivals in the country, Spoleto USA is a counterpart to the arts festival held in Spoleto, Italy, which was founded by composer Gian Carlo Menotti. The Charleston festival offers opera, dance, chamber music, theater, symphonic music, jazz, solo voice, choral performance, visual arts and special events, including conversations with the artists—more than 120 offerings in total. Venues include the Gaillard Auditorium and the historic Dock Street Theatre in Charleston, as well as less-conventional locales such as Middleton Place and Mepkin Abbey Monastery.
Late May-early June.

OLD CITY MARKET
Market Street, between Meeting and East Bay Streets
This alfresco market, said to be open every day since 1782, was a former slaughterhouse (but because this is Charleston, it has an impressive edifice that looks like the Parthenon). Today it's brimming with tourists looking to buy everything from chewy taffy to the famous sweetgrass baskets that Gulla women have been weaving for generations.
Daily 10 a.m.-sunset.

OLD EXCHANGE AND PROVOST DUNGEON
122 E. Bay St., Charleston, 843-727-2165, 888-763-0448; www.oldexchange.com
Completed in 1771, the Royal Exchange and Custom House is one of the most historically significant buildings of Colonial and Revolutionary America. The upper levels were designed to accommodate heavy export and import trade and as a place to conduct business, and the lower level held common prisoners, pirates and suspected rebels. In 1788, South Carolina delegates gathered in the building to ratify the U.S. Constitution. George Washington was a guest of honor here at a grand ball in 1791.
Admission: adults $8, seniors and children 7-12 $4, children 6 and under free. Daily 9 a.m.-5 p.m.

ST. PHILIP'S EPISCOPAL CHURCH
142 Church St., Charleston, 843-722-7734; www.stphilipschurchsc.org
Established in 1670, this is the oldest congregation in Charleston and the first Episcopal Church in the Carolinas. Today's building was completed in 1838. During the Civil War, its bells were removed and converted into cannons for the Confederacy. New bells were placed in the steeple on July 4, 1976.
Daily.

WHERE TO STAY

★★★ANCHORAGE INN
26 Vendue Range, Charleston, 843-723-8300, 800-421-2952; www.anchoragencharleston.com
Afternoon tea, English toiletries and period furnishings make for a sophisticated

stay at this inn in the downtown historic district.

19 rooms. Complimentary breakfast. Business center. $61-150

★★★★CHARLESTON PLACE

205 Meeting St., Charleston, 888-635-2350; www.charlestonplace.com

This popular hotel is located in the middle of the historic district, just a stone's throw from Old City Market and King Street, where you'll find the city's best shopping. The enormous 3,000-piece Murano crystal chandelier hanging in the middle of the Georgian open-armed staircase in the lobby is the centerpiece of this buzzing hotel, where people are always zigzagging the Italianate white marble lobby perusing the upscale shops, having drinks in the handsome lounge, and heading to the popular Charleston Grille for a bite before retiring to rooms draped in lace, chintz and damask.

440 rooms. Restaurant, bar. Business center. Fitness center. Spa. $251-350

★★★CHARLESTON'S VENDUE INN

19 Vendue Range, Charleston, 843-577-7970, 800-845-7900; www.vendueinn.com

With its polished pine floors, Oriental rugs, period furniture and other historic accents, this romantic inn offers a memorable Charleston stay. Many of the individually decorated rooms overlook the Charleston Harbor and Waterfront Park.

65 rooms. Restaurant, bar. Complimentary breakfast. Fitness center. $61-150

★★★FRANCIS MARION HOTEL

387 King St., Charleston, 843-722-0600, 877-756-2121; www.francismarioncharleston.com

Originally opened in 1924, this European-style hotel was named for an American Revolution war hero who evaded British troops by winding through swampland. Rooms are cozy, but the hotel's amenities and its prompt, courteous service make for a comfortable stay.

230 rooms. Restaurant, bar. Fitness center. Spa. $151-250

★★★HARBOUR VIEW INN

2 Vendue Range, Charleston, 843-853-8439, 888-853-8439; www.harbourviewcharleston.com

Enjoy spectacular vistas of Charleston's East Harbor from this historic inn. Located near some of the city's best restaurants, rooms have four-poster beds, flat-screen TVs and plush beds with luxe linens.

57 rooms. Business center. $151-250

★★★HILTON CHARLESTON HARBOR RESORT AND MARINA

20 Patriot's Point Road, Charleston, 843-856-0028, 888-856-01028; www.charlestonharborresort.com

This luxurious resort sits on an 18-hole private championship golf course, a private beach and a 450-slip marina. Beautiful sunsets across the Charleston Harbor and the historic skyline, with many antebellum buildings and churches, are visible from most rooms. Water sports from charter fishing to parasailing are available.

129 rooms. Restaurant, bar. Pool. Beach. Golf. $151-250

★★★MARKET PAVILION HOTEL

225 E. Bay St., Charleston, 843-723-0500, 877-440-2250; www.marketpavilion.com

This hotel has become the place to stay—or at least have a drink—in Charleston. People crowd the lobby restaurant, Grill 225, for a juicy steak dinner, and then everyone is headed upstairs to the swanky rooftop pool and bar for cocktails and a spectacular view of Charleston and its dark waters. Beautifully appointed guest rooms have four-poster beds, cashmere blankets, marble baths and fluffy bathrobes.

66 rooms. Restaurant, bar. Complimentary breakfast. $251-350

★★★PLANTERS INN
112 N. Market St., Charleston, 843-722-2345, 800-845-7082; www.plantersinn.com

This polished Relais and Chateaux property, located in the heart of the historic district, has more of a boutique hotel feel, while still offering plenty of old-fashioned charm. The original building, constructed in 1884, was a dry goods supply company; it became a hotel in 1983 and underwent a $4 million renovation in 1997. Rooms have high ceilings, four-poster beds with teddy bears, marble bathrooms and furniture from Baker's historic Charleston collection. Book a junior suite—they're much larger than the regular rooms and have extra large bathrooms. Sweet tea is always available in the comfy lobby, with its velvet couches and oil paintings of historical figures. You'll also find a quiet courtyard with palm trees and a fountain. Rooms facing the courtyard have loggias and rocking chairs.

64 rooms. Restaurant. Complimentary breakfast. $151-250

★★★RENAISSANCE CHARLESTON HOTEL HISTORIC DISTRICT
68 Wentworth St., Charleston, 843-534-0300; www.renaissancehotels.com

The Renaissance Charleston offers some splendor in the middle of the city's historic district. Guest accommodations feature baths with granite vanities, beds with plush down comforters and fluffy pillows, plus extras like wireless Internet access and PlayStations. The hotel's signature restaurant, Wentworth Grill, serves fresh, seasonal Southern-influenced cuisine perfect for business meetings or a dinner.

166 rooms. Restaurant, bar. Fitness center. Pool. Spa. $151-250

★★★WENTWORTH MANSION
149 Wentworth St., Charleston, 843-853-1886, 888-466-1886; www.wentworthmansion.com

Once a private home, this stunning mansion in the city's historic center has hand-carved marble fireplaces, ornate plasterwork and Tiffany stained-glass

WHAT IS THE BEST OVERALL HOTEL IN CHARLESTON?

Charleston Place claims a great spot in the historic district. The rooms draw on the city's rich history for its traditional colonial-style décor. Perks like a saltwater pool with a retractable roof, a full-service spa and upscale shops make it very now.

windows. Guest rooms offer gas fireplaces and charming views. A full European breakfast is served on the sun porch each morning, and the Rodgers Library is a great spot for evening drinks.

21 rooms. Restaurant. Complimentary breakfast. $251-350

RECOMMENDED

BARKSDALE HOUSE INN

27 George St., Charleston, 843-577-4800, 888-577-4980; www.barksdalehouse.com

Built as a town house in 1778 by wealthy Charlestonian George Barksdale, this stately bed and breakfast is filled with period furnishings and modern conveniences.

14 rooms. Complimentary breakfast. No children under 10. $61-150

BATTERY CARRIAGE HOUSE INN

20 S. Battery, Charleston, 843-727-3100, 800-775-5575; www.batterycarriagehouse.com

Hidden within the flowering gardens of the Steven-Lathers Mansion, an exquisite private home, this 1843 bed and breakfast offers private entrances, romantic décor and a view of Charleston Harbor.

11 rooms. Complimentary breakfast. No children under 12. $61-150

THE GOVERNOR'S HOUSE INN

117 Broad St., Charleston, 843-720-2070, 800-720-9812; www.governorshouse.com

A National Landmark, this inn is the former home of Edward Rutledge, national statesman, patriot and youngest signer of the Declaration of Independence who later served as a U.S. senator and governor of South Carolina. Rooms and common areas are exquisitely detailed.

11 rooms. Bar. $251-350

INDIGO INN

1 Maiden Lane, Charleston, 843-577-5900, 800-845-7639; www.indigoinn.com

Housed in an 1850 warehouse once used to store indigo for dying textiles, this colorful inn is in the middle of the historic district, just one block from City Market.

40 rooms. Complimentary breakfast. $61-150

KINGS COURTYARD INN

198 King St., Charleston, 843-723-7000, 866-720-2949; www.kingscourtyardinn.com

This three-story antebellum Greek Revival-style structure was built in 1854 and remains one of the gems of Charleston's historic district.

44 rooms. Restaurant, bar. Complimentary breakfast. $61-150

MAISON DU PRE

317 E. Bay St., Charleston, 843-723-8691, 800-844-4667; www.maisondupre.com

The main house dates to 1804. Located in historic downtown, adjacent to the Gaillard Auditorium, this inn is decorated in period furniture and art made by the family that runs it.

15 rooms. Complimentary breakfast. $61-150

MEETING STREET INN

173 Meeting St., Charleston, 843-723-1882, 800-842-8022; www.meetingstreetinn.com

Each room in this classic, single-house inn opens onto the piazza and courtyard.

Rooms are individually decorated with period furniture.

56 rooms. Bar. Complimentary breakfast. $61-150

VICTORIA HOUSE INN

208 King St., Charleston, 843-720-2946, 866-720-2946; www.thevictoriahouseinn.com

Built in the late 1880s, this Romanesque-style Victorian house now serves as a lovely inn. Located in the downtown historic district, the inn offers lavish amenities such as a bedside champagne breakfast.

22 rooms. Complimentary breakfast. $61-150

WHERE TO EAT

★★★CAROLINA'S

10 Exchange St., Charleston, 843-724-3800, 888-486-7673; www.carolinasrestaurant.com

Located on a quiet, sleepy stretch of Exchange Street, Carolina's is the place to go for honest, straightforward low-country cuisine. The restaurant is divided into three distinct dining areas: the romantic Sidewalk Room, the relaxed Bar Room and the Perditas Room, an homage to the restaurant that used to occupy this space. Perditas' famous fruits de mer dish is always on the menu, alongside standout items such as the jumbo lump crab cake and the pan-roasted lamb rack.

American. Lunch, dinner. Reservations recommended. Bar. $36-85

★★★CHARLESTON GRILL

Charleston Place Hotel, 224 King St., Charleston, 843-577-4522; www.charlestongrill.com

The Charleston Grill is a clubby spot in the Charleston Place Hotel. Stained-glass French doors, dark wood-paneled walls and marble floors create a classy Old World atmosphere. Rich dishes like shrimp and catfish hoecakes with fried oysters and tartar rémoulade provide a hint of the kind of low-country fare served at this sophisticated restaurant. Live jazz draws locals.

American. Dinner. Reservations recommended. Outdoor seating. Children's menu. Bar. $86 and up

★★★CIRCA 1886

149 Wentworth St., Charleston, 843-853-7828; www.circa1886.com

Located behind the historic Wentworth Mansion, this restaurant offers classic Charleston charm. The 280-bottle wine list complements the local cuisine on the menu, which talented chef Marc Collins creates using regional ingredients. Try the Carolina crab cake soufflé, a cheese course made from Appalachian raw cow milk cheese, or the catfish with lobster and white cheddar grits. Desserts are traditional and rich, from gingerbread pudding with orange blossom honey ice cream to sweet potato-butterscotch soufflé. The classic presentation of each dish adds an elegant flourish to the meal. The staff is polished and friendly.

American. Dinner. Closed Sunday. Reservations recommended. Bar. $36-85

★★★CYPRESS: A LOW-COUNTRY GRILLE

167 E. Bay St., Charleston, 843-727-0111; www.magnolias-blossom-cypress.com

This restaurant offers a daring take on classic low-country food—traditionally defined by hearty dishes with plenty of rice, shrimp and unique seasonings. The wood-burning grill adds additional flavor to entrées like reconstructed lamb T-bone.

American. Dinner. Reservations recommended. Children's menu. Bar. $36-85

WHICH
CHARLESTON
RESTAURANTS
SERVE THE BEST
LOW-COUNTRY
CUISINE?

Carolina's:
When you want straight-forward low-country cuisine, Carolina's is the place to eat. It serves dishes like crab cakes along with fixings like grits and collard greens.

Charleston Grill:
This sophisticated spot in the Charleston Place Hotel serves delicious low-country fare, with live jazz often playing in the background.

Circa 1886:
Homey low-country food gets an upgrade at this restaurant. Crab is transformed into a crab cake soufflé and catfish is mixed with lobster and white cheddar grits.

Cypress:
A Lowcountry Grille:
Cypress elevates low-country meals. Take, for example, the rib-eye with pimento mac and cheese, ham cracklings and bone marrow steak sauce.

★★★HIGH COTTON

199 E. Bay St., Charleston, 843-724-3815; www.high-cotton.net

"High cotton" is an old Southern saying that means "living large." The menu at this casually elegant restaurant echoes that sentiment with boldly flavored dishes such as cornbread-crusted flounder with sweet pea and corn succotash, or bourbon-glazed pork with white cheddar-jalapeño grits.

American. Lunch (Saturday), dinner, Sunday brunch. Children's menu. Bar. $16-35

★★★MAGNOLIA'S

185 E. Bay St., Charleston, 843-577-7771;
www.magnolias-blossom-cypress.com

This Charleston landmark livens up Southern favorites. The down south egg roll is stuffed with collard greens, chicken and tasso and served with red pepper purée, spicy mustard and peach chutney, while the pan-fried chicken livers come with caramelized onions, country ham and a Madeira sauce. For lunch, try the delicious slow-cooked barbecue mini-sandwiches served on super soft buns with jalapeño-peach coleslaw.

American. Lunch, dinner, Sunday brunch. Bar. $16-35

★★★MCCRADY'S

2 Unity Alley, Charleston, 843-577-0025; www.mccradysrestaurant.com

You can almost picture the Rutledges having a drink and talking politics at this handsome restaurant located down a romantic alley in a brick structure built back in 1788. It was originally a tavern before it was abandoned; it was restored to its former glory in 1982, with a few modern touches added, including a sky light and leather banquettes. The menu complements this fresh take. Chef Sean Brock's intoxicating dishes include beef tenderloin with beets, garden onions and smoked hollandaise; halibut with lemon-truffle emulsion; and scallops marinated in mango vinegar, avocado, crispy rice and chamomile. The tome of a wine list includes many hard-to-find varieties. The bar is a sophisticated spot for a glass of wine and a cheese plate, or one of the unusual deserts such as peanut butter cake with popcorn ice cream and salted caramel.

International. Dinner. Reservations recommended. Bar. $36-85

★★★★PENINSULA GRILL

112 N. Market St., Charleston, 843-723-0700;
www.peninsulagrill.com

Located in the Planter's Inn, this restaurant has the sophisticated feel of an urban eatery without losing sight of its Southern charm. The menu is inventive, offering boldly flavored dishes spiced up with low-country accents like collards, hushpuppies, grits and black-eyed peas. Chef Robert Carter's famous coconut layer cake is worth the splurge. There's also a champagne bar menu of decadent little treats like oysters, lobster, foie gras, caviar and duck pâté.

American. Dinner. Reservations recommended. Outdoor seating. Bar. $36-85

★★★SOCIAL WINE BAR

188 E. Bay St., Charleston, 843-577-5665; www.socialwinebar.com

Social Wine Bar's collection of wine extends beyond wine titans Napa Valley and Burgundy, France. Here, you'll find bottles from Spain and Italy to pinots from Oregon's Willamette Valley and syrahs from France's Cotes du Rhone. Why go to West Coast vineyards when they can come to you? Social Wine Bar even offers a selection of choice sake. With such a dizzying array of wine from which to choose, any vino lover in Charleston will have to make a stop at this popular venue that serves not only wine but also sophisticated, tapas-style small plates. Try the warm spinach salad with grilled pears or the rich oxtail rillette napoleon from the "hot" menu to start.

American. Dinner, late-night. $36-85

RECOMMENDED

ANSON

12 Anson St., Charleston, 843-577-0551; www.ansonrestaurant.com

This popular low country restaurant in an old warehouse with plantation shutters and gold ballroom chairs is popular with visitors and Charlestonians alike, who come to feast on such favorites as cornmeal-dusted okra and chicken done three ways: barbequed, fried and marmalade. The chefs use fresh local seafood and produce, often organic, and the menu changes seasonally. You'll also find a nice selection of wines at this Charleston charmer.

Southern. Dinner. Bar. Children's menu. Reservations recommended. $36-85

BASIL

460 King St., Charleston, 843-724-3490; www.basilthairestaurant.com

Charlestonians consider Basil restaurant the finest place to get their Thai food fixes. They praise Basil's deep-fried duck and zesty pad thai. And we're not talking mere take-out Thai here. Basil serves up sophisticated fare that stays true to its roots, thanks to chef Suntorn Cherdchoongarm, who insists on cooking everything from scratch and using freshly made sauces. At Basil, you'll find traditional curries, both green and red, along with savory chicken satay and spicy volcano shrimp. Don't forget to start off with the fresh Basil Roll, wrapped in light, soft rice paper and filled with crisp lettuce, bean sprouts, shrimp and, of course, tender leaves of fragrant basil.

Thai. Lunch (Monday-Friday), dinner. $36-85

CRU CAFÉ

18 Pinckney St., Charleston, 843-534-2434; www.crucafe.com

A guy who buys a place crossing Motley Street and calls it Cru Café has to be one cool cat. This tiny café located in an old Charleston single house is nothing to look at, but don't let that stop you. Make a reservation—even for lunch. The place is packed with people who come to sample owner and chef John Zucker's inventive, fresh cuisine. Try the crunchy calamari salad with slaw and sesame dressing; along with one of the tasty sandwiches and a crisp, cool glass of wine, and you have the perfect lunch. If you're sharing, consider the creamy four-cheese macaroni, which arrives at your table bubbling hot. Dinner offers pasta and risotto, an à la carte grill, and entrées such as poblano and mozzarella fried chicken. Afterall this, you might just want a bite of something sweet, like strawberry bread pudding or cheesecake with fresh berries. Rock on.

American. Reservations recommended. $36-85

LA FOURCHETTE

432 King St., Charleston, 843-722-6261; www.lafourchettecharleston.com

This bistro on Upper King has locals pouring in for its signature pommes frites fried twice in duck fat. This method transforms ordinary hand-cut fries into perfectly delectable, crispy frites that are served with housemade mayonnaise for dipping. Cozy, dimly lit and convincingly Parisian, La Fourchette keeps it charmingly modest with a 40-seat dining room and a simple, authentically French menu. Start with a classic salade vert made of Boston lettuce to whet your appetite before the fries and finish off with a steaming bowl of mussels cooked in white wine or the coquilles St. Jacques, a dish of rich chopped scallops in baked cream.

French. Dinner. $16-35

FIG

232 Meeting St., Charleston, 843-805-5900; www.eatatfig.com

Fig stands for "Food Is Good" and that pretty much sums up the experience at this deliciously simple restaurant. Chef Mike Lata's philosophy involves combing the best products and technique to extract pure flavor. Witness the local radishes with artisanal butter and braised short ribs with parsnip purée, garden carrots and red wine. The minimalist décor with long banquettes and a communal table sets the mood. Desserts like the olive oil cake with mascarpone and grapes are also just plain, well, good.

American. Dinner, late-night. Reservations recommended. $36-85

SLIGHTLY NORTH OF BROAD

192 E. Bay St., Charleston, 843-723-3424;
www.slightlynorthofbroad.net

Better known as SNOB, this rollicking restaurant located in a 19th-century brick warehouse turns out such satisfying dishes as carpaccio of beef with pecorino and grilled bread and crab cakes over a sauté of okra, corn, grape tomatoes and yellow squash.

Southern. Lunch, dinner. Bar. Children's menu. $16-35

LOW COUNTRY

South Carolina's Low Country includes all of the coastal towns that tourists flock to for an on-the-beach vacation. The region is also home to sprawling plantation estates, important historic spots and terrific golf courses. The second-oldest town in the state, Beaufort is the unofficial capital of Low Country and is filled with antebellum homes and churches. Georgetown sits on the shore of Winyah Bay, and offers historic plantations, gardens and beaches. Murrells Inlet calls itself the state's seafood capital. Besides restaurants, there is a beautiful stretch of beach in the area known as the Grand Strand with amazingly well-preserved marshland and coastline. Summerville has a quintessentially Southern charm and history. More than 700 homes and buildings are on the National Register of Historic Places.

Of course, the region also includes popular resort destinations. Year-round resort island Hilton Head attracts all travelers, from families who want an easy, kid-friendly atmosphere to high-end vacationers. Hilton Head, reached by a bridge on Highway 278, is bordered by one of the few remaining unpolluted marine estuaries on the East Coast and is the largest sea island between New Jersey and Florida. The island has 12 miles of beaches, numerous golf courses and tennis courts, swimming, miles of bicycle paths, horseback riding, four nature preserves and deep-sea, sound and dockside fishing

Kiawah Island is one of the richest natural environments on the eastern seaboard and a beautiful little island to visit just outside Charleston. Named for the Native Americans who once hunted and fished here, the island is separated from the mainland by the Kiawah River and a mile-wide salt marsh. Separate resort areas and private residential neighborhoods ensure a minimum of automobile traffic and leave much of the island untouched.

On Kiawah, sunny days are filled with great golf, good food and happy outdoor fun. The accommodations are top-notch and the tennis and golf are world-class (scores of tournaments have taken place here, including the Ryder Cup).

There's also 10 miles of glorious white-sand beach that some say is the best anywhere. Rent a bike and cruise around the island, taking in the ocean breezes and the beautiful homes. You'll find many tours to explore the wildlife.

WHAT TO SEE

BEAUFORT
JOHN MARK VERDIER HOUSE MUSEUM
801 Bay St., Beaufort, 843-524-6335; www.historic-beaufort.org

This Federal-period house built in 1790 was once known as the Lafayette Building because the Marquis de Lafayette is said to have spoken here from the piazza in 1825.

Admission: $5. Monday-Saturday 11 a.m.-4 p.m.

ST. HELENA'S EPISCOPAL CHURCH
505 Church St., Beaufort, 843-522-1712; www.sthelenas1712.org

Tombstones from the surrounding burial ground became operating tables when the church was used as a hospital during the Civil War.

Tuesday-Friday 10 a.m.-4 p.m., Saturday 10 a.m.-1 p.m.

HIGHLIGHT

WHAT ARE THE TOP THINGS TO DO IN LOW COUNTRY?

EXPLORE THE SAVANNAH NATIONAL WILDLIFE REFUGE

The 25,000-acre refuge is mostly made up of bottomland hardwoods, but it also offers a road where you can see wildlife like waterfowl and songbirds.

VISIT THE PATRIOTS POINT NAVAL AND MARITIME MUSEUM

This is a must for Navy buffs. The museum features the famed World War II aircraft carrier the *U.S.S. Yorktown*, along with a number of other vessels and displays.

PRACTICE YOUR GOLF SWING

Resort cities like Hilton Head, Myrtle Beach and Kiawah Island are renowned for their top golf courses. Go play a round or two on one of the many courses.

GEORGETOWN

HAMPTON PLANTATION STATE PARK

1950 Rutledge Road, McClellanville, 843-546-9361; www.discoversouthcarolina.com

This restored 18th-century mansion was the center of a large rice plantation. Guided tours go on the hour.

Grounds: Memorial Day-Labor Day, daily 9 a.m-6 p.m.; rest of the year, Thursday-Monday 9 a.m.-6 p.m. Mansion: Memorial Day-Labor Day, daily 11 a.m.-4 p.m.; rest of the year, Thursday-Monday 1-4 p.m.

HOPSEWEE PLANTATION

494 Hopsewee Road, Georgetown, 803-546-7891; www.hopsewee.com

This preserved 1740 rice plantation house on the North Santee River marks the birthplace of Thomas Lynch Jr., a signer of the Declaration of Independence.

Admission: adults $15, children 5-17 $7.50; ground only $5. March-October, Monday-Friday 10 a.m.-4 p.m.; rest of year, Thursday-Friday 10 a.m.-4 p.m.; and by appointment.

PRINCE GEORGE WINYAH CHURCH

708 Broad St., Georgetown, 843-546-4358; www.pgwinyah.org

The English stained-glass window behind the altar was originally a part of St. Mary's Chapel for Negroes at Hagley Plantation on Waccamaw. The church has been in continuous use since it was constructed, except during the American Revolution and the Civil War.

Memorial Day-October, Monday-Friday 11:30 a.m.-4:30 p.m.

TOWN CLOCK BUILDING
633 Front St., Georgetown

The tablet marks the landing of Lafayette at North Island in 1777. Federal troops came ashore on the dock at the rear of the building in an attempt to capture the town.

HARDEEVILLE
SAVANNAH NATIONAL WILDLIFE REFUGE
1000 Business Center Drive, Hardeeville, 912-652-4415; www.fws.gov

More than half of the 29,000 acres consists of bottomland hardwoods reminiscent of the great cypress and tupelo swamps that once extended along the Carolina and Georgia low country. Argent Swamp can only be reached by boat; wild azaleas, iris, spider lilies and other flowers bloom in succession, beginning in spring. Laurel Hill Wildlife Drive is open to cars and allows viewing of wildlife, especially waterfowl from December to February. Migrating songbirds are abundant in spring and fall. The Tupelo-Swamp Walk (mid-March-September) is best for bird-watchers and photographers.
Daily.

HILTON HEAD
DAUFUSKIE ISLAND RESORT GOLF
421 Squire Pope Road, Hilton Head, 843-341-4810, 800-648-6778; www.daufuskieresort.com

Rates for both resort guests and day players are relatively low for the two 18-hole courses on the property (the Melrose, designed by Jack Nicklaus, and the Bloody Point, designed by Tom Weiskopf and Jay Morrish), both of which offer challenging holes and great views of the Atlantic Ocean.

HARBOUR TOWN GOLF LINKS
Sea Pines Resort, 32 Greenwood Drive, Hilton Head Island, 888-807-6873; www.seapines.com

Pete Dye designed the courses, featuring the designer's signature red-and-white-striped lighthouse, which serves as a backdrop for the course's 18th hole. The par-71 layout is less than 7,000 yards from the back tees, but the fairways can be narrow and the greens small. Two other courses at the resort, Ocean and Sea Pines, add 36 more holes to the offerings.

MOUNT PLEASANT
PATRIOTS POINT NAVAL AND MARITIME MUSEUM
40 Patriots Point Road, Mount Pleasant, 843-884-2727; www.patriotspoint.org

This is an amazing assemblage of naval equipment and lore, appropriately located in Charleston Harbor. The star is the famed World War II aircraft carrier, the *U.S.S. Yorktown*. Onboard the Yorktown are numerous displays, including the Congressional Medal of Honor Society's museum and headquarters, the World War II Fast Carrier exhibit, the Battle of Midway Torpedo Squadrons memorial and a World War II cruiser room. Other vessels include the *Savannah*, the world's first nuclear-powered merchant ship; the *Laffey*, a World War II destroyer; the *Clamagore*, a World War II submarine; and the *Ingham*, a Coast Guard cutter.
Admission: adults $18, seniors and military personnel $15, children 6-11 $11, children 5 and under free. Daily 9 a.m.-6:30 p.m.

HIGHLIGHT

WHERE'S THE BEST GOLF ON KIAWAH ISLAND?

Thoughtfully developed on a barrier island of coastal South Carolina only 21 miles from historic Charleston, Kiawah Island Golf Resort lies along 10 miles of one of America's most beautiful white-sand beaches, with its romantic tidal marsh. This 10,000-acre island has five championship courses that were designed by the world's leading golf course architects for all levels of play, and where scores of tourmanents have taken place, including the 1991 Ryder Cup. In 2012, Kiawah Island Golf Resort will host the 94th PGA Championship, earning them the right to say they're only among four courses in the country to host all of the major PGA Championships. A visit here and you'll easily understand why. You could spend weeks playing the courses on this ultra-exclusive island with fine restaurants and luxury accommodations. When you're not on the fairways, rent a bike and tour the island. Sunny days are filled with great golf, good food and happy outdoor fun.

THE COURSES

THE OCEAN

Designed by Pete Dye, this course, which will host the PGA Championship in 2012, will forever be famous as the setting for the movie *The Legend of Bagger Vance* and the dramatic cliffhanger that occurred at the 1991 Ryder Cup, known as the "War by the Shore," when Bernhard Langer's six-foot putt slid by the hole and the United States claimed a one-point victory. The Ocean stretches three miles and features 10 holes that run along the Atlantic Ocean, the only course in the Northern Hemisphere that can claim that distinguishing trademark. The 7,296-yard, par-72 layout mimics the links of England and Scotland, and thanks to winds that blow off the Atlantic, yardage can vary. Played from the extreme back tee on every hole, the course measures 7,937 yards. Greens fees: The steep fee of the Ocean Course ($239-$320) includes a "complimentary" cart and forecaddie or caddie, but that doesn't include a tip. The pro shop will remind you of that at check-in with a card that recommends caddie tips of $65 per bag ($25 for forecaddies). Walking-only policy before noon. If you choose to walk, you're not required to take a caddie, but be advised: Walkers who opt to go it alone must carry their bags as no push carts are available.

TURTLE POINT

Opened in 1981, Turtle Point doesn't have all that artificial mounding that became popular later on in that over-the-top decade. Instead, the design by Jack Nicklaus effortlessly blends into the spectacular landscape. At 6,914 yards from the back markers with five par-4s stretching 420 yards or longer, this course will definitely test your skills. A tip: The 412-yard 15th is the toughest so prepare yourself—the small green is covered by dunes and can be a real bear when the wind is blowing. Be sure to check out the new clubhouse afterward; it was opened in 2002 when the entire course was renovated.

OSPREY POINT

This course, designed by Tom Fazio and completed in 1986, is a real Southern treat. The beautiful course features saltwater marshes, giant oaks and fragrant magnolia trees, and is a heck of a tough course to play. Fazio's par-72 layout stretches 6,871 yards from the back tees. You'll also find lots of strategic short par-4s, in addition to a pair of 3s longer than 200 yards and a 453-yard, par-4 ninth. The course includes a driving range and a clubhouse.

COUGAR POINT

The new Gary Player-designed course features a par-72 layout stretching 6,861 yards from the back tees. The course has four great finishing holes, beginning with the par-5 15th hole that will have you on the edge of your game. The piece de resistance is the par-4 18th hole. The course is perhaps most well known for three-holes midway through, which border the tidal marsh and offer golfers amazing views of the Kiawah River and the peaceful marshes. From here, you might also spot some of the wildlife Kiawah is a haven for, including wading birds, pelicans and osprey.

OAK POINT

This Scottish-American style course, designed by Clyde Johnston, features a par-72 layout that is a challenge for any golfer. The fairways are on the grounds of an old cotton plantation bordering Haulover Creek and the Kiawah River. Golfers can take in the saltwater marshes and forests filled with pine trees and ancient oaks while they go for that hole-in-one. The new clubhouse overlooking the 18th hole is a great place to recap the day's events.

GREENS FEES

Greens fees for all courses other than Ocean: Rates range from $87 to $215, including cart. The resort encourages golfers to play two rounds a day with deep second-round discounts ($110-$160 for the Ocean Course; $50-$70 for the other four courses).

INSTRUCTION

The Tommy Cuthbert Golf Learning Center will no doubt help you improve your game— and it's not a bad way to spend a day here in Kiawah, either, especially a rainy one. The facility includes the latest in video swing analysis, private instructional areas, covered hitting bays and Astroturf putting surface. A brand new pro shop offers club fitting and is stocked with the best golf equipment. The center has men's and women's locker rooms with showers, and more.

MURRELLS INLET
BROOKGREEN GARDENS
1931 Brookgreen Drive, Murrells Inlet, 843-235-6000, 800-849-1931; www.brookgreen.org

On the site of former rice and indigo plantations, these gardens contain more than 500 pieces of American sculpture, boxwood, massive moss-hung oaks and native plants, as well as a wildlife park with native animals. Creek and all-terrain vehicle excursions take visitors through forests, creeks, old plantation homes and rice fields.

Admission: adults $12, seniors $10, children 4-12 $6, children 3 and under free. Daily 9:30 a.m.-5 p.m.

HUNTINGTON BEACH STATE PARK
16148 Ocean Highway, Georgetown, 803-237-4440; www.southcarolinaparks.com

The marsh boardwalk lets you get close to nature in this 2,500-acre parkland. There is fishing and surfing, along with numerous hiking trails.

Daily.

MYRTLE BEACH
BAREFOOT RESORT
4980 Barefoot Resort Bridge Road, North Myrtle Beach, 843-390-3200, 800-320-6536; www.barefootgolf.com

Maybe the best place in Myrtle Beach to play golf, Barefoot Resort features four courses designed by some of the sport's biggest names—Davis Love III, Tom Fazio, Greg Norman and Pete Dye all took a piece of the land and crafted courses.

BROADWAY AT THE BEACH
1325 Celebrity Circle, Myrtle Beach, 843-444-3200, 800-386-4662; www.broadwayatthebeach.com

This 350-acre complex, billed as the largest venue of its kind in South Carolina, features a wide variety of shops, dining and nightclubs. Also onsite are a 16-screen movie theater, an IMAX theater, a NASCAR SpeedPark, a miniature golf course, a water park and an aquarium. Broadway at the Beach is also home to the Myrtle Beach Pelicans, a Class A affiliate of the Atlanta Braves.

SUMMERVILLE
FRANCIS BEIDLER FOREST
336 Sanctuary Road, Summerville, 843-462-2150; www.audubon.org

Located in the heart of the Low Country, this 11,000-acre site in Four Holes Swamp encompasses the largest remaining virgin stand of bald cypress and tupelo gum trees in the world. Oak, ash and blackgum also grow here, as do 300 varieties of wildlife and numerous flowers, ferns, vines and other plants. A National Audubon Society sanctuary, the forest is named for a lumberman who championed conservation on both public and private lands. A 6,500-foot boardwalk into the swamp leads out from and back to the visitor center.

Tuesday-Sunday 9 a.m.-5 p.m.

OLD DORCHESTER STATE HISTORIC SITE
300 State Park Road, Summerville, 843-873-1740; www.southcarolinaparks.com

This 325-acre park is on the site of a colonial village founded in 1697 by a group representing the Congregational Church of Dorchester, Mass. By the time the war was over, the town had been abandoned. Overlooking the Ashley River, the site today includes remnants of a fort, a cemetery and the bell tower of St. Georges Parish Church. Archaeological excavations are ongoing.

Thursday-Monday 9 a.m.-6 p.m.

WHERE TO STAY

BEAUFORT

★★★BEAUFORT INN

809 Port Republic St., Beaufort, 843-379-4667; www.beaufortinn.com

Built in 1897, this romantic low country inn offers rooms, suites and a private two-bedroom cottage. The dining room has seasonal Southern cuisine and an extensive wine list.

21 rooms. Restaurant. Complimentary breakfast. No children under 8. $251-350

★★★THE RHETT HOUSE INN

1009 Craven St., Beaufort, 843-524-9030, 888-480-9530; www.rhetthouseinn.com

One block from the Intracoastal Waterway is the Rhett House Inn, a plantation dating back to 1820. It has rooms decorated with floral fabrics, fireplaces, four-poster beds and antiques.

17 rooms. Complimentary breakfast. No children under 5. $151-250

HILTON HEAD

★★★CROWNE PLAZA

130 Shipyard Drive, Hilton Head Island, 843-842-2400, 800-334-1881; www.cphiltonhead.com

Located in Shipyard Plantation, this 11-acre resort is a paradise for golfers and tennis players. The beachfront location is set on miles of sandy oceanfront great for trying out sailboats, boogie boards and beach trikes.

340 rooms. Restaurant, bar. Beach. $151-250

★★★DAUFUSKIE ISLAND RESORT AND BREATHE SPA

421 Squire Pope Road, Hilton Head Island, 843-341-4820, 800-648-6778; www.daufuskieresort.com

The full-service resort, which has vacation cottages and villas, offers a range of activities, from 36 holes of golf to horseback riding, croquet and tennis.

192 rooms. Restaurant, bar. Pool. Spa. Beach. $151-250

WHAT ARE THE MOST LUXURIOUS HOTELS?

The Sanctuary at Kiawah Island:
You'll find a sanctuary at this oceanfront hotel, whether it be on one of the five nearby championship golf courses, in the superb spa or on the beach.

Woodlands Inn:
This plantation appoints its rooms with indulgences like fireplaces, steam-heated towel racks and Jacuzzis. To get pampered, visit the day spa.

★★★HILTON HEAD MARRIOTT BEACH AND GOLF RESORT

1 Hotel Circle at Palmetto Dunes, Hilton Head Island, 843-686-8400, 800-228-9290; www.hilton-headmarriott.com

This beachfront Marriott is at Palmetto Dunes, within walking distance of the Shelter Cove Marina shops and attractions. Nicely appointed rooms plus beach access and several pools provide reasons to stay within the resort's walls.

513 rooms. Restaurant, bar. Pool. Beach. $61-150

★★★HILTON OCEANFRONT RESORT HILTON HEAD ISLAND

23 Ocean Lane, Hilton Head Island, 843-842-8000, 800-845-8001; www.hiltonheadhilton.com

Enjoy the widest beach on the island at this luxe, self-contained resort. Manicured gardens and lagoons adorn the property.

324 rooms. Restaurant, bar. Pool. Beach. $251-350

★★★★THE INN AT HARBOUR TOWN

32 Greenwood Drive, Hilton Head Island, 866-561-8802; www.seapines.com

With 5,000 acres of pristine coastal expanse at your disposal, there's little reason to stay inside. That is, until you enter the understated elegance of the Inn at Harbour Town at The Sea Pines Resort. This boutique-style inn mixes Southern sophistication—a personal butler to cater to your every whim— with casual charm to ensure a restful and pleasure-packed stay. The tastefully decorated guest rooms are surprisingly spacious with in-room refrigerators, work desks and balconies overlooking the racquet club or sprawling golf course. Active sorts can fill their day with a tennis match on one of the 23 courts or a bike ride over more than 15 miles of paved trails (bicycle rentals are complimentary). Getting off the plantation is equally sweet with the historic Harbour Town lighthouse and numerous independent boutiques and restaurants only a short walk from the inn. Don't be surprised if the staff remembers your name throughout your visit; it's simply considered good old Southern hospitality here.

60 rooms. Restaurant, bar. Business center. Fitness center. Pool. Golf. Tennis. $151-250

★★★★THE INN AT PALMETTO BLUFF

476 Mount Pilla Road, Bluffton, 843-706-6500, 866-706-6565; www.palmettobluffresort.com

This low-country inn, a sister to California's famed Auberge du Soleil, delivers luxury accommodations, fine dining and pure relaxation in a riverfront setting. Rooms offer plenty of extravagant touches, such as plasma televisions, wet bars with Sub-Zero refrigerators and deep soaking tubs. Enjoy the Jack Nicklaus-designed golf course or the full-service spa. The River House restaurant serves Southern-influenced recipes such as she-crab bisque laced with aged sherry and cast-iron fried quail with bacon, eggs, arugula and warm ricotta pudding.

50 rooms. Restaurant, bar. $351 and up

★★★MAIN STREET INN

2200 Main St., Hilton Head Island, 843-681-3001, 800-471-3001; www.mainstreetinn.com

The Main Street Inn is a beacon of sophistication. The 34 rooms are individually designed, yet all feature luxurious velvet and silk linens, unique artwork and distinctive furnishings. Afternoon tea is a daily tradition.

34 rooms. Complimentary breakfast. No children under 12. $61-150

★★★THE WESTIN RESORT, HILTON HEAD ISLAND

2A Grasslawn Ave., Hilton Head Island, 843-681-4000; www.westin.com

This self-contained beachfront resort is a standout with its roster of leisure activities ranging from golf, tennis and swimming to a fully stocked Reebok gym with yoga, Pilates and fitness machines. Rooms have plush beds with fluffy duvets, soaking tubs and balconies.

412 rooms. Restaurant, bar. Pool. Spa. Beach. $151-250

KIAWAH ISLAND

★★★★★THE SANCTUARY AT KIAWAH ISLAND

1 Sanctuary Beach Drive, Kiawah Island, 843-768-6000, 877-683-1234; www.thesanctuary.com

This grand resort resembling an old Southern estate is the place to stay on Kiawah Island, thanks to its spectacular beachfront setting, fine dining and a first-class spa. The gorgeous lobby with creaky walnut floors and handcrafted rugs is set up like a wealthy great aunt's living room, with intimate seating areas, limestone fireplaces and wood cabinets full of porcelain knickknacks. Large windows look out to the perfectly manicured lawns and the beach right beyond. Two large staircases and murals depicting the island's wildlife flank the elegant space. Rooms (be sure to ask for an ocean view) have a breezy traditional feel with their early American furniture, four-poster beds, large tubs, colorful drapes and plantation shutters. The café next to the pool is a great spot for lunch, and the lounge off the lobby is perfect for a cocktail after a day on the golf course. With five championship courses just outside its door, the Sanctuary hotel at Kiawah Island is a natural choice for golfers. The elegant resort also offers fine dining and a first-class spa. Throw in some Southern hospitality, which they do, and you won't want to leave.

255 rooms. Restaurant, bar. Pool. Spa. Beach. $351 and up

MYRTLE BEACH

★★★THE CYPRESS INN

16 Elm St., Conway, 843-248-8199, 800-575-5307; www.acypressinn.com

This 12-room bed and breakfast in the quiet town of Conway is located alongside a quaint marina. Go deep-sea fishing or simply walk the beautiful stretches of South Carolina beaches, located only 15 minutes away.

12 rooms. Complimentary breakfast. Spa. $61-150

★★★EMBASSY SUITES

9800 Queensway Blvd., Myrtle Beach, 843-449-0006, 800-876-0010;
www.kingstonplantation.com

Modern and inviting, this Embassy Suites is close to Myrtle Beach's restaurants, water parks and shopping. The hotel itself has six outdoor pools, golf and tennis.

385 rooms. Restaurant, bar. Complimentary breakfast. Pool. $151-250

★★★HILTON MYRTLE BEACH RESORT

10000 Beach Club Drive, Myrtle Beach, 843-449-5000, 877-887-9549; www.hilton.com

This waterfront hotel has great views of the Atlantic Ocean and inviting guest rooms decorated in bright hues of gold, blue, green and terra cotta. Nearby activities include the shops at Broadway at the Beach, the NASCAR Speedway, and the Palace Theater, as well as many dining options.

385 rooms. Restaurant, bar. Pool. Beach. Golf. $251-350

★★★SHERATON MYRTLE BEACH CONVENTION CENTER HOTEL

2101 N. Oak St., Myrtle Beach, 843-918-5000; www.starwoodhotels.com

Situated in the center of Myrtle Beach, within walking distance to the Broadway at the Beach shopping area, this contemporary Sheraton offers an ideal location. The hotel's signature beds come with down comforters and pillow-top mattresses.

402 rooms. Restaurant, bar. Business center. Fitness center. Pool. $151-250

PAWLEYS ISLAND

★★★LITCHFIELD PLANTATION

King's River Road, Pawleys Island, 843-237-9121, 800-869-1410;
www.litchfieldplantation.com

This former plantation house from the 1750s has been beautifully restored and converted into an elegant country inn. Guests will find uniquely decorated rooms with private baths, and suites with antique sleigh beds, fireplaces and double Jacuzzis. The resort has direct beach access via Litchfield Plantation's beach club on Pawleys Island, plus onsite dining at the Carriage House Club.

38 rooms. Restaurant, bar. Complimentary breakfast. Pool. $151-250

SUMMERVILLE

★★★★★WOODLANDS INN

125 Parsons Road, Summerville, 843-875-2600, 800-774-9999;
www.woodlandsinn.com

The 1906 Greek Revival-style Main House has casual, refined and lavishly appointed guest rooms created by interior designer David Eskell-Briggs. Guests can dip their toes in the pool, volley on the two clay tennis courts, play croquet matches on the lawn and ride bikes to the nearby town of Summerville. Sandalwoods Day Spa features Aveda products in all of its treatments. The Dining Room turns out delicious dishes in a cozy space.

19 rooms. Restaurant, bar. Business center. Pool. Spa. Tennis. $251-350

WHERE TO EAT

HILTON HEAD

★★★HARBOURMASTER'S OCEAN GRILL

1 Shelter Cove Lane, Hilton Head Island, 843-785-3030;
www.oceangrillrestaurant.com

Located on the waterway entrance to Shelter Cove Harbour, this restaurant offers creative and sumptuous seafood cuisine, along with exceptional service, unmatched ambience and dramatic views.

Seafood. Dinner. Closed January. Reservations recommended. Outdoor seating. Children's menu. Bar. $36-85

★★★RED FISH

8 Archer Road, Hilton Head Island, 843-686-3388; www.redfishofhiltonhead.com

Red Fish offers a menu of unique Caribbean dishes made with creatively blended housemade seasonings, vegetables and tropical fruits. Grilled grouper, Latin ribs and crispy Ashley Farms free-range brick chicken are among many enticing menu choices. An extensive wine list has more than 1,000 bottles. Warm terra-cotta walls accented with framed pictures and dark wood chairs set around white-clothed tables add to the casual atmosphere.

Caribbean. Lunch, dinner. Reservations recommended. Outdoor seating. Children's menu. Bar. $16-35

KIAWAH ISLAND
★★★★THE OCEAN ROOM
1 Sanctuary Beach Drive, Kiawah Island, 843-768-6253, 877-683-1234; www.thesanctuary.com

Plates sparkle at this fine-dining steakhouse with starters such as lobster bisque and foie gras torchon with brioche French toast, and entrées such as a 14-ounce rib-eye; and Scottish salmon with baby spinach, baby potatoes and house-cured pancetta. Or enjoy a five-course tasting menu with wine pairings. If you're feeling especially indulgent, order a side of the black truffle pommes frites (you won't be disappointed). You can also sit at the bar and order from the snack menu with items like the braised short ribs egg rolls, and caramel fondue for dessert.

Seafood, steak. Dinner. Reservations recommended. Bar. $36-85

MYRTLE BEACH
★★★THE PARSON'S TABLE
4305 McCorsley Ave., Little River, 843-249-3702;
www.parsonstable.com

Not only can you get a juicy roast prime rib at The Parson's Table, but you can eat it inside a church, too. The location remains very much the same structure that it was in 1885, when Little River Methodist Church was built. The cherished establishment first opened its church doors as a restaurant in the late 1970s and has been serving exquisite American steak-house fare ever since. The restaurant's décor is positively Southern-charm antique, complete with dark wooden walls, stained-glass windows and an original Tiffany glass lamp in the main dining room. The Parson's Table offers a thorough wine list as well as a good seafood selection on top of the traditional beef.

American, steak. Dinner. Closed Sunday. $36-85

★★★SEABLUE TAPAS
503 Highway 17 North, North Myrtle Beach, 843-249-8800; www.seablueonline.com

SeaBlue Tapas is in a shopping center across the street from a Home Depot and a TGIF, but step inside its doors and you're suddenly transported into ultra-chic, impossibly cool blues. The bar, the walls and the glowing aquarium all emanate blue light. At times, you'll feel like you're in an underwater lounge instead of a restaurant. As for the tapas, try the SeaBlue shrimp and grits, sizzling in a garlicky sauce, or the braised baby-back ribs. If you need a break from all that blue, try the Raspberry Flirtini.

American. Dinner. Closed Sunday $36-85

SUMMERVILLE
★★★★★THE DINING ROOM AT THE WOODLANDS
Woodlands Inn, 125 Parsons Road, Summerville, 843-308-2115, 800-774-9999;
www.woodlandsinn.com

Perfecting the atmosphere of Southern charm, the Dining Room offers menus that change daily and feature flavorful regional American dishes. Chef Sean Diehl and his staff showcase local ingredients. Standout dishes include hay-smoked duckling with crispy pomme darphin and Maine lobster with morels and English pea-acquerello risotto. With wine pairings by the sommelier and desserts like chocolate Napoleon with fleur de sel caramel, the end of a meal is as memorable as the beginning.

American. Breakfast, lunch, dinner, Sunday brunch. Reservations recommended. Outdoor seating. Jacket required at dinner. Bar. $86 and up

RECOMMENDED

PAWLEYS ISLAND
CARRIAGE HOUSE CLUB
Kings River Road, Litchfield Plantation, Pawleys Island, 843-237-9322; www.litchfieldplantation.com

Set in the serene backdrop of the Litchfield Plantation, the brick structure that houses the Carriage House Club restaurant is a Southern jewel to be sure. The former English carriage house is now a choice establishment for classic gourmet cuisine with a Southern twist. Must-orders are two chef specialties: the Carriage House grouper, lightly battered and served with a beurre blanc sauce and the goat cheese-Dijon mustard-crusted rack of lamb. If that doesn't do you in, take a look at the dessert list, which features good ol' pecan and key lime pies.

American. Breakfast, dinner. Closed Sunday-Monday. $36-85

SPAS

HILTON HEAD
★★★★SPA AT PALMETTO BLUFF
The Inn at Palmetto Bluff, 476 Mount Pilla Road, Bluffton, 843-706-6500, 866-706-6565; www.palmettobluffresort.com

Plantation shutters, willowing white drapery and the surrounding verdant countryside heighten the serenity of true Southern hospitality. Treatments for golfers include the Masters (hydrating massage and facial for sun-damaged skin) and the 20th Hole (private steam and sports massage). Everyone—not just golfers—will destress with treatments such as the aromatherapy massage, which uses a personalized mix of flower-, herb- and root-based essential oils.

KIAWAH ISLAND
★★★★★SPA AT THE SANCTUARY
Sanctuary at Kiawah Island, 1 Sanctuary Beach Drive, Kiawah Island, 843-768-6340; www.thesanctuary.com

Located inside the Sanctuary at Kiawah Island, the Spa resembles a grand Southern seaside mansion. Inside the hospitable staff greets guests with herbal tea and fresh fruit before leading the way to one of 12 rooms for nature-based treatments, which feature botanical extracts, natural enzymes and a signature Southern touch. If exercise is on your mind, head downstairs to the fitness center, which features the latest cardiovascular and resistance equipment, a 65-foot-long indoor pool, and Pilates and yoga studios.

WHERE TO SHOP

MYRTLE BEACH

BAREFOOT LANDING
4898 Highway 17 S., Myrtle Beach, 843-272-8349, 800-272-2320; www.bflanding.com

With a mixture of specialty shops and factory stores, Barefoot Landing appeals to a variety of shoppers. Shops include Ron Jon Surf Shop, Chico's, Crazy Shirts, Izod, Sunglass Hut, White House/Black Market and more. There are also more than a dozen eateries and a variety of entertainment options, including the House of Blues, Carolina Vineyards Winery and a video arcade.
Daily, hours vary by season.

INDEX

NORTH AND SOUTH CAROLINA

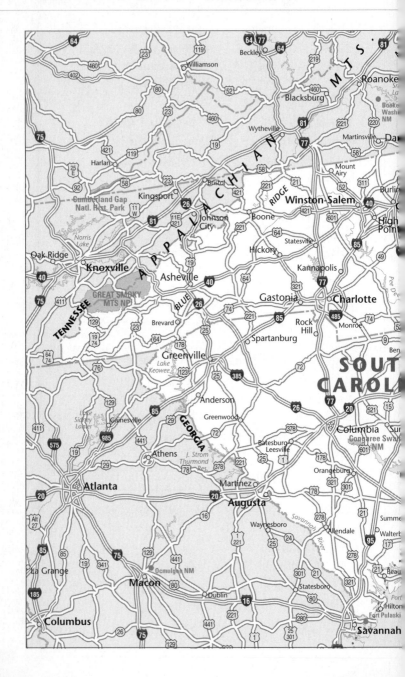

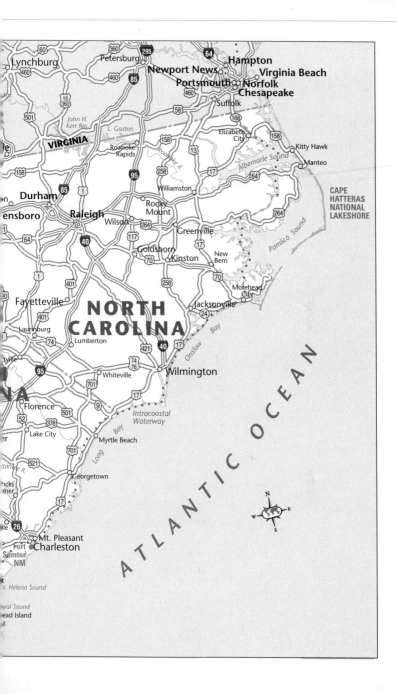

GEORGIA

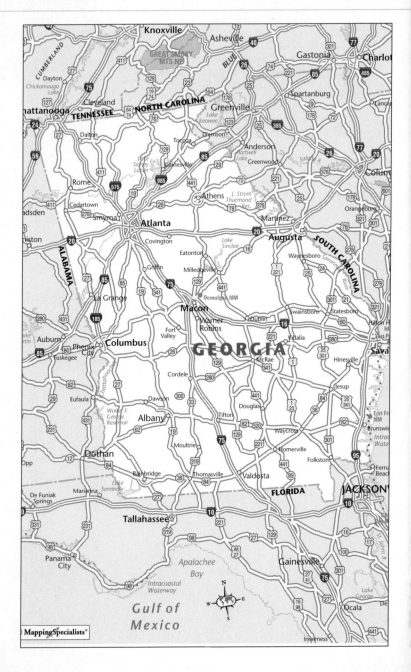

NOTES

NOTES

NOTES

NOTES

NOTES

NOTES

NOTES

052631521

NOTES